Catholic Social Teaching
in Global Perspective

GREGORIAN UNIVERSITY STUDIES
IN CATHOLIC SOCIAL TEACHING

Catholic Social Teaching in Global Perspective

Edited by
Daniel McDonald, SJ

ORBIS BOOKS

Maryknoll, New York 10545

Founded in 1970, Orbis Books endeavors to publish works that enlighten the mind, nourish the spirit, and challenge the conscience. The publishing arm of the Maryknoll Fathers and Brothers, Orbis seeks to explore the global dimensions of the Christian faith and mission, to invite dialogue with diverse cultures and religious traditions, and to serve the cause of reconciliation and peace. The books published reflect the views of their authors and do not represent the official position of the Maryknoll Society. To learn more about Maryknoll and Orbis Books, please visit our website at www.maryknollsociety.org.

Manufactured in the United States of America.
Manuscript editing and typesetting by Joan Weber Laflamme.

Library of Congress Cataloguing-in-Publication

Gregorian University studies in Catholic social teaching : Catholic social teaching in global perspective / edited by Daniel McDonald.
    p. cm.
    ISBN 978–1–57075–896–6 (pbk.)
    1. Christian sociology—Catholic Church. 2. Catholic Church—Doctrines. 3. Christianity and culture. I. McDonald, Daniel, S.J.
    BX1753.G69 2010
    261—dc22

2010017127

This volume is dedicated to my parents, C. E. and Marialyce, who showed me that social justice was not just an abstraction, but that it could be realized by paying attention to my world and fighting injustice when I recognized it. In schooling me about that, they opened my eyes to realize that the world was significantly bigger than my own backyard.

Contents

Introduction

Daniel McDonald, SJ

"When I return to my homeland next month, how best can I apply the social teaching of the Catholic Church to my culture?" Such was a challenge from one of our students at the Gregorian University as she prepared to leave Italy after three years in academic formation at the Faculty of Social Science. She had engaged in careful study of CST alongside her studies in economy and development. Her question was not theoretical. She was about to return to her homeland and was asking me for a serious conversation on how she might connect her studies to the burning justice issues in her culture. She was looking for a discussion that would help bring some integration to her work as a lay woman in her diocese, or at least a beginning of that discussion. Implicit in her question was also a methodological query about how to approach this in a structurally positive way.

To say that my response was inadequate would be generous. So accustomed to thinking within a Western frame of reference, I really did not understand her culture in such a way that I could engage her in any substantive conversation. I pride myself on the reality that I learn about other cultures because it is part of what I consider my duty in teaching students from 126 different countries. What I faced was a most concrete experience of the difference and the distance between knowledge and understanding. I retreated into a safe haven and asked questions based on Joe Holland's and Peter Henriot's blueprint for social analysis.[1] While this was a helpful response in that moment and possibly safer because I only had to ask systematic questions, the reality was that I could not enter into a serious collaborative and evaluative discussion with this student. As I recall, I comforted myself in a quasi-colonial fashion that she would be in interaction with others within her similar context and the truth would emerge as the team she worked with sorted out the best practices and approaches to Catholic Social Teaching in their part of the world.

The value of that moment, that memory, and an inadequate response is the real focus of this volume. Her direct question occasioned a deeper reflection on culture, the Catholic Church, and the role of CST in addressing varying cultural and geographical contexts. When our students return to their countries, they are a long way from Rome. These graduates are loyal Catholics who are trying to transform their Roman educational experience into capital for their homelands. The gift they have received they wish to give. But they wish to frame this educational gift within their local and national contexts. Their challenge is to discover the meaning of application of CST within their cultural situation. This is their desire, their hope. They are receiving the call to action challenge of Paul VI in his 1971 apostolic letter *(Octogesima Adveniens)*. That is, they desire to examine these social teachings of the church within their own cultural context.

As the second in this new series on the social teaching of the Catholic Church, this volume hopes to provide a stimulus for conversations in various geographical and cultural contexts.[2] The question put to the authors of this work was: How can you reflect on your particular continent and its "culture" in order to best apply—including strategies and methodologies if appropriate—CST in your area of the world? Part of this challenge might be how your culture can best understand CST and what might be the best approach to apply CST in your particular cultural understandings. The authors were asked not to focus on one particular document but to apply the principles of CST to their nation or area of the world and to tease out how their culture might best understand, act on, and accomplish such applied understandings. What follows is the result of that request and challenge. The latitude given in the question is also attended to in the various responses. The authors focused their presentations in different ways, and it is precisely this richness that gives us a glimpse into more global considerations worth thinking about as church. My fear was that I would have to somehow justify looking at more narrow worlds, and this would return readers to a less global reflection. What in fact emerged was a much more expansive understanding of various cultures alongside the profound gift that CST offers this world. What also emerges is a challenge to see the real invitation of globalization within an expanding notion of culture. In these essays we move beyond ideas of isolated nations to examining spheres of local and global influence and some new insights about how CST has a decidedly global appeal. Focused reflection on the aspirations of this treasury of the church can be realized in different cultures when local application moves alongside, is influenced by, and may indeed bring something to these church teachings. The effect can be significant in places where Christianity is a minority; it also can be re-understood and revitalized in places traditionally Christian and Catholic. In this way we see a new engagement with the church's teachings on justice when embraced at the local and international levels.

Another question emerged in the process of reflecting on my student's question. In what ways might we need to think about justice, in what ways might we need to expand our ideas of justice, and in what ways might we need to include more in our notions of justice as we reflect on a more global world? In wanting to understand those questions more precisely and to focus these more squarely, for example, I asked Tom Hughson to lend his help, and a resulting essay challenges us to think in more comprehensive categories and with greater precision about the nature and meaning of social justice and the common good in relation to culture. His reflection on this issue offers a most interesting invitation to consider the role of what Bernard

Lonergan and Robert Doran have called the reflexive dimension of culture in reference to CST, a perspective open to various international and cultural contexts. His decidedly inclusive understanding of justice and the common good can speak not only to different cultures but to the integrated habits possible in reflexive culture. His reflection moves beyond an analysis that often remained simply critical of globalizing economies and technology, and a certain type of ethic that can be so particularized as to be isolating. What, we can ask anew, does social justice mean during the new infancy experiences of this more interconnected world? What might it mean to consider theoretical understandings about culture and justice in applying CST in so many differing contexts? Hughson proposes that these ideas cannot be considered or conceived within only one cultural context and that CST cannot be complete in any context apart from further consideration of culture, especially reflexive culture.

This volume comes at an interesting time. In November 2009 *Primo Rapporto sulla Dottrina Sociale della Chiesa nel mondo (First Report on the Social Teaching of the Church in the World)* was published, while the present volume was under way.[3] The *Primo Rapporto* provides an overview on what, where, and how Catholic Social Teaching is being applied on five continents. It gives information and an orientation to what is happening with CST on the global stage. It provides interesting reading and a global update on continents, their struggles, and where CST brings real challenges to world cultures. The *Primo Rapporto* can easily be read alongside this work and offers its own contribution of information to all people interested in justice in the framework of Catholic faith.

When reading this volume, it is helpful to remember some very basic ideas that arose in conversation with contributors Sandie Cornish and David Freeman. They rightly pointed out that Catholic Social Teaching develops through dialogue with the people, places, and events of history. It is not a purely abstract and theoretical discipline, but rather part of applied moral theology. It calls for attentiveness to the movement of the Spirit in the world and responsiveness to the signs of the times. Everything has the potential to reveal something of God to us, and so we pay careful attention to reality, including our social, cultural, and political reality. In framing this, they pointed out that CST at the international level has historically been grounded primarily in Western European experience. Its development as a useful guide for action in our globalized world demands more than ever that greater attention be paid to the full range and diversity of human experiences. To do less would seem to suggest, at least implicitly, that God is active only in certain experiences, or that some peoples and places count more than others.

Perennial principles in applying the word of God to social problems may take root in and be expressed through every culture, and each such particular experience can enhance humanity's understanding both of reality and of God's call to us through it. Reflecting on how CST has been understood in each continent, how it has guided action, and how the local teachings have evolved can thus provide insights that are useful beyond one specific context. Each continent's thought and action can likewise be enriched by reflection on experiences from other local contexts.

The original plan was to have this volume represent a functionally global world by including a chapter from each of the following continents or cultural spheres of influence: Africa, Asia, Australia, Western and Eastern Europe, India, North America and Latin America (the latter including all countries south of the United States). For a variety of reasons, it is hoped that the chapters from highly significant Eastern European and Latin American contexts can be included in a later volume under another rubric. For the time being, the documents issued in September 1968 by the Conference of Latin American Bishops at Medellín, Colombia, still seem worth consideration for their richness. The fifth General Conference of the Latin American and Caribbean Bishops (CELAM), which met in Aparecida, Brazil, in 2007, likewise brought forth a rich examination of social truth built on the Medellín sense of consciousness both social and magisterial. Continuing these traditions can frame new discussions about Latin America and application of CST. In

Eastern Europe the Ukrainian Catholic University in Lviv is very active. Its Institute of Religion and Society formally seeks to work as a mediator between secular and religious viewpoints. In particular, the institute engages in dialogue that will help any number of social institutions learn from the experience of the Catholic Church, in particular from CST. The institute's approach and documents can be mined for a context emerging out of the former Communist bloc.

The chapters are presented in alpha-geographical order after a perspectival chapter by Thomas Hughson, SJ, as follows:

Africa: David Kaulemu posits a relational question about politics, economy, and culture that proclaims respect for life in African culture and in the principles of CST. He brings together a discussion on the spiritual, cultural, and moral crises facing Africa and suggests how CST could be critical in finding a solution to them. In particular, CST carries the insight that can universalize common values and move Africa away from provincialism to a more universal and integrative sense of values in its cultural and moral experience. He suggests how to build this integration and how this transformation might be accomplished.

Australia: Sandie Cornish and David Freeman provide an account of CST in Australia, the only continent that doubles as a single country. They identify the paradox of the simultaneous presence and absence of CST within the soul of Australian Catholicism and Australian public life. CST is acknowledged by most church leaders—ordained and lay—as integral rather than discretionary for the practice of the faith, and core precepts of CST can be detected leaking into key Federal Parliamentary debates. Yet CST remains profoundly marginal within the lives and intellectual universe of many Catholic laypeople, however noble and tirelessly generous to others they may be. Cornish and Freeman identify some of Australia's principal CST turning points of the past three decades, developments that indicate both the problems and solutions that frame the present and provide intimations of new possibilities. Their brief digest of hope-filled signs of the times includes the details of two contemporary responses to new subjectivity, the Jesuits' Faith Doing Justice website in Sydney, and the Edmund Rice Institute for Social Justice in Fremantle, Western Australia. **East Asia: Agnes M. Brazal** presents a sustained reflection on the idea of harmony as it emerges in East Asian culture and as it is incorporated into the First Bishops' Institute for Interreligious Affairs on the Theology of Dialogue. In broad outline this harmony carries a sense of the intellectual and the affective, the religious and artistic, the personal and societal. The themes of solidarity, the common good, justice, collaboration, balance—all are treated, and she builds her arguments for an integrated world in the challenges of care for the earth, facing dualities, the prophetic dimension of Christianity in East Asia, and the preferential option for the poor. As in all searches for harmony, she ends with a challenge to the twin dimensions of this world: the personal and the structural.

Europe (Western): Johan Verstraeten enters the world of Catholic Social Teaching from a Western European perspective. There are fundamental long-term issues that need addressing in Western Europe, especially the economy and technology. With these as important social and cultural issues, he argues for a methodology requiring a reading of the signs of the times. But this must be done in such a way that these social issues and their resultant associations in culture touch the history, meaning, and implications of CST. He argues for an integration of the influence of the Catholic Church's official social teaching on the European context and points out the influence that the "organic model" has had in generating a dialogic conversation between culture and the church's teaching. It is here that the dynamic of culture and CST is reflexive, effective, but not without difficulties. No longer wielding direct influence on the political worlds and government intervention, where can the church be a voice? His insight is most helpful in calling Europe to rediscover church teaching in the midst of its contemporary social challenges.

India: Joseph (Jeewendra) Jadhav deals with how the social teaching of the church could be practically applied in the field. The methodology of the social teaching of the church encompassing the principles of see-judge-act is followed. This methodology is applied in the rural district of Ahemadnagar in the state of Maharashtra, India, where 80 percent of the population is involved in agricultural activities and remains in these rural villages close to or on their own farms. The author himself was involved in implementing the social teaching of the church in this context. The techniques are based on the judicial utilization, conservation, and regeneration of natural resources, keeping in mind the concerns of the church. At a time of rising concerns regarding personal and political responsibility for protecting the environment, his application is a compelling example. This methodology for Comprehensive Watershed Development was developed after much trial and error. This methodology has been implemented successfully for the overall development of the peoples and is an example for possible replication in similar circumstances. It is an application based on the multiplier effect of Catholic Social Teaching.

North America: John Coleman, SJ, examines Canada and the United States for some of the cultural components he indicates are important in discussing applied approaches to Catholic Social Teaching. Demonstrating the historical importance of such areas as the political and legal arenas and the ways these have provided grist for some direct applications of CST in North America, he shows how the process of applying these teachings of the church in the practical circumstances have provided a particularly North American stamp to CST. He studies a variety of differing cultural approaches in the United States and Canada and assesses the similar-dissimilar historical and contemporary geographical needs alongside the variety of adaptations of CST in North America. After a deft presentation of historical applications within these two cultural approaches, he moves on to new horizons for applying these documents in the present social and cultural context: grassroots groups, political groups, and education groups. He points out what these groups are doing and how their methods can aid the further development and application of CST.

Notes

[1] See Joe Holland and Peter Henriot, SJ, *Social Analysis: Linking Faith and Justice* (Maryknoll, NY: Orbis Books, 1983).

[2] The first volume, *The Social Teaching of the Church: Some Global Challenges*, was published in Italian as *Dottrina Sociale della Chiesa: alcune sfide globali* (Naples: Il Pozzo di Giacobbe, 2010).

[3] *Primo Rapporto*, ed. Giampaolo Crepaldi and Stefano Fontana (Siena: Edizioni Cantagalli s.r.l., 2009).

Contributors

Agnes M. Brazal is president of DaKaTeo (Catholic Theological Society of the Philippines), past coordinator of the Ecclesia of Women in Asia, and professor of Maryhill School of Theology. She co-edited the anthologies *Transformative Theological Ethics: East Asian Contexts* (2010), *Faith on the Move: Toward a Theology of Migration in Asia* (2008), and *Body and Sexuality: Theological-Pastoral Perspectives of Women in Asia* (2007) (finalist, 27th National Book Award for Theology and Religion). She obtained her licentiate and doctorate in sacred theology at the Katholieke Universiteit Leuven.

John A. Coleman, SJ, a sociologist and ethicist, was for many years the Charles Casassa Professor of Social Values at Loyola Marymount University, Los Angeles. Coleman is the author of *An American Strategic Theology* (1982), *One Hundred Years of Catholic Social Teaching* (1991), *Globalization and Catholic Social Thought* (2005) and *Christian Political Ethics* (2007).

Sandie Cornish works with the Australian Jesuits in research, policy, planning, and formation for their social ministries, and leads the web-based Faith Doing Justice project. She teaches occasionally in the fields of missiology and social ethics with member institutes of the Sydney College of Divinity. She played a significant role in each of the major research and consultation activities of the Australian Bishops' Committee for Justice, Development, and Peace during the late 1980s and 1990s, and has held the positions of national executive officer of the Australian Catholic Social Justice Council and coordinator of the Hong Kong–based Asian Centre for the Progress of Peoples.

David Freeman is director of the Edmund Rice Institute for Social Justice in Fremantle, Western Australia. The institute works across social justice education, research, advocacy and solidarity work. Freeman is a Councillor of the Australian Catholic Social Justice Council, the advisory body to the Australian Catholic Bishops Conference. Freeman's formative intellectual influences are Catholic social teaching, the social sciences, and the Jocist see-judge-act method. He was formerly Australian president of the Young Christian Students movement and a Praesidium member of its World Council. He has taught Catholic Social Teaching in the masters' program at the University of Notre Dame Australia, and sociology and/or political science at Murdoch, Melbourne, and La Trobe universities and Ormond College. He has been a Fulbright Scholar and visiting fellow at Harvard University.

Thomas Hughson, SJ, director of graduate studies in the Department of Theology at Marquette University, served as religious superior and acting dean at the Pontifical Biblical Institute-Jerusalem 1986–1989. Recent publications include "Interpreting Vatican II: 'A New Pentecost,'" *Theological Studies* (March 2008), and "From a Systematics of History to Communications: Transition, Difference, Options," in *Meaning and History in Systematic Theology: Essays in Honor of Robert M. Doran, SJ* (2009). "Social Justice in Lactantius's *Divine Institutes*: An Exploration" is forthcoming in a Leuven Institute for Catholic Social Thought volume. A monograph appropriating classical Christology as a resource for Catholic social thought is under way.

Joseph (Jeewendra) Jadhav, SJ, is a professor in Catholic social teaching on the Faculty of Social Sciences at the Pontifical Gregorian University in Rome. He has studied psychology and social work with a specialization in rural development at the Centre for Studies and Research Development of Ahemadnagar College of Pune University. He worked in social development activities and as a field officer and promoter for the Social Centre Ahemadnagar. He was a consultant for the Watershed

Development Programs and regional promoter for the Indo-German Watershed Development Program for Nashik District in Maharashtra from 1991 to 1997.

David Kaulemu is the regional coordinator for eastern and southern Africa of the African Forum for Catholic Social Teaching (AFCAST). Before taking up this post, he was a lecturer of philosophy and chair of the Department of Religious Studies, Classics, and Philosophy at the University of Zimbabwe. He has taught, researched, facilitated workshops, and published on social ethics, development, and Christian social teaching. He has been an international visiting scholar at the Department of Philosophy of the University of Aberdeen, the Woodstock Theological Center at Georgetown University, and the Council for Research in Values and Philosophy at the Catholic University of America.

Johan Verstraeten holds a PhD in religious studies from the Catholic University of Leuven (Belgium), where he is currently professor of social ethics and director of the Centre for Catholic Social Thought at the Faculty of Theology. He has been director of the Centre for Ethics at that university (1990–2000), and director and chair of the European Ethics Network (1996–2002). He serves on the editorial boards of *Business Ethics: A European Review*, *The Journal of Catholic Social Thought* and *Ethical Perspectives*. He publishes primarily on Catholic social thought and on leadership. He co-edited *Catholic Social Thought: Twilight or Renaissance* (2000) and *Scrutinizing the Signs of the Times in the Light of the Gospel* (2005).

Acronyms and Abbreviations

ACR	Australian Catholic Relief (became Caritas Australia)
ACSJC	Australian Catholic Social Justice Council
ACU	Australian Catholic University
AFCAST	African Forum for Catholic Social Teaching
AMECEA	Association of Member Episcopal Conferences in Eastern Africa
APRM	African Peer Review Mechanism
AU	African Union
BCJDEP	Bishops' Committee for Justice, Development, Ecology and Peace (Australia); originally the BCJDP
BCJDP	Bishops' Committee for Justice, Development, and Peace (Australia)
BECs	basic ecclesial communities
BIRA	Bishops' Institute for Interreligious Affairs
CCJP	Catholic Commission for Justice and Peace (Australia)
COMECE	Commission of the Bishops' Conferences of the European Union
CSSA	Catholic Social Services Australia

ERC	Edmund Rice Centre (Sydney)
ERISJ	Edmund Rice Institute for Social Justice, Fremantle
FABC	Federation of Asian Bishops' Conferences
IMBISA	Inter-Regional Meeting of the Bishops of South Africa
MDGs	Millennium Development Goals
NAPCC	National Action Plan on Climate Change
NEPAD	New Partnership for Development
OAU	Organization of African Unity
OPW	Office for the Participation of Women (Australia)
TAC	Theological Advisory Committee (FABC)
UNDA	University of Notre Dame Australia
YCS	Young Christian Students
YCW	Young Christian Workers

1.

Social Justice and *Common Good*

What Are They For?

Thomas Hughson, SJ

> *There is beauty in this world and there are the humiliated.*
> *We must strive, as difficult as it may be, not to be unfaithful*
> *to either one.*
>
> —ALBERT CAMUS (PARAPHRASE)

Are the categories *social justice* and *common good* an untroubled heritage or an obsolete disadvantage for the development of CST?[1] Does their silence on culture weaken them in the face of postmodern circumstances bringing the importance of cultures to the fore? Would an alternative formula such as *sociocultural justice* be preferable because it indicates a link with culture and more clearly implies a common good inclusive of a cultural dimension in and beyond social, economic, and political structures? Are they permanent, immobile residents in the lexicon of CST? Is there room in CST for conceiving and formulating the significance of culture in and for a just social order?

Inquiry toward an answer will focus on a specific set of documents. The documents make up the literature of official papal and episcopal CST (collected in a volume such as O'Brien and Shannon's *Catholic Social Thought*), plus subsequent papal encyclicals, statements from episcopal conferences, and the synchronic *Compendium of the Social Doctrine of the Church*.[2] The aim is not an encyclopedic survey of documents or a distillation of what can be proposed as basic themes but rather raising a plausible hypothesis about a missing element in CST.

Testing basic terms and concepts in a given field of discourse can be fruitful for more reasons than conceptual precision that improves verbal definitions. In this case, problematizing the language and conceptuality of social justice and the common good looks to their relationship with culture. Is there a link between the concepts of a common good owed to Aquinas and renewed after Leo XIII's *Aeterni Patris* and ambient cultures? Broaching this topic presupposes that almost eighty years of usage since *Quadragesimo Anno* have not so woven the language of social justice into CST that entertaining possible revision threatens to unravel the whole fabric.

Terms at Issue

In 1931 social justice was new to papal social teaching but had already appeared in the mid-nineteenth century from theologian Luigi Taparelli D'Azeglio.[3] In 1937 Pius XI clarified social justice in *Divini Redemptoris* as pertaining, first of all, to the economic order. Each individual, whether employer or worker, had an obligation to contribute to a common good in the economic realm. But making a contribution depended on the prior fact that, as Pius XI put it, "each individual in the dignity of his human personality is supplied with all that is necessary for the exercise of his social functions" (*Divini Redemptoris*, no. 51). The wealthy and powerful had means at their disposal that equipped them for "exercise of . . . social functions." So emphasis fell on what would bring about conditions—a just wage, lessening unemployment, decent working conditions, freedom to organize, reform or transformation of the economy to insure a proportionate redistribution of wealth—enabling workers to exercise their social functions.

Social justice adapted Aquinas's idea of general justice, also called legal justice insofar as laws promote it, to modern conditions. General justice concerned obligations to the common good of society incumbent on its individual members: "The virtue of a good citizen is general justice, whereby the person is directed to the common good."[4] General or legal justice was about people's actions in relation to a common good, not just to each individual's good. What is the common good? According to *Gaudium et Spes*, the common good "embraces the sum of those conditions of social life by which individuals, families, and groups can achieve their own fulfillment in a relatively thorough and ready way" (no. 74). Contributing to and benefiting from these "conditions of social life" is a matter of general or social justice, which, like any kind of justice, is other directed.[5] An orientation beyond an individual, family, or group to the common good can be immanent in all manner of virtuous acts, including distributive and commutative justice.[6] Social justice, then, has the first and defining aspect of being an active contribution to the common good of temporal society.[7]

Why disturb this language? Identifying the provenance of the question will clarify the direction of the reflection. Asking about the longevity of categories stems from commitment to CST and to a Christian social agenda. The question does not express aversion to movements, ideas, labors, initiatives, organizations, and people inside and outside the church seeking social justice. Far from it and to the contrary. Stating admiration for Scandinavian social democracies and for a social approach to democracy in Germany and France can prevent confusion between interrogating standard items in the vocabulary of CST and a retrograde resistance to the meanings and referents of social justice and common good. Still, why interrogate those items? Are they not doing just fine? Do they not stand more in need of popular communication, explanation, reception, and application than of theoretical reexamination? From what specific grounds does an interrogation arise?

The starting point for a sense of something problematic, some doubts about the advisability of sustaining the language of *social justice* and the *common good*, was conversation with two eminent professors. Both John Atherton, emeritus from the Department of Religions and Theology at the University of Manchester and former Canon Theologian of Manchester Cathedral, and George Newlands, emeritus dean of the Faculty of Divinity at the University of Glasgow, wondered, each in a distinct way and for different reasons, about a modern Christian social agenda continually formulated in the familiar vocabulary of social justice and common good.

Professor Newlands wasn't sure about social justice and the common good as an axis for a wide, ecumenical social agenda. Instead, it might be more productive for theological reflection, in systematics too and not only in social ethics, to make a turn to human rights. The human rights agenda invites consensus across the churches, fosters dialogue with non-theological disciplines, and grounds cooperation between Christian and other groups dedicated to human rights. Systematic theology, in addition to Christian social ethic, can enrich Christian commitment to human rights by expounding how human rights involve Christology and theological anthropology as premises. A turn to human rights can give new life and new language to a fatigued social justice agenda.[8]

Two themes threaded through Professor Atherton's doubts about *social justice* and the *common good*."[9] One, taking account of Manchester as the epicenter of the Industrial Revolution, and within a framework of critical analysis of defects in capitalism and a proposal for transforming them, was a distancing from insufficient admission, whether by Britain's old and new Labor Party or by Christians committed to social justice, of material benefits from capitalism. The other was concern about dangers to minorities in advocating the common good as a basic principle in a pluralistic society. Atherton shares this misgiving with Iris Marion Young, and both are close but not identical to John Rawls's liberal critique of a common good to which John Coleman has responded.[10]

The two professors' friendly doubts interrupted social justice language for a project I tentatively had titled "Christ and

Social Justice." Their unexpected views were welcome. They planted an interesting doubt. Eventually the question detached from the conversations and took on a life of its own, so that I am not seeking to reconstruct their views in order to reply to them but to answer a question they stimulated.

Once embarked on reconsidering the language of CST, another problem surfaced. *Social justice* had connotations in CST that it lacked when a topic for philosophy and the social sciences. When the same terms mean different things in two different realms of discourse, equivocation occurs and communication fails. David Miller states, "In the writings of most contemporary political philosophers, social justice is regarded as an aspect of distributive justice."[11] The editors of a recent, valuable anthology observe that "issues of social justice, in the broadest sense, arise when decisions affect the distribution of benefits and burdens between different individuals or groups."[12] To be sure, benefits and burdens go beyond the economics into society and the political order.

CST has a concept of social justice broader and subtler in several respects. CST does not simply incorporate the results of one or another academic discipline because it looks to what can be called the overall health of a society. Social health—whether flourishing or declining, serving its people well or ill—depends on a loosely coordinated but interrelated functioning of social, economic, cultural, religious, and political institutions. John Rawls called these the "major institutions" of a society, and designated their cumulative interaction the "basic structure" of a society.[13] Social health is a society's basic structure in a condition of flourishing, gauged by the well-being of the most vulnerable, marginalized, and poor. The criteria and processes of distribution are at stake as well as the quality of the outcome in terms of the dignity and flourishing of the person.

Finally, faith keeps the virtue of social justice with reference not only to moral values, norms, actions, virtues, and a just social order, but also to human dignity and the meaning of the human. And as with the whole of morality, faith locates social justice within the divine/human relationship. In fidelity to the divine/human relationship, CST keeps conscience and knowledge accountable to God, revelation, and lived faith in full respect for the human and civil right to religious liberty. Religious liberty matters because in a pluralist society not all accept a tie between religion and social justice.[14]

Clearly, *common good* and *social justice* carry important, defensible content that can be put into dialogue with other usages. However, interdisciplinary dialogue, dialogue among religious groups, and entry by faith-based groups into public life all would benefit from maximum clarity and agreement on terminology. The fact of different meanings in different discourses raises a question about formulation. Are the terms *social justice* and *common good* commonly understood in their variant meanings in different kinds of discourse? Might it be advisable and productive to find substitutes for these terms that could travel across discourses more easily? Pius IX had no qualms about leaving behind Aquinas's "general justice" by introducing "social justice."

From these several kinds of misgivings emerges a larger problematic that goes beyond the language of CST. Has CST taken adequate account of cultural context generally, and in particular has CST opened its invaluable content to theories and understandings of culture? For the sake of discussion, then, I propose that *social justice* and the *common good* be put into the position of being under reexamination to see whether they helpfully meet new conditions. A maximum or a minimum outcome is possible. A maximum conclusion will be to modify, revise, or abandon the language of social justice and common good. A minimal conclusion will be to retain the familiar language with new insistence on its inseparability from culture.

Public Theology

Of course, political and liberation theologies already have coined new descriptive and normative languages for much of what CST promotes under headings of social justice and common good.

And yet, beside liberation and political theologies another ecumenically potent current of social theology has emerged, a descendant of practical theology called public theology.[15] Public theology has absorbed an option for the poor from liberation theology and engages in socio-critical analysis somewhat in line with political theology,[16] and like them, public theology too considers privatized religion an unacceptable status quo. Public theology also typically proceeds on the principle of a conditional, critical, continually examined grant of legitimacy to both democracy and capitalism.[17] Its goal is authentic and effective Christian participation in a democratic polity in the situation of a predominantly middle-class economy.

Contrarily, two schools of thought, Radical Orthodoxy, associated with John Milbank, and perspectives championed by Stanley Hauerwas, object strenuously to any such grant of legitimacy to modern nation-states and so renounce public theology. The critique extends all the way to protesting the distinction and priority of civil society to the state. William T. Cavanaugh from the Hauerwas school abhors the fact that "'political theology' and 'public theology' have assumed the legitimacy of the separation of the state from civil society, and tried to situate the Church as one more interest group within civil society."[18] This line of thought has something but not everything to contribute in dialectical tension with public-theological endorsing of, for example, laws, institutions, and policies protective of the human and civil right to liberty in matters of religion, and with seeking the reform not the eradication of capitalism.

Kenneth and Michael Himes quote David Hollenbach's well-received statement that public theology represents an "effort to discover and communicate the socially significant meanings of Christian symbols and tradition" in the form of "theological reflection which examines the resources latent within the Christian tradition for understanding the church's public role."[19] In succinct fashion the Himeses confirm that "public theology wants to bring the wisdom of the Christian tradition into public conversation to contribute to the well-being of the society."[20]

"Public theology," states Lutheran theologian Robert Benne, "refers . . . to the *engagement* of a living religious tradition with its public environment—the economic, political, and cultural spheres of our common life."[21] Benne explains that a religious tradition's knowledge "*interprets* the public world in the light of the religious tradition. It may be used to persuade the world of the cogency of its vision of how things ought to be in the public spheres of life."[22] "An important way in which churches (as distinguished from individual bishops, pastors and lay leaders) engage in public theology is by publishing or in some other manner communicating their distinctive, official positions on public matters."[23]

CST, irreducible to social ethics, belongs to this mode of public theology by which a church tradition interprets the public world. Contrarily, Benne as an individual academic theologian puts the highest priority not on church teaching about public matters but on individuals forming their own personal responses instructed by participation in word and sacrament without reference to official statements, public positions, and policies such as CST.

Theologians have taken up public theology in reference to facts, interpretations, practices, and theories that start at regional levels yet have a scope that opens to national and international realities.[24] The concerns of public theology in the modes of both church teaching and academic theology inspire the ensuing discussion of CST. It has to be admitted that only a few efforts in academic public theology have addressed the reality of cultures.[25] By and large, public theology from individual theologians no less than CST has focused on social practice.

Critical review of social justice and common good with an eye to culture will be an indispensable consideration for CST on one condition. That condition has to do with emergent realizations of how economic, political, and social structures involve a people's culture.[26] Insofar as the traditional social question on the ground has been changing in the direction of a higher priority for culture, to that extent CST has to take greater theoretical account of culture, even to the point of reexamining familiar CST vocabulary.

Though not the only factor raising the profile of culture, thought about economic globalization involves practical and theoretical attention to many cultures touched by globalization. Globalization, a topic on the agenda of CST, stirs an interest in cultures insofar as mobility of capital, technology, labor, and ideals affects local mores, traditional relationships, and world views.[27] I agree with Kenneth Himes that to counteract a false universalism built into globalization CST must "shift its focus: whereas in the past CST had been primarily directed at issues of economics and secondarily of politics, the new context of globalization will force the tradition more to issues of culture and identity."[28] At the same time, I do not think the issue of culture can be tied to the question of cultural identity for persons, groups, or a society except on the premise that identity can be mixed, and need not be "pure."

Then too, pluralist societies increasingly pose the problem of some members, groups, or nations that are being excluded from access to full participation in economic and political life because cultural differences predefine and pre-position them as marginalized, as second-class citizens. Benedict XVI's *Caritas in Veritate* speaks about international development facing "the prospect of a world in need of profound cultural renewal" (no. 21) and recognizes that there are "immaterial or cultural causes of development and underdevelopment" (no. 22).

Marginalization also flows from racism. Postulating several races distinguished by skin color and a few facial features is a cultural habit of perception, not biological, genetic fact. Racism is a cultural bias that blocks full access to participation in social, economic, and political life.[29] A society cannot then receive the contribution from a racial minority to economic and political life. But access to an economy and to citizenship does not necessarily eradicate racism, because racism infects a culture first of all. Overcoming assignment of some members of a society to second-class citizenship because of perceived cultural apprehension of racial differences involves changes in culture, not just adjustments in economic, social, and political institutions. The Pontifical Council of Justice and Peace adverts to a cultural dimension in racism in referring to a partial remedy, education that belongs to the realm of culture.[30] May it not be timely to think about revising or moving beyond social justice and the common good as if they were separate from cultures? One alternative, without discarding distinctions among the economy, social cohesion, and political institutions, is to envision a flourishing culture as part of the goal for which a just social order exists. Culture is that for whose sake social justice is sought. A just social order is the means, a people flourishing in their cultural activities is the end.[31] Beginning in prayerful gratitude for CST supports projecting a possible line of its development. Comparison of that possibility with postconciliar CST begets ideas and judgments with a critical edge. Critical is not hostile. Nonetheless, respect for transparency advises setting forth a guiding hermeneutical principle.

From Above or from Below?

CST has drawn upon scripture, tradition, reason, and historical experience in developing an ongoing, faith-based response to the modern "social question" broadly understood. Paul Misner and Marvin Krier Mich, among others, have detailed the historically knowable contribution of a multitude of local pastoral and lay initiatives to the emergence of CST, at least since *Rerum Novarum*.[32] As Lonergan observes, the good is always concrete. I infer that this means the social good is also local, grassroots, historically situated, and if formulated, then in a given language. Like the good and the social good, so too suffering is always concrete, in all people to some extent, yet at times more grievous in some individuals and groups with names and addresses. Not surprisingly, then, "social Catholicism" has taken its rise in response to human suffering of various kinds and has generated organized local lay and pastoral initiatives in the church's grassroots.

Consequently, there is reason to agree with John Coleman in approving Gordon Zahn's proposal that the official writings of

CST, including postconciliar CST, be read "from below" as responses to prior Catholic social movements, and I would add again, as responses to peoples' suffering, which evoked the movements in the first place.[33] Yet, and noting Coleman's refusal to dismiss CST,[34] there also is reason to think that CST documents published "from above," besides whatever original theoretical or pastoral thought they add to content "from below," also contain three new meanings that have to do less with how CST comes about than with its role and impact in the church.[35] Supposing the extreme that all content in CST came from prior social movements so that papal and episcopal CST simply ratified material "from below," even then the three new meanings would justify reading CST "from above" as well as "from below."

One new dimension of meaning has to do with further testing of various local, regional, or national movements against the background of the whole international church seen "from above" and in light of a practical tie to the tradition of apostolic authority. Official approval of ideas and practical orientations originating "from below" lends increased credibility to their positive connection with the word of God, the Holy Spirit, scripture, tradition, and reason. Papal and episcopal CST, not always a main source of new ideas, exercises a maximum degree of responsibility for conserving the heritage of gospel faith and ecclesial structures so that what survives testing can be widely and confidently received throughout the church as valid appropriation and application of scripture and tradition.

Somewhat similarly, during Vatican II the worldwide episcopacy as well as popes John XXIII and Paul VI tested and approved the direction of liturgical, biblical, and lay apostolic renewals already under way. Conciliar debates and votes of approval for the documents incorporated some already developed theological themes. The prior initiatives and theological perspectives thereby came onto a new level of authorization "from above" that approximated (at least in principle) a panoptic appreciation for insights arising in many local churches, peoples, nations, languages, cultural contexts, and emergent situations in the whole, international church. The episcopate and the Petrine office carried out what is a little like an official (from above) substantiating of what (from below) had been a strong working hypothesis.

What also accrues to content received "from below" is participation in what Bernard Lonergan designated an "effective function of meaning."[36] The sources of meaning are all conscious acts and their intended contents, both transcendental and categorical. Meaning is often associated with symbols and interpretations, ideas and definitions, values and decisions, truths and history. Lonergan distinguishes an effective from a cognitive function of meaning. Effective meaning is operative not explanatory; it is not primarily a grasp of intelligibility, a judgment of truth, or an appreciation of a good.

Effective meaning resides in intelligent directives, commands, persuasion, and coordination of human activities whether, for example, by CEOs and shift foremen of mining companies, political leaders at all levels, producers and directors of films and plays, the chief engineer on a construction project, or the pilot of an airliner. Authorized directives guide cooperative actions toward agreed purposes not attainable without coordinated activity by many individuals. The communication of directives does not occur in grunts and idiosyncratic gestures but in words and physical expressions functioning as carriers of common meaning that function toward producing economic, civic, and political effects from human work. Work is "meaning-full" activity. There is meaning apart from theory, proposition, and definition.

An emergency situation illuminates the distinction between cognitive and effective functions of meaning. The captain of a fire brigade on the scene of a blazing apartment house coordinates and directs actions among trained firefighters toward the socially agreed, foreknown purposes of saving lives and extinguishing the conflagration. Without exercise of directive authority by the on-site captain, each firefighter could well act according to a different plan, or none, for rescuing the residents and fighting the fire. Under pressures of time, seeking a consensus or a multiplicity of uncoordinated efforts would spell disaster. So there has to be someone in charge to coordinate the whole effort. The captain is the one who strategizes and deploys the resources. The resources include technology. Now the captain may or may not grasp the physics and chemistry in the diffusion of heated gases and the rates of oxidation in various building materials. The degree of scientific comprehension will not matter apart from training and experience. It is enough that the captain knows how to put personnel and material resources to the best use. That too belongs to cognitive meaning. The act of communicating directives and work carried out according to them are meaning in a primarily effective function that manifests practical intelligence. Putting theoretical and practical cognitive meaning to work invests communicating directives and the work with effective meaning. Communicating the directives and the work are meaningful human activities whose full intelligibility does not reduce to prior ingredients. Meaning functions effectively in the captain's communicating of directives and in the organized activities they guide.

By analogy, CST receives prior content "from below," like the fire captain's prior theoretical and practical knowledge from sources beyond himself. When CST subsumes and communicates preexisting content in publication "from above," then the ideas and practical orientations "from below" are drawn into an effective function of meaning apart from any new cognitive meaning a pope or his writing assistant may add, which again may be substantial. The summing up, arranging, and communicating of content "from below" invests it with new effective meaning. It has become meaning operative in an authoritative guiding influence, somewhat like effective meaning in a fire captain's communication to fire fighters directing and coordinating their efforts. Content that had been cognitive and locally effective meaning enters into an internationally effective function of meaning.

Now, adding an effective function of meaning in CST to papal verification of authenticity to Christian sources results in a reevaluation of supposing an antagonism defines the difference between reading "from above" and "from below." Instead, neither vantage point excludes the other. They differ and generate varying perspectives but are not locked into irreconcilable conflict. They can be conceived as two interpretative perspectives on CST derived from differing positions within the church as institution. Tension, not contradiction, characterizes their co-possibility as situated modes of attention to CST. A dialectic obtains not a synthesis but contraries able to be complementary. Reading from both vantage points sets in motion an interaction between local or regional origins "from below" and international reception of CST "from above."

CST and Culture

Arguably theology is undergoing a turn to culture.[37] To what has theology been turning? What, that is, has CST been ignoring? A definition of culture represents an option among alternatives. The church at Vatican II, the academy, and individual theologians have jettisoned a classicist ideal of culture as one timeless universal achievement in the Christian West that serves as a normative gauge for degrees of human realization by which to measure all other societies and cultures in all eras and places. In this view the evolved West is the future of all peoples, the end of their progress and the end of histories. That ideal and definition are no longer an option for the church, CST, or theology.

By contrast, a typically modern or empirical idea of culture comes from anthropology, has footings in observation and research, differentiates culture from nature, sees a culture as humanly constructed, varying from one bounded social group to another, embracing the totality of a group's way of life, and shaping members of that group. A culture is a synchronic, unitary whole of interrelated parts guided by the "meaning dimension of social life" that forms social behaviors and produces a social order on the basis of "a community of meaning."[38] Staking no claim to the universal normativity of any culture, yet presupposing a common humanity able to be disengaged from the weight of a heritage or tradition,[39] this idea is an option. At Vatican II the church made an option for this ideal and definition. The option was not out of the blue. Sporadic remote preparation took place in the form of new insights on evangelizing. For example, a 1659 directive from the Congregation for the Propagation of the Faith had urged bishops in China not to import France, Spain, or Italy, just the faith.[40] That appreciation of a difference between faith and a European nation's reception of it broadened to become the principle of not identifying the gospel with Western cultures. The eighteenth-century distinction and ensuing practices opened a Western door to the spiritual giftedness of non-Western cultures and religions, eventually evident in Vatican II's *Nostra Aetate.*

More proximate to Vatican II, Allen Figueroa Deck points out, popes from Leo XIII to Pius XII were the very portals through which an anthropological concept of culture entered Catholic social thought.[41] Vatican II firmly held to a modern idea of culture. For instance, *Gaudium et Spes* commented that in cultures, "different styles of living and different scales of values originate in different ways of using things, of working and self-expression, of practicing religion and of behavior, of developing science and the arts, and of cultivating beauty" (no. 53). Figueroa Deck judges that Vatican II made an anthropological concept of culture the "integrating or architectonic principle for understanding the church's mission and social teaching today."[42] Paul VI's *Evangelii Nuntiandi* and John Paul II's *Redemptoris Missio*, as well as postconciliar theologies of mission bear out this assessment.[43] Inculturation of the gospel in each cultural context, in light of a modern idea of culture, became a theological mainstay.

For example, in discussing inculturation Marcello De Carvalho Azevedo exemplifies a postconciliar option for the modern idea of culture. Culture, he states, is "the set of meanings, values, and patterns which underlie the perceptible phenomena of a concrete society, whether they are recognizable on the level of social practice . . . or whether they are carriers of signs, symbols, meanings and representations, conceptions and feelings that consciously or unconsciously pass from generation to generation."[44] Social practice here includes material culture and technology, along with social, economic, and political activities.

His analysis of culture began to go beyond the absence of historical process in the modern idea of culture by describing signs, meanings, feelings, and concepts transmitted from one generation to the next. His idea of culture had merit, and I worked with it in a 1993 discussion of social justice as cultural change.[45] But there are limits to the modern concept of culture, and subsequent critiques have expanded on them to the point of advancing a more complicated, postmodern notion of culture(s) that leaves the theological ideal of inculturation in a condition as problematic as an unqualified modern idea of culture has become.

The modern, anthropological idea of culture was, critiques pointed out, inattentive to historical process; conceived a culture as an unchanging, internally consistent whole; presumed a consensus on it within it; ignored human agency in how a culture was socially regulative; and treated each culture as a self-contained social monad ideally impervious to influences from other cultures.[46] The postmodern anthropological idea complicates the modern idea by closer and more detailed reference to historical processes. In each culture contentious, heterogeneous, decentralized, internally contradictory ideals, meanings, and practices continually shift in degrees of consolidation and interact with other cultures.

Negotiating meanings involves a struggle for power but not necessarily coercion.[47] The personal and social result is that cultural identity has been conceived as a "hybrid, relational affair, something that lives between as much as within cultures."[48] Creoles, exiles, expatriates, and *mestizos/as* become exemplars of this kind of cultural identity.[49] "Pure" identities are not suspect, are not received as necessarily descriptive or normative. Cultural and personal identities can be too solid, too fixed, too complete, over-determined by memories, functioning as negations of others. Postmodern ideas on culture dissolve an assumption that an educated elite can define its culture for everyone, once and for all.[50] Along with suspicion about a clear, solid definition of a "pure" identity in any culture comes respect for sometimes messy, vulgar, often inspired popular culture as a primary zone in which faith and a culture meet.[51]

Analyses

Nevertheless a distinction made by Azevedo and by Lonergan too deserves continued acceptance despite trailing a modern ideal of culture. Each distinguishes two levels or components in a culture. The two levels are not a class-based division between an aristocracy and commoners, *proles* and an elite, but a function-based differentiation. The first level or component consists in people's activities participating in the everyday operation of the main institutions (economy, state, family, schools, and so on) of a society. Azevedo calls these activities "social practice," and I will keep this phrase. Social practice is where social justice does or does not come to personal and public structural realization.

Still, Bernard Lonergan offers an understanding of the second level of a culture better able to understand social justice not only embedded in social practice but also in front of it as a goal. "In front of" means the world projected by affirmation of social justice and the common good, and more broadly by CST. The second level of culture, the reflexive component, lies beyond and in front of attainment of social justice.

Lonergan analyzes culture as the common meanings of a society as a continual resultant from a communicative process that arises in common experience. However, interfering group biases, organized obtuseness, and other obstacles beset the interplay in and between each of these steps so that nothing is automatic. To the contrary, cultural common meanings exist only in a contentious dialectic between progress and decline.[52] Common meanings constitutive of a society are not a fixed, permanent set whose only historical dynamism is to pass from generation to generation. Instead, a culture is common meanings in constant circulation from personal and historical experience of major and minor events that may be celebrated in song, all the way to collective decisions that mark turning points, and then back again to experience, halting often to assimilate whatever historical events (for example, the end of an empire) intervene to challenge common societal self-understandings previously held (for example, Western classicism, non-Western subalternity).

True, Lonergan sometimes describes common meaning as if there is a settled consensus within a group or society and in that respect has a modern idea of culture.[53] However his larger analysis of meaning releases his idea of culture from modern limits. He treats meaning as a dynamic, historically contingent process with plenty of conflicting elements that are fodder for the method of a theological specialty he names *dialectic*. His attention to the complex nature and historically concrete dialectic in the common meaning that constitutes any society's culture gives Lonergan's account affinity with postmodern ideas of culture as a contested, internally diversified process of producing and circulating meanings within any group, society, or subculture.

Like Azevedo, Lonergan divides culture into two elements. The first coincides with Azevedo's "social practice," conceived as sets of common meanings, values, images, commitments, and motives operative in a particular people's ordinary social, economic, political, and technological activities. Lonergan parts company over the second level or component of culture, which does not coincide with Azevedo's "signs, symbols, meanings and representations . . . that pass from generation to generation." Lonergan includes "scientific, scholarly, philosophic and theological understanding of the everyday."[54] This is the reflexive level of culture inhabited by the natural and social sciences, philosophy, humane letters, history, and critical studies of all sorts. Humane learning, the sciences, philosophy, and critical studies of everyday meanings and values occur on the reflexive level. This seems to be the locale of the fine arts too.

Azevedo captures well the difference between social practice and the rest of a folk culture, but his second level of culture does not deal adequately with whatever exceeds folkways or a common-sense heritage. So I will adopt Lonergan's "reflexive culture" as the second level of a culture, keeping Azevedo's "social practice" for the first.

Robert Doran emphasizes interaction between the two levels or components of culture, everyday social practice and reflexive culture.[55] His account of culture proceeds from Lonergan's integral scale of ascending values: vital, social, cultural, personal, religious.[56] Personal, cultural, and social values are realized in a tension between two poles. The personal subject exists and develops in dialectic between the limits of neural exigencies and self-transcendence in modes of intentional consciousness. Culture exists and develops in dialectic between constitutive cosmological and anthropological meanings. Society as community exists and progresses in a dialectical tension between intersubjective spontaneity and the acts and products of practical intelligence. The social order, economy, and political organization of a society come from practical intelligence.

Society's everyday operations, shaped by more and less social and distributive justice in providing conditions within which people can attain vital values (nutrition, clothing, shelter, health, vigor, and a capacity for physical action), are infused with cultural meanings. The culturally infused social operations are culture as social practice. Social practice is culture as operative, constituting, embodied, inherited, and taken for granted in acts and structures of a social, economic, technological, and political sort.

How can social practice be shaped by and then come to embody social justice? Doran notes that the reflexive level of a culture can influence cultural meanings operative in social practice. In fact, a crucial nexus obtains between social practice and reflexive culture. Changing social practice toward a more just order depends significantly on meanings from the reflexive level of culture entering into the polity. One sort of influence on social practice that reverses unjust conditions comes from "prolonged and difficult theoretical and scientific work."[57] But only a cultivated interiority can maintain a creative tension between practicality and intersubjective spontaneity essential to a successful social order. A flourishing society has a communal integrity, the outcome of suppressing neither practical intelligence (political, economic, technological) nor intersubjective spontaneity (friends, family, neighbors, groups with common interests) but keeping both alive and interactive at the same time. The reflexive level of a culture tends to subvert ethnocentrism and nationalism that can be carried along and instantiated in practicality and intersubjective spontaneity.

Applying Doran's analysis, social justice pertains to practical intelligence as the source and sustenance of institutions and structures. Moreover, the

> cultural values in general of a healthy society are constituted by the operative assumptions resulting from the pursuit of the transcendental objectives of the human spirit: of the beautiful in story and song, ritual and dance, art and literature; of the intelligible in science, scholarship, and common sense; of the true in philosophy and theology; and of the good in all questions regarding normativity.[58]

The cultural values, the operative assumptions, and their origin in human self-transcendence are present in social practice and on the reflexive level of culture.

Members of a society active on the reflexive level originate the interpretative perspectives, critical standards, new ideas, and future prospects that lead to reshaping the structural products of practical intelligence. For social practice to become socially just, then, may well and on a case-by-case basis depend on keeping practical intelligence in economic activities, political activities, use of technology, and social interactions open to theoretical, artistic, scientific, philosophical, theological meanings flowing from freedom, autonomy in inquiry, and creativity on the reflexive level of culture. This allows practical intelligence to stay actively in tension with intersubjective spontaneity without overwhelming it. From time to time one task of practical intelligence in its political office is to mediate these reflexive meanings into the polity to shape policies that affect the economy and the use of technology. So a first step in social analysis is to see how open the acts and products of practical intelligence are to meanings from reflexive culture. Checking practicality on whether it is open or closed represents an indirect, long-term approach to social justice that underscores the essential role of culture, especially reflexive culture, in a society's common good. A society that has given over its social order, its social practice, so completely to a closed practicality and so to a predominantly instrumental outlook, will not be moved easily, if at all, to regard as a valid goal persons, their well-being, and the structures that foster well-being for all members of society.

There is a possible hyper-pragmatic blindness that inverts right order by seeing and acting as if the economy and polity ought to be served rather than serve, since persons and their well-being already have been predefined as means instrumental to practical ends such as producing and consuming as, it would be thought, legitimately manipulated citizens. In such a condition reflexive culture is marginalized and deprived of public influence.

Then art, philosophy, and theology along with the natural and social sciences, humane learning, and scholarship are all measured, for example, exclusively by their utility to the operations of a free-market economy and democratic polity. To the extent that this sort of situation prevails, to that extent advocacy of a just social order involves clarifying the danger of allowing market forces to be understood as if they were processes as natural, inalterable, and universal as gravity.

However, Doran's analytic concepts need one clarification. His concept of practicality seems to be equivalent to instrumental reason, *techné*, its products, and attainments.[59] Practicality, he points out, needs to be receptive to theory and reflexive culture because intentional consciousness also has to do with intelligibility, value, truth, beauty, and the whole human good. But beyond that valid point it needs to be said that the nature of practicality also encompasses what traditionally was designated *phronesis* (prudence) and *poésis* (art). Canny prudential judgments expressed in attitudes and sayings, creativity in artisanal crafts, popular art, and music belong to what Lonergan and Doran identify as intersubjectivity in tension with instrumental reason.[60] They locate acts and outcomes from *phronesis* and *poésis* in intersubjective spontaneity not in practicality. But just that locating seems to me to surrender practicality to instrumental reason by accepting an exclusion of *phronesis* and *poésis* from practicality.

Practicality, then, has its own internal dimensions beyond instrumental reason and has its own source of spontaneity. That slight adjustment in the meaning of practicality allows locating the point of origin for what the field of cultural studies calls popular culture in practicality. Popular culture is not folk culture. The milieu and communication of popular culture are mass media, not generation-to-generation tradition. This means that hopes for advancing more just social practice have to listen to, take account of, and learn from popular culture as well as from reflexive culture. Instrumental reason as practicality also has to come to respect ideas, values, and feelings expressed by *phronesis* and *poésis* in popular culture.

That clarification of Doran's analysis permits refinement of the inquiry up to this point. CST by and large has ignored how movement toward just social practice depends on two factors, reflexive culture "from above" and popular culture "from within" practicality. Social practice is where social justice comes to realization. Yet CST considers neither the reflexive level of culture nor popular culture as potential sources of change toward social justice. The humanism espoused by CST holds a still vacant place for reflexive culture, it is true, but less clearly for popular culture.

Observations

A first observation comes in the form of grateful recognition that in promoting social justice and a common good, CST consistently has taught about culture as social practice, albeit without adverting to this as a mode of culture. At the same time, CST and Catholic thought generally have not addressed the idea and reality of cultural postmodernity extensively because of preoccupation with affirming religious transcendence in integral humanism and integral development.

What does it mean and why is it important to point out that CST ignores the cultural dimension of social practice, reflexive culture, and popular culture? That is, it is not enough that Paul VI, John Paul II, and Benedict XVI steadfastly have protested against understanding the human person and the development of peoples *(progressio)* in terms purely of economic and political structures justly arranged.[61] The protest implies prior affirmation of ulterior human dimensions. Yet typically, reference to the ulterior dimensions has taken the form of a defining and irreplaceable witness to religion, apart from discussion of the reflexive level of culture or of popular culture. The reflexive level, not to mention popular culture, plays, for example, but a relatively minor role in the *Compendium of the Social Doctrine of the Church.*[62]

True, the *Compendium* as a whole presents many principles supportive of a just social order as embodying cultural meanings and of reflexive culture as fulfillment of a just social practice. For example, there is a central affirmation of the dignity of the human person, a starting point in "integral and solidary humanism";[63] a reference to Paul VI's idea of "development" as having an important cultural dimension;[64] attention to the human person;[65] and recognition that culture involves the "integral perfection of the person and the good of the whole of society."[66] Culture turns up in the *Compendium* as a basic dimension of human social existence, but science, art, and humane learning are situated in perspectives of evangelizing strategies, of refuting philosophical errors, and of correcting ethical shortcomings.

There is little or no celebration of unpredictable creativity and no engagement with postmodern cultural conditions of pluralism internal to most societies. Culture emerges as a troubling realm not fully identical with economic, political, and social life that somehow is indivisible from those dimensions. Nevertheless, the *Compendium* hints at a larger intuition about the importance of the symbolic part of reflexive culture for CST. A full-color photographic reproduction of Ambrogio Lorenzatti's 1338–39 *Allegory of Good Government* graces the front, spine, and back of the volume.[67] Might the maxim against judging a book by its cover be ignored in this case?

Social Catholicism in the form of liberation theology has not ignored cultural contexts and world views in addressing the situation of the poor, or that political theology did not arise from, address, and develop theoretical antidotes to a contextual problem of authoritarianism. These and other currents "from below" aside, CST "from above," with notable exceptions in Asian and African bishops' conferences, has not advanced too far in elucidating how a just social order embodies and also provides support for a particular culture, particularly the reflexive component. Postconciliar CST has attended to culture as social practice but not much to a just social practice as embodying cultural meanings and even less in reference to reflexive culture or popular culture. More common is a binary contrast between those who exalt immanent economic, political, and social realities and the church's defense of a transcendent, constitutive human relationship with God. The only absence CST usually points to in secular discussions and plans for social, political, and economic development is an absence of religion due to a closed and truncated secularism that denies human and divine transcendence. There seems to be no intrinsic reason why CST may not initiate analysis and discussion on the cultural finality inherent in social, political, and economic social practice.

Finality toward Reflexive Culture

Finality is an immanent tendency toward an end, goal, or outcome that completes and perfects whatever has the tendency. In an Aristotelian four-cause analysis, that end or outcome is the final cause in addition to material, efficient, and formal causes of an entity's natural activities that express what it is. A society can be thought of as enough like an entity to bear the asking of a question about what it is for, to what does it tend, what is its final cause? And a commonly accepted answer in CST is that the finality of a society lies in the flourishing of its members as persons. Social justice and common good in a society are not entities but states of affairs, institutional arrangements, and qualitative ingredients of a society. So social justice and the common good share in a society's finality toward the human flourishing of its members.

But social injustice in the day-to-day operation of institutional arrangements prevents that flourishing for all or some. Accordingly, social justice measured by the common good shares in and promotes the end of a society, which is the flourishing of its members. This means that social justice and the common good are not complete ends in themselves, though to be achieved they must be sought. Yet they remain intermediate to an end beyond themselves that they do not and cannot produce. They have society's end, human flourishing, as their final cause, so they have a finality in fostering and tending toward that social goal.

Consequently, discussion now shifts to what could be called a modified eudemonistic perspective on social justice and the common good. The reason for shifting is to highlight incompleteness in social justice and a common good taken by themselves as if comprising a self-contained agenda. Both are for something beyond themselves, human flourishing, or to use a phrase preferred by Atherton, "human well-being," or a phrase from Pope Benedict XVI's *Caritas in Veritate*, "transcendental humanism." Social justice and a common good are part of that picture, not the whole of it.

Now, a eudemonistic ethic attends to the way choices mold a person or society. Besides a direct object in matters external to the person or society, choosing has an interior effect in forming an individual or a social character. To act in accord with social justice, to participate in the major institutions of a society, to promote a common good that makes a contribution possible from all—these result in an individual's habit of justice and in a society having a shared ethos of social justice. This interior effect correlates with external effects in the public life of a society. The interior effect is the eudemonistic aspect of social justice and the common good. Social justice, like any virtue, can be appreciated as its own reward insofar as persons becoming socially just persons participate in a just social order that fulfills a person's and a society's capacity to become and to be just.

Modification of this perspective consists in emphasizing that the virtue of social justice prepares for further modes of virtue and a range of public effects above and beyond the economic and the political. Those capacities, modes, and effects lie in the realm of culture, above all in reflexive culture. Artists, poets, playwrights, novelists, musicians, academic specialists and teachers, researchers, scientists, philosophers, the best journalists all exemplify this range of further, cultural effects. A modified eudemonistic ethic looks to intrinsic connections between practices and institutions realizing the virtue of social justice and activities of a cultural sort. This pertains both to those whose commitment to solidarity leads them to promote social justice likely to benefit others more than themselves and those seeking social justice as redress for their own suffering.

Those bringing about justice find in a just economic and political order not the fullness of life but a platform for cultural activity, starting with family life, friendships, neighbors, education, and in some societies a folk culture. Their exercise of social justice through participation in the main institutions of a society opens onto broader and deeper realizations of their own and others' human existence and dignity. Social justice underlies and facilitates but is not the substance of those further realizations. This is all to say that access by the poor, marginalized, and vulnerable to participation in economic, social, and political life—a goal or end of social justice—is not an end in itself. Nor is a character formed in social justice a complete, self-sufficient point of human arrival. Access to and growth in culture is part of what justice serves but cannot produce.

Conclusion

Social justice in social practice is not a complete end in itself but is a way station to fuller individual and social self-realization. Of course, social justice cannot be a means if it has not first been an end sought and attained to some degree. But all social practice and no reflexive culture would have made even Jesus in his humanity a dull boy, not the vibrant, topical, attractive, liberating, and whole-making public figure to whom the New Testament bears witness. Social justice is a means toward cultural creativity in and beyond economic activities. That finality belongs to social justice as an inner momentum toward humane living characterized by being more than having (though having enough allows for fuller realization of being).

Nor is a society's "common good" an end in itself. A substantive, effective, and normative common good remains a set of conditions ("the sum total of social conditions which allow people, either as groups or as individuals, to reach their fulfillment more fully and more readily"[68]) facilitating but not automatically producing people's exercise of personal freedom in cultural creativity and a humane life. The *Catechism of the Catholic Church* teaches that the common good "should make accessible to each, what is needed to lead a truly human life: food, clothing, health, work, education, culture, and so on" (no. 1908).[69] Culture at the level of both social practice and reflexive culture belongs to the common good of a society.[70] This is an important affirmation of education and culture over and above food, clothing, health, and work. Apparently, the *Catechism* distinguishes social practice (food, clothing, health, and work) from the reflexive level of culture (education and culture) and does not refer to popular culture. The distinction has not incited further teaching on influence from the reflexive part of culture on social practice.

The *Compendium* explains that the common good is not an "end in itself; it has value only in reference to attaining the ultimate ends of the person and the universal common good of the whole of creation."[71] This forthright assertion nevertheless also elides attention to reflexive culture as a distinct zone short of the ultimate ends of the person (God, mediated in religion) and yet not comprised within social, economic, and political structures. A *Compendium* description of social justice ("Social justice concerns . . . the social, political, and economic aspects and, above all, the structural dimensions of problems and their respective solutions"[72]) contains no reference to culture.

Both "social justice" and a "common good," then, are incomplete attributes of a "good life," of human flourishing or human well-being. The role of reflexive culture as opposed to the distinctly religious and eternal has been tacit rather than extensively addressed in a constructive way. Popular culture has been marginalized. Small yet frequent critiques of negative features in contemporary cultures (materialism, relativism, consumerism, and so forth) do not add up to an engagement with either reflexive or popular culture, or for that matter with the cultural dimension of social practice.

Insofar as social justice and a common good are operative in a society, they embody some of that society's common meanings and thereby constitute social practice in a cultural dimension. But they both share finality toward an ulterior temporal good that is popular and reflexive culture. As real but partial signs and instruments of inherently social realizations of human dignity, they have an immanent tendency toward facilitating that further cultural dimension. If that finality can be conveyed in the language of social justice and the common good, then well and good; explanation of those terms in their intrinsic orientation beyond themselves in culture will suffice. But if not, then they may need revision or conceptual genetic engineering like that occurring in altering Aquinas's general justice so it became social justice.

Again thankfully, CST has borne constant witness to a vision of humanity, a theological anthropology not confined to social, economic, and political capacities, activities, and structures, and in so doing conceives social, economic, and political realities in reference to a human meaning, a "transcendental humanism"

(*Populorum Progressio*, no. 16; *Caritas in Veritate*, no. 18) both open to God and possessed of its own kind of human transcendence. Catholic personalism permeates CST. Clarity on the significance of the person individually and in social existence has led to CST arranging in right order relations among immanent social, political, and economic structures.

Notes

[1] CST belongs within the larger field of social Catholicism. See, for example, Paul Misner, *Social Catholicism in Europe: From the Onset of Industrialization to the First World War* (New York: Crossroads, 1991). Social Catholicism includes Catholic social thought. See David J. O'Brien and Thomas A. Shannon, eds., *Catholic Social Thought: The Documentary Heritage* (Maryknoll, NY: Orbis Books, 2005; J. S. Boswell, F. P. McHugh, and J. Verstraeten, eds., *Catholic Social Thought: Twilight or Renaissance?* (Leuven: Peeters, 2000); and Francis P. McHugh, *Catholic Social Thought Renovating the Tradition: A Keyguide to Resources* (Leuven: Peeters, 2008). Catholic social tradition is the historical longitude of social Catholicism. See Judith A. Merkle, *From the Heart of the Church: The Catholic Social Tradition* (Collegeville, MN: Liturgical Press, 2004); and Kathleen Maas Weigert and Alexia K. Kelly, eds., *Living the Catholic Social Tradition: Cases and Commentary* (Lanham, MD: Sheed and Ward, 2005).

[2] Pontifical Council on Justice and Peace, *Compendium of the Social Doctrine of the Church* (Rome: Libreria Editrice Vaticana, 2004; Washington DC: USCCB Publishing, 2005).

[3] See Christine Firer Hinze, "*Quadragesimo Anno*," in *Modern Catholic Social Teaching: Commentaries and Interpretations*, ed. Kenneth Himes, 151–74 (Washington DC: Georgetown University Press, 2004), 167.

[4] Thomas Aquinas, *Summa Theologiae* 2a2ae, Q. 58, art. 6, trans. David Hollenbach, in *The Common Good and Christian Ethics* (Cambridge: Cambridge University Press, 2002), 195. See the translation, introduction, notes, and glossary by Thomas Gilby, OP, *Justice*, vol. 37 in the Blackfriars' *Summa Theologiae* (2a2ae. 57–62) (New York: McGraw–Hill, 1975), Q. 58, art. 6. Hollenbach's translation is clearer than Gilby's ("this last [virtue . . . of a good citizen] is general justice, which governs our acts for the common good"), 35.

[5] Aquinas remarks that "the rightness of other moral virtues is not determined apart from the frame of mind of the person acting," adding that justice has its rightness "even abstracting from the temper in which it

is done" [*qualiter ab agente fiat*], Hollenbach, vol. 37, *Summa Theologiae* 2a2ae, Q. 57, art. 1.

⁶ Jean-Yves Calvez, SJ, "Social Justice," in *The New Catholic Encyclopedia* (Palatine, IL: Jack Heraly and Associates, 1981), 2:319.

⁷ Hollenbach explains and applies general or social justice to the split between affluent suburbs and struggling inner cities in "Poverty, Justice, and the Good of the City," chap. 7 in *The Common Good and Christian Ethics*, 173–211, esp. 190–200.

⁸ See George Newlands, *The Transformative Imagination* (Aldershot, England: Ashgate Publishing, 2004); idem, *Christ and Human Rights: The Transformative Engagement* (Aldershot, England: Ashgate Publishing, 2006).

⁹ See John Atherton, *Marginalization* (London: SCM Press, 2003); idem, *Transfiguring Capitalism: An Inquiry into Religion and Global Change* (London: SCM Press, 2008).

¹⁰ John A. Coleman, SJ, "The Future of Catholic Social Thought," 522–44, in Himes, *Modern Catholic Social Teaching*, 538–41.

¹¹ David Miller, *Principles of Social Justice* (Cambridge, MA: Harvard University Press, 1999), 2.

¹² Matthew Clayton and Andrew Williams, eds., *Social Justice* (Malden, MA: Blackwell, 2004), 1.

¹³ John Rawls, *Theory of Justice* (Cambridge, MA: Belknap Press, 1999; original 1971), 6–7. See also John Rawls, *Justice as Fairness: A Restatement*, ed. Erin Kelly (Cambridge, MA: Belknap Press, 2001), 39–57.

¹⁴ Shivesh C. Thakur argues against religious concern for social justice because "religion's ultimate goal, namely the transcendental state of spiritual salvation or liberation . . . must regard earthly matters as 'ultimately inconsequential'" (*Religion and Social Justice* [New York: St. Martin's Press, 1996], 44). In *When Love Is Not Enough: A Theo-ethic of Justice* (Collegeville, MN: Liturgical Press, 2002), Mary Elsbernd and Reimund Bieringer comment in relation to the Johannine portrayal of embodiment that "if bodies matter, justice has to be concerned about concrete, tangible realities" (65). As the Presbyterian Church USA said in a 1954 statement of theological principles for social action, "Religion is about life in its wholeness" (Presbyterian Church USA, "Theological Basis for Social Action . . . 1954 statement," chap. 1 in *Compilation of Social Policy*).

¹⁵ "The relationship between the concerns of practical theology and the category of 'public theology'" was the main theme for the 2003 International Academy of Practical Theology at Manchester University, as explained by Elaine Graham and Anna Rowlands, editors of the proceedings, in *Pathways to the Public Square: Practical Theology in an Age of Pluralism* (Münster: Lit Verlag, 2005), 3.

¹⁶ John de Gruchy adverts to a transition from the languages of European political theology and Latin American liberation theology to public

theology once apartheid officially ended in South Africa. Then theology, beyond advocating emancipatory participation in abolishing apartheid, acquired not only a task of seeking faith's light on active participation in a pluralist democracy, nor only of legitimating democracy, but of bringing "a vision that pushes democracy towards a greater expression of what we believe is God's will for the world." See John W. de Gruchy, "From Political to Public Theologies: The Role of Theology in the Public Life of South Africa," in *Public Theology for the Twenty-first Century: Essays in Honour of Duncan B. Forrester*, ed. W. J. Storrar and A. R. Morton, 45–62 (London: T&T Clark Ltd, 2004), 59.

[17] Sebastian Kim, editor of the *International Journal of Public Theology*, says that "public theology is a deliberate use of common language in a commitment to influence public decision-making, and also to learn from substantive public discourse. It involves academic theologians in developing categories that are capable of affecting the ethical conscience of the political community. Public theology is an engagement of living religious traditions with their public environment the economic, political, and cultural spheres of common life" (Editorial, *International Journal of Public Theology* 1, no. 1 [2007]: 1–2).

[18] William T. Cavanaugh, *Theopolitical Imagination* (New York: T&T Clark, 2002), 3.

[19] Kenneth R. Himes, OFM, and Michael J. Himes, *The Fullness of Faith: The Public Significance of Theology* (New York: Paulist Press, 1993), 4, quoting David Hollenbach, "Editor's Conclusion" in David Hollenbach, Robin Lovin, John Coleman, and J. Bryan Hehir, "Theology and Philosophy in Public: A Symposium on John Courtney Murray's Unfinished Agenda," *Theological Studies* 40 (December 1979): 714.

[20] Himes and Himes, *The Fullness of Faith*, 5.

[21] Robert Benne, *The Paradoxical Vision: A Public Theology for the Twenty-first Century* (Minneapolis, MN: Fortress Press, 1995), 4.

[22] Ibid., 8.

[23] De Gruchy remarks that "it is necessary to talk now about public theolog*ies*, rather than *a* public theology, both within the global postcolonial context and within our new multicultural democracy in South Africa" ("From Political to Public Theologies," 56).

[24] Among Catholic theologians see, for example, Robert W. McElroy, *The Search for an American Public Theology: The Contribution of John Courtney Murray* (New York: Paulist Press, 1989); Thomas Hughson, SJ, *The Believer as Citizen: John Courtney Murray in a New Context* (New York: Paulist Press, 1993); Himes and Himes, *The Fullness of Faith*; Mary Doak, *Reclaiming Narrative for Public Theology* (Albany: State University of New York Press, 2004); and William J. Collinge, ed., *Faith in Public Life* (Maryknoll, NY: Orbis Books, 2008).

[25] One is Jean-Guy Nadeau, "Public Theology in Pop Culture: Critical Uses and Functions of the Bible in Rock Music and Metal," in Graham and Rowlands, *Pathways to the Public Square*, 157–69.

[26] See a proposal for a cultural approach to social justice in Joseph P. Fitzpatrick, SJ, "Justice as a Problem of Culture," *Catholic Mind* 76 (1978): 10–26. My summation of his approach to an option for the poor: "J. Fitzpatrick had approached this theme in arguing that, 'the heart of the problem of justice is culture,' because judgments on an acceptable amount of food, the way to dress, and decent dwelling-places have a cultural aspect. Customs, manners, relationships, attitudes toward family, work, and the future all have cultural meanings and values. In regard to economic arrangements therefore, it becomes necessary to ask, 'what do they mean in terms of human interests, in terms of human destiny, in terms of what human life means?'" (Hughson, *The Believer as Citizen*, 111).

[27] Vincent Miller discusses homogenization and heterogenization in "Where Is the Church? Globalization and Catholicity," *Theological Studies* 69, no. 2 (June 2008): 412–32.

[28] Kenneth Himes, "Globalization with a Human Face: Catholic Social Teaching and Globalization," *Theological Studies* 69, no. 2 (June 2008), 281.

[29] On systemic distortion embedded in social structures and institutions, see Bryan Massingale, "James Cone and Recent Catholic Episcopal Teaching on Racism," in *Theological Studies* 61, no. 4 (December 2000): 700–730. Black liberation theologian James Cone reiterated a longstanding challenge to white Protestant and Catholic theologians in the United States to tackle white supremacy as a theological problem in "Black Liberation Theology and Black Catholics: A Critical Conversation," *Theological Studies* 61, no. 4 (December 2000): 731–47. See also Laurie M. Cassidy and Alex Mikulich, eds., *Interrupting White Privilege: Catholic Theologians Break the Silence* (Maryknoll, NY: Orbis Books, 2007).

[30] Pontifical Council for Justice and Peace, *Contribution to World Conference against Racism, Racial Discrimination, Xenophobia, and Related Intolerance* (Durban: August 31–September 7, 2001): "The international community is aware that the roots of racism, discrimination and intolerance are found in prejudice and ignorance, which are first of all the fruits of sin, but also of faulty and inadequate *education*."

[31] For a liberationist approach that looks to a cultural outcome, see Ada María Isasi-Díaz, "Creating a Liberating Culture: Latinas' Subversive Narratives," in *Convergence on Culture: Theologians in Dialogue with Cultural Analysis and Criticism*, ed. Delwin Brown, Sheila Greeve Davaney, and Kathryn Tanner, 122–39 (New York: Oxford Press, 2001).

[32] Misner, *Social Catholicism in Europe*, Marvin Krier Mich, *Catholic Social Teaching and Movements* (Mystic, CT: Twenty-Third Publications, 1998).

[33] Coleman, "The Future of Catholic Social Thought," 524–25.

[34] Some recent applications of CST include Thomas Massaro, SJ, *Living Justice: Catholic Social Teaching in Action* (Franklin, WI: Sheed and Ward, 2000); and John P. Hogan, *Credible Signs of Christ Alive: Case Studies from the Catholic Campaign for Human Development* (Lanham, MD: Sheed and Ward, 2003). Helpful studies are Charles E. Curran, *Catholic Social Teaching 1891–Present: Historical, Theological, and Ethical Analyses* (Washington DC: Georgetown University Press, 2002); Elsbernd and Bieringer, *When Love Is Not Enough*; and Kenneth Himes, *Modern Catholic Social Teaching*.

[35] It is no longer inside information that at papal request Oswald Nell-Breuning, SJ, drafted much of *Quadragesimo Anno.* with Pius XI adding material on a corporatist economy. Nell-Breuning brought "social justice" from the work of his mentor, Heinrich Pesch, into *Quadragesimo Anno.*

[36] Bernard Lonergan, *Method in Theology* (New York: Seabury Press, 1972), chap. 3.

[37] See Kathryn Tanner, *Theories of Culture: A New Agenda for Theology* (Minneapolis, MN: Fortress Press, 1997); and Brown, Davaney, and Tanner, *Convergence on Culture*.

[38] Tanner, *Theories of Culture*, 32.

[39] Ibid., 36–37. Tanner associates this presupposition with "the Enlightenment project of freeing human society from the dead weight of tradition or custom" (37).

[40] Stephen B. Bevans, SVD, and Jeffrey Gros, FSC, *Evangelization and Religious Freedom: Ad Gentes, Dignitatis Humanae* (New York: Paulist Press, 2009), 41.

[41] Allen Figueroa Deck, SJ, "Culture," in Judith A. Dwyer ed., *The New Dictionary of Catholic Social Thought* (Collegeville, MN: Michael Glazier, Liturgical Press, 1994), 256–61 at 260–61.

[42] Ibid., 257.

[43] For example, positive connections between (a modern idea of) culture and mission are evident in Paul VI's *Evangelii Nuntiandi* and John Paul II's *Redemptoris Missio* (see Bevans and Gros, *Evangelization and Religious Freedom*).

[44] Marcello de Carvalho Azevedo, *Inculturation and the Challenge of Modernity* (Rome: Gregorian University Press, 1982), 10.

[45] Hughson, *The Believer as Citizen*, 108–12.

[46] Tanner, *Theories of Culture*, chap. 3.

[47] See Sheila Greeve Davaney, "Theology and the Turn to Cultural Analysis," 3–16, in Brown, Davaney, and Tanner, *Convergence on Culture*, 6.

[48] Davaney, in Brown, Davaney, and Tanner, *Convergence on Culture*, 57–58.

[49] See Virgilio Elizondo, *Galilean Journey: The Mexican-American Promise* (Maryknoll, NY: Orbis Books, 1993), and a later modification of

his insight in "Jesus the Galilean Jew in Mestizo Theology," *Theological Studies* 70, no. 2 (June 2009): 262–80.

50 Robert Jackson remarks that "it also needs to be recognized that minority cultures, religions, and ethnicities are themselves internally pluralistic, and the symbols and values associated with their various constituent groups are open to negotiation, contest, and change." Robert Jackson, *Rethinking Religious Education and Plurality: Issues in Diversity and Pedagogy* (London: RoutledgeFalmer, 2004), 130, as quoted in Thomas Hughson, "Beyond Informed Citizens: Who Are 'The Wise'?" in *Forum on Public Policy* 2, no. 1 (2006): 176.

51 See Nadeau, "Public Theology in Pop Culture," 157–69; also Tom Beaudoin, *Virtual Faith: The Irreverent Spiritual Quest of Generation X* (San Francisco: Jossey-Bass, 1998); David Dark, *Everyday Apocalypse: The Sacred Revealed in Radiohead, the Simpsons and Other Pop Culture Icons* (Grand Rapids, MI: Brazos Press, 2002); Craig Detweiler and Barry Taylor, *A Matrix of Meanings: Finding God in Pop Culture* (Grand Rapids, MI: Baker Academic, 2003); Gordon Lynch, *Understanding Theology and Popular Culture* (Oxford: Blackwell Publishing, 2005).

52 Lonergan, *Method in Theology*, 356–66.

53 Ibid., 301–2.

54 Robert Doran, summarizing Lonergan in *What Is Systematic Theology?* (Toronto: University of Toronto Press, 2005), 174.

55 See Robert Doran, *Theology and the Dialectics of History* (Toronto: University of Toronto Press, 1990), esp. chaps. 4, 11, and 16; and idem, *What Is Systematic Theology?*

56 Lonergan, *Method in Theology*, chap 2, section 2 on feelings and section 3 on the notion of value.

57 Doran, *Theology and the Dialectics of History*, 98.

58 Ibid., 98–99.

59 Ibid., 359–77.

60 Ibid., 359–60.

61 Paul VI remarked that "development . . . cannot be restricted to economic growth alone. . . . It must be well rounded; it must foster the development of each man and of the whole man" (no. 14). John Paul II stated that "development that does not include the cultural, transcendent, and religious dimensions of man and society . . . is even less conducive to authentic liberation" (*Sollicitudo Rei Socialis*, no. 7). John Paul II's *Laborem Exercens* included "scientific or artistic" activities in the category of work (no. 18).

62 John Paul II launched the Pontifical Council for Culture in 1982. The Pontifical Council for Justice and Peace produced the *Compendium of the Social Doctrine of the Church*. The beautiful book cover notwithstanding, there is little to suggest collaboration on the *Compendium*.

63 *Compendium*, Introduction, nos. 1–19, 1–7.

⁶⁴ Ibid., no. 98, 45.

⁶⁵ Ibid., nos. 105–59, 49–70.

⁶⁶ Ibid., no. 556, 242.

⁶⁷ Ibid., "Cover Art," unnumbered flyleaf following p. 446. Also see the Pontifical Council for Culture publication "*Via Pulchritudinis*: Privileged Pathway for Evangelization and Dialogue," available on the Vatican website.

⁶⁸ *Compendium*, no. 164, 72, quoting *Gaudium et Spes* and other sources.

⁶⁹ Interdicasterial Commission for the *Catechism of the Catholic Church*, English translation by Libreria Editrice Vaticana, United States Conference of Catholic Bishops (Liguori, MO: Liguori Publications, 1994). See nos. 1905–27, referring to *Gaudium et Spes*, no. 26. On social justices see nos. 1928–49.

⁷⁰ The UN Declaration on Human Rights states that "(1) Everyone has the right freely to participate in the cultural life of the community, to enjoy the arts and to share in scientific advancement and its benefits" (art. 27). Vatican II speaks about "a right to culture" and a duty to develop oneself and to so assist others (*Gaudium et Spes*, no. 60).

⁷¹ *Compendium*, no. 170, 75.

⁷² Ibid., nos. 201, 89–90.

2.

Building Solidarity for Social Transformation through the Church's Social Teaching

David Kaulemu

The question of how the Church ought to be at once faithful to Christ and an effective sign and instrument of him in the world or worlds of today continues.

—JOSEPH A. KOMONCHAK

Introduction

Africa urgently needs fundamental transformation in various respects. Its politics, economics, and cultures and how all these different realms relate to one another can be transformed in ways that will lead to the respect of life and dignity of all God's creation, social justice, peace, and human and ecological flourishing. Of course, Africa's transformation cannot be an isolated process. It requires and entails fundamental transformation at the global level. This essay's focus is Africa. Key to Africa's transformation are the spiritual, moral, and cultural frameworks and sensibilities that are capable of facilitating the necessary changes and adjustments. We have tried economic and political structural adjustment programs with little success. It is time we commit ourselves to moral/cultural/spiritual adjustment efforts to accompany our political and economic reforms. This would involve looking seriously but critically at ways to widen and deepen African social imaginaries.

What various African communities imagine and feel about themselves is critical to how they relate to themselves and to others in the political, economic, and social spheres. What is needed is the retrieval, deepening, and widening of African traditional moral sensibilities in order to find them their rightful place in African modernity. This means reconciling various ethnic sensibilities and also reconciling them with the demands of modern politics and economies. This process will have to reject aspects of ethnic traditions that demonize others. Modern development theories have so far worked on the assumption that they can ignore African traditional social imaginaries and simply transpose modern political and economic institutions over them. Most African political leaders have themselves believed this way.[1] The results have been disastrous.[2] The church too has historically made the same mistakes until the Second Vatican Council, when there was a change in the Catholic social imagination.

This new sensibility that is beginning to inform CST can facilitate the development of a culturally inclusive spirituality, humane habits of thought, and democratic cultural practices appropriate to the development of new African societies capable of participating confidently in dialogues at global levels. The African Forum for CST (AFCAST) was formed to recognize and take advantage of this potential in CST for the transformation of the African church and society. As a network of experts on CST, it aims at building solidarity informed by the church's social teaching to transform Africa and the rest of the world. AFCAST, however, uses strategies that avoid the formation of new organizations. It works with already existing organizations, institutions, and systems, encouraging them to strengthen those aspects of the social teaching that best express their goals and to interrogate the theory and practice of the social teaching with the view to informing it with relevant African experiences.

Facts, Values, and the Battle for Naming and Defining

African peoples have made tremendous progress toward freeing themselves from suffering caused by natural and human forces. Since 1957, when Ghana achieved national independence, country after country emulated this example. Today, most countries in sub-Saharan Africa are proudly politically independent. Yet the continent is still characterized by famine, wars, conflicts, disease, oppression, exploitation, and little respect for human life and human dignity. The continent is rich in human and natural resources, yet most people live in poverty. Sub-Saharan African countries have received so much aid that has "done so much ill and so little good."[3] Alex de Waal analyzes the history of the role of humanitarian organizations in Africa and concludes that from the 1980s, aid agencies in Africa grew in number and power and yet "actual existing humanitarianism is a disappointment."[4] Sub-Saharan Africa remains the epicenter of the HIV and AIDS pandemic. It is also important to mention in this context that the presence and teaching of the church in Africa has not prevented the occurrence of conflicts, wars, and genocides. Aylward Shorter observes,

> In Africa the year 1994 will be forever remembered as the year of genocide, when between half a million and a million people were massacred in the tiny overpopulated African country of Rwanda. By any standards it was a country that was massively Christian. More than 60% of the population was Catholic, and Church authorities boasted of the high rates of church attendance and frequent reception of the sacraments.[5]

Many of Africa's political leaders have been Catholic, yet their rule has not reflected respect for CST. Mobuto Sese Seko is the most notorious. Robert Gabriel Mugabe is the most contemporary African political leader who, apart from overseeing the Gukurahundi[6] and Murambatsvina programs, embarked on a land reform program with little evidence that he had read the Catholic Church document *Toward a Better Distribution of Land*, written by the Pontifical Council for Justice and Peace in 1997. More important, there is little evidence that as a faithful Catholic he is committed to establishing a regime that respects the values and principles of CST. These principles include respect for life, respect for the dignity of persons, and respect for the right to participate in the activities of one's community. Mugabe's regime struggles to appreciate the rights of people to choose their own leaders and to search genuinely for the common good.

The late Julius Nyerere is probably the most progressive Catholic African leader to have taken seriously traditional African sensibilities. Yet he failed to relate them systematically to CST. Had the church helped him to benefit from the richness of CST in his reflection on African socialism, the world would have benefited much more from him. His work will certainly be important for inculturating CST and widening African traditions' sensibilities.

A number of books that claim that something can be done about Africa's woes have been published recently.[7] Global economic organizations such as the World Bank, the World Trade Organization, and the International Monetary Fund continue to modify their technically minded strategies and to express confidence that they will work.[8] In September 2000 the Millennium Development Goals (MDGs) were signed by 150 world political leaders. The leaders pledged to (1) eradicate extreme poverty and hunger (2) achieve universal primary-school enrollment (3) promote gender equality and empower women (4) reduce child mortality and improve maternal health (5) combat HIV/AIDS, malaria, and other diseases (6) ensure environmental sustainability, and (7) develop a global partnership for development by 2015. Other activities to support the MDGs were initiated. Some of them are enumerated by William Easterly as follows:

Gordon Brown and Tony Blair put the cause of ending poverty in Africa at the top of the agenda of the G8 Summit in Scotland in July 2005. Bob Geldof assembled well-bands for "Live 8" concerts on July 3, 2005, to lobby the G8 to "Make Poverty History" in Africa. Veterans of the 1985 Live Aid concert, such as Elton John and Madonna, performed, as did a younger generation's bands, such as Coldplay. Hundreds of thousands marched on the G8 Summit for the cause. Live 8's appeals for helping the poor and its dramatizations of their sufferings were moving, and it is great that rock stars donate their time for the needy and desperate.[9]

In Africa itself there have been countless efforts to address the various challenges since political independence. There have been experiments from Kwame Nkhruma's pan-Africanism, Nyerere's Ujamaa, Kenneth Kaunda's humanism, Gerry Rawlings's military coups, and Samora Machel's and Do Santos's communism to Mugabe's fast-track land reform.

The problems of Africa are defined and understood differently. Many of the solutions proposed assume that the problems are technical problems that need technical solutions. Most assume that these problems are of an economic nature. The slogan is "Fix the economics and everything else will fall into place." Whether it is what William Easterly calls the grand "planners," such as Joseph Stiglitz, Jeffrey Sachs, or the World Bank, or the "searchers," such as Muhammad Yunus and Easterly himself, the approach is to postulate economic techniques to fix Africa's problems.

Local efforts have been more politically than economically oriented. The fathers of African liberation had the slogan, "Seek ye the political kingdom and everything else shall be added unto you." Political kingdoms were achieved but very little else in the direction of justice, peace, and prosperity. Today, African leaders have immersed themselves in the science of political engineering, inventing different types of political technologies to transform Africa—from Daniel Arapi Moi's Nyayoism in Kenya,

Yowere Museveni's Movement and the banishment of political parties in Uganda, failed attempts to build one-party states in Tanzania, Zambia, Malawi, Zimbabwe, Mozambique, and Angola, attempts to maintain African traditional kingdoms in Swaziland and Lesotho, to various versions of Western-inspired democracy in Botswana and South Africa.

In general these approaches have been reductionist and exclusivist, and that is why they have either failed or still face serious viability and legitimacy problems. In most of the countries of the regions of eastern and southern Africa, the majority of people are still apathetic regarding their country's political and economic processes. Many of them have up to 70 percent unemployment rates. Informal and rural activities and relationships sustain the lives of most African peoples whose efforts and thinking are not considered in the formal national arrangements. Many of the activities that sustain African peoples have either been criminalized or made expensive to carry out. For example, many African communities were divided by colonial boundaries and now they are required to possess passports in order to see their relatives across borders.

In response, many African peoples live their lives in spite of their governments. They cross borders without passports and buy and sell without declaring duty to revenue authorities. The meaning of government is lost to them. More important, the government approaches have failed because they have not asked wider questions about the cultures, spiritualities, and moral motivations underlying the people who are supposed to implement and live with the innovative political and economic experiments suggested.

Redefining Africa's Problems

Some of the suggested technical solutions to African problems we probably do need. But the social, political, and economic challenges we are facing in Africa are really symptoms of deeper spiritual, cultural, and moral crises. These spiritual, cultural, and moral crises explain the deep divisions, conflicts, corruption, injustice, and retarded human development that undermine the environment. CST could be critical in finding solutions to these challenges because CST shares many values with African cultures and communities. They share the emphasis on the social nature of human beings, the importance of community, and the values of social solidarity and the common good. However, CST has the ability to help African cultures to universalize these values and go beyond African tendencies toward provincialism. CST can expand the African cultural/moral experience.

The terms *spiritual*, *cultural*, and *moral* are here being used in a very wide sense to refer to how people look at themselves and at fellow humans, the environment, and the Creator. This wide sense includes their sense of identity, their emotional responses to fellow humans, to animals, to the environment, and to God. Basically, it is about their emotional intelligence and social imagination. It is this spirituality, this morality, and this sensibility that inform how people will organize economic, political, and social structures, systems, institutions, organizations, and processes. It is about the spiritual and ethical assumptions of society, that is, what values are in place in order to inform and facilitate other activities like economics, politics, and social struggles. When political and economic activities threaten these basic ethical values, society runs the danger of cutting off the branch on which it is sitting. Adam Smith, often regarded as the economist and philosopher of the capitalist free-market economy, recognizes that the market cannot work without assuming certain values as the moral basis of society. For him, sympathy and justice were social virtues without which economics and indeed politics could not succeed, hence, his book *Theory of Moral Sentiments*. In the case of African societies, a general comprehensive ethical/spiritual framework appropriate for the post-colonial modern society and sensitive to the traditional African imagination simply does not exist. It is this required framework that CST can help to develop.

To be fair, some efforts have already gone into this project. I made reference to the work of Nyerere, which I think needs to be expanded and updated. Kwame Nkrumah's pan-Africanism can be useful in helping Africans transcend their local divisions and conflicts. Unfortunately, the history of pan-Africanism has been at best ambiguous. While it has contributed a lot toward liberation from colonialism, it has also acted as an ideology that has so far worked at the level of African leaders as they maintain their hold on power while oppressing and dividing their own people in their respective countries. The limitations the old pan-Africanism, which informed the Organization of African Unity (OAU), were recognized by some of the new leaders of Africa. Presidents Thabo Mbeki of South Africa, Olesugun Obasanjo of Nigeria, Abulaziz Bouteflicka of Algeria, Abdulaye Wade of Senegal, John Kuofor of Ghana, and Joakim Chissano of Mozambique called it "the new African Agenda." It helped the move from OAU to establish the African Union (AU). The AU has established a development plan called New Partnership for Development (NEPAD) and has introduced the African Peer Review Mechanism (APRM) to promote democratic practices by African governments. AU regards Africa's subregional bodies as the building blocks of implementing the new pan-Africanism of the AU.

While some positive developments have been achieved, even some new pan-Africanist leaders have failed and have sometimes even resisted regional economic integration and failed to abide by the democratic guidelines established by the AU and to be monitored by the APRM. Regional integration has been explained in the following words,

Regional integration is creating a common approach, complete with institutions, by states in a region, around economic, political or societal issues. It is about liberation, self-determination, peace, security and development. Integration is transformational and calls for a radical approach bringing together disparate states. This transformation depends heavily on regional cohesion in securing societal integration within a region; it builds regional awareness and identity. It requires regional interstate co-operation and co-ordination, as well as interstate civil society coop-eration and co-ordination. But co-operation should not be confused with regional integration and unification. Regional cooperation is merely part of the process that leads to regional integration and unification.[10]

Civil-society organizations working in the regions of eastern and southern Africa have recognized the need for regional integration and have noted that the limited integration efforts have so far followed "the traditional model of state-dominated and elite-driven approaches." They go on to call for a new paradigm that invites civil society to "engage governments and interstate bodies and foster regional integration processes." "The new paradigm calls for a people-centered, participatory approach."[11] The new pan-Africanism is certainly incisive and an advance over its predecessor, yet it is still stuck in the technological fix. The new paradigm still stops at looking for techniques and strategies to facilitate people's participation and to create space for people's voices to be heard. This is how the strategies are explained and justified:

> The cost of non-engagement is to leave Africa's interstate bodies as mere extensions of governmental interests; not to engage is to leave these institutions untransformed and undemocratized. The challenge is transformation and this can only happen by means of critical independent engagement by civil society. Such a transformative paradigm could be found in a deliberative policy-making approach. Deliberative policy-making is about the challenge to citizens and civil society actors in engaging and influencing government decision-making processes. Deliberative policy-making is about civil society actors grabbing the mandate to participate and play oversight and representative roles in governance and decision-making. It seeks to bring about a new paradigm in governance and policy-making by making these accessible to marginalized and poor sectors of society. It teaches us that public participation in public

policy decision-making is not a favor by governments to citizens; it is right, and governments have a duty to effect it. This new paradigm calls for accessibility, openness and representation, and a move away from policy and governance processes dominated by governmental and NGO elites and the organized. Deliberative policy-making seeks to give a voice to the voiceless. Thus the organized sectors of civil society and those with access to resources must engage in initiatives to ensure that the poor, marginalized and unorganized have access and can participate. It must be conceded that we have weak institutions, mechanisms, and structures for public participation in decision-making processes on the continent and in the region. Executive policy-making processes in Africa still remain inaccessible; even today there is very little public engagement.[12]

The passage above does not raise the question of what content the marginalized and the poor will bring to this decision-making process and to the institutions and mechanisms for participation. It does not raise the issue of the values, the concepts of identity, and the ethical framework that the marginalized work with. Surely people do not come to modern institutions as *tabula rasa*. What if the failure of development experiments in Africa is because of the intellectual, emotional, and spiritual baggage the people of Africa bring to these experiments? To put the same point in another way, what if failure results because the development process has not reconciled itself to the African mental and spiritual landscape?

But, of course, it is not only the poor and marginalized who bring mental and emotional content to the institutions, structures, mechanisms, and processes of participation. Government leaders and the civil-society players themselves have various conceptualizations of themselves and of others. They also bring with them institutional demands. Civic organizations have identified "government institutional interests" that inform their way of proceeding regarding the question of integration. The same can be said of civil-society organizations, NGOs, and humanitarian organizations. Alex de Waal argues in the context of famine relief that

> contemporary international humanitarianism works, but not for famine vulnerable people in Africa. High-profile "debased" humanitarianism works to extend the institutional reach of relief agencies, to create an attractive narrative for the media and to provide a political alibi for Western governments. The future of famine prevention does *not* lie with today's international relief agencies, until they have radically reformed. On the contrary, while fighting famine remains entrusted to today's humanitarian international, famine will continue.[13]

Carol Lancaster confirms this point and explains that those who give aid bring their way of thinking to the processes and structures facilitating their relationship with others:

> Nearly all aid-giving governments have as one of the stated goals of their aid programs promoting development abroad, reflecting the humanitarian values and economic interests of their publics. However, most governments also pursue other goals with their aid, including diplomatic, commercial, and national cultural goals.[14]

De Waal and Lancaster give us reasons for not pinning too much hope for the development of Africa on the aid from outside Africa, for they say that those who give aid bring more than humanitarianism and altruism to the aid-giving process. In fact, the aid-giving gesture can be used as an alibi for other interests. Of course, they do not call for the abolition of aid or humanitarianism.[15] Indeed, even taking into account that aid may come with strings attached, used the right way, it can still make some positive difference. But what do Africans bring to the table of development? One thing is clear. The institutional and structural interests from Africa do not seem to be very well organized or well coordinated. The institutions and structures that exist do not seem to have taken seriously, let alone facilitated the participation of the African peoples with their social imaginaries. This is not a cry for an African ideology but a call for creating space so as to make sense of the African predicament and encourage an appropriate ethical response that informs African intellectual and emotional responses consistent with various Africa experiences, past, present, and future. As it is, African societies are characterized by multiple siege mentalities. They are ethnic, racial, and sometimes national. Ethnic divisions run deep. But the ethnicity is created and re-created. Some of it was invented and encouraged by colonialism.[16] Yet it has molded many people's understanding of reality and informs their emotional responses. Modernization processes (such as urbanization, education, employment in modern institutions, participation in modern democratic processes, and Christianization) have not positively engaged African social imaginaries that include ethnicity and cultural, intellectual and spiritual tools. It is therefore not surprising that modern development and democratization efforts are undermined by what has been identified as corruption, ethnic conflicts, apathy, and various forms of illegality.

Some Positive Examples from Africa

Shorter points out that the Special Assembly for Africa of the Synod of Bishops "pledged the Catholic Church to undertake a closer dialogue with realities of Africa, so that Christianity could more effectively come to terms with the continent's social, cultural and economic ambiguities."[17] The Synod itself concluded that the transformation of Africa depends primarily on this experience, which, in turn depends on welcoming "the Good News to the roots of our cultures."[18] AFCAST tries to create opportunities for African experiences to dialogue with CST. Through specially designed workshops, seminars, and lectures, attempts are made to take seriously "the roots of African cultures."

The roots of African cultures are in the myths, rites, and incantations that reveal their religious and social imagination through rituals. Shorter argues, "For the mystery of Christ to become credible to contemporary Africa, it must appeal to the African religious imagination."[19] He traces this imagination not only in rituals but through African literature. It can also be found in African historical and anthropological narratives as well as in poetry, oral culture, theater, and film. To say this, however, is not to say that the roots of African cultures are perfect. Like any culture in the world, these roots have their fair share of tendencies toward evil. The church has great potential for helping African cultures transcend themselves. The Catholic Church in Africa is beginning to recognize "the resources of evangelization and inculturation, and the imaginative expression of the Christian faith within Africa's cultural tradition.[20] Yet the bulk of the work is still to be done. The advances in the development of African liturgy in the Democratic Republic of Congo are only the beginning. My own observations of the church in Ghana give me hope. I noted with admiration how the church in Ghana and in West Africa in general has gone a long way to reconcile the African social, religious, and African traditional healing practices with the Christian faith. A lot has to do with the maturity of the local church and the local clergy. Yet even in West Africa, where ethnicity can be a blessing, it still has been shown to be a curse.

What can African churches do to support one another? There is great need for the institutions and organizations of the African church to learn from one another and to support one another. Closer contacts among bishops' conferences and regional bodies need to be fuelled. AFCAST, through its members, has tried to use those contacts. Our members are active in IMBISA and AMECEA and in the bishops' conferences of our respective countries. Our members are supportive of the church structures and church personnel in research, training, and information dissemination. More important, they are keen to support the African church in contributing to the development of the CST, making sure that the teaching is informed by African experiences.

Paradoxes of African Modernity

Pre-colonial African Imaginaries

Sociologists Peter L. Berger and Thomas Luckmann have demonstrated how "reality is socially constructed"[21] through the dialectical processes of "externalization, objectification and internalization."[22] Explaining these processes Berger writes:

> Externalization is the ongoing outpouring of human being into the world, both in physical and the mental activity of men. Objectification is the attainment by the product of this activity (again both physical and mental) of a reality that confronts its original producers as a facticity external to and other than themselves. Internalization is the reappropriation by men of this same reality, transforming it once again from structures of the objective world into structures of the subjective consciousness. It is through externalization that society is a human product. It is through objectification that society becomes a reality *sui generis*. It is through internalization that man is a product of society.[23]

Berger goes on to demonstrate how "the socially constructed world" refers to the ordered experiences that give meaning to reality for that society. "A meaningful order, or *nomos*, is imposed upon the discrete experiences and meanings of individuals."[24] Komonchak describes how Lonergan develops this idea to conclude that "human knowledge of the world, then, is a common, public fund, which has developed over the ages and in which one first shares by sharing the common sense of one's own community."[25] In this sense "the real world is not the world of the individual's immediate experience," because meaning goes beyond experience to understanding and judgment. For Lonergan, understanding and judgment are higher levels of processing knowledge in order to give it meaning useful in human action and organization. The world, therefore, is mediated by meaning that is socially processed and constructed.

> For the world mediated by meaning is a world known not by the sense experience of an individual but by the external and internal experience of a cultural community, and by the continuously checked and re-checked judgments of the community. Knowing, accordingly, is not just seeing; it is experiencing, understanding, and believing. The criteria of objectivity are not just the criteria of ocular vision; they are the compounded criteria of experiencing, of understanding, of judging, and of believing. The reality known is not just looked at; it is given in experience, organized and extrapolated by understanding, posited by judgment and belief.[26]

In Africa, as in other societies, myth, magical rites, incantations, and ceremonies play their part in the process of knowing. African myths and rites are repositories of knowledge, emotions, ethical values, and spiritual wealth accumulated over many years and through many experiences. Myths are narratives constructed to deal with the fears, hopes, anxieties, and pains of communities. Rituals help to revisit those experiences, tracing accumulated layers of experiences in responding to physical and social environments. Both myths and rituals perpetuate the mediation of meaning even in the midst of modernity.[27] Failure to engage African rituals in order to revisit and reconstruct accumulated knowledge as well as emotional and spiritual wisdom misses opportunities for evangelization, genuine dialogue, and the invitation to shared imaginaries. The failure positively to engage African imaginaries means that some Africans have continued to reconstruct and therefore perpetuate pre-colonial "imagined communities" and have found little reason or meaning in investing fully in new African imagined communities. Hence, we still have pre-colonial mentalities embedded in modern African institutions, structures, organizations, and processes.

By systematically devaluing African traditional imaginaries, colonial administration and the church forced African communities to take up siege mentalities and encouraged them not to embrace fully the myths, rituals, ceremonies, and symbolic meanings of modernity. They missed opportunities for expanding existing social imaginaries and creating new imagined communities that would embrace multiethnic and multiracial groups necessary for the construction of modern societies. These are missed opportunities for creating comprehensive solidarity. Settler communities continued to see themselves as European, even as their cultures became less and less European. Most African communities withdrew into themselves and focused on defending their threatened existence as they were encouraged to harbor suspicion of other groups through divide-and-rule tactics. These fears and suspicions often erupt into anger and hatred in work places, during party-political campaigns, and in urban residential areas, including squatter camps. Traditional mentalities are constantly recruited to socially disruptive projects.[28] This creates difficult challenges for peace and democracy in Africa.

There have been demands from the international community to interrogate cultures in developing countries for purposes of rooting out sources of "international terrorism." Rituals are being developed for investigating, identifying, interrogating, disclosing, and diffusing rituals of war. Unfortunately, the rituals used are themselves violent and therefore will bring out the worst of the interrogated cultures. CST has sometimes redirected the spotlight onto Western cultures to reveal their need for transcendence and salvation.

Colonial Inventions of African Imagination

A lot has been written already about how colonial powers contributed to the invention of tribalism or ethnicity as a popular ideology in Southern Africa. Leroy Vail identifies three factors: (1) the existence of a group of intellectuals to formulate the ideology (European missionaries, anthropologists, and historians);

(2) use of African intermediaries (local intellectuals and "traditional" leaders); and (3) the real need for some values in times of social change and disruption of communities. Ethnic ideologies defined the cultural characteristics of members of various ethnic groups. These were used to divide and rule. For example, some groups would be identified as smart and hardworking, and others as lazy and evil. Various groups were identified as having qualities suitable for working in specific industries, such as the hospitality industry, the police and army, fields, or mines. Missionaries provided cultural symbols that were organized into African cultural identities. Most African languages were first transcribed by missionaries, who also wrote the grammar of those languages. They also provided researched written history of African societies and created ethnic boundaries by specifying local customs.

Mission schools encouraged ethnic identities in African pupils and produced educated local Africans who became the new force in shaping the new ethnic ideologies. Veil explains that the use of African intermediaries was more prevalent in British colonies, where a strategy called indirect rule was used. It was the strategy of using traditional structures of authority that were modified and subsumed under colonial authority. This was desirable because using traditional African leaders was less expensive. It was also strategic, since maintenance of tribal groups prevented the emergence of detribalized Africans who were dangerous to colonial administration. Indirect rule gave opportunities to African political authorities to enhance some personal power and also created opportunities for African intellectuals and European missionaries to collaborate with newly recognized African chiefs. But chiefs who did not collaborate were deposed.

Ethnic ideology appealed to the African petty bourgeoisie because of its promise for leadership in the newly defined "tribe" and as interpreters of African traditions. Their collaboration with chiefs covered up class distinctions that were beginning to appear. The ideology protected the African petty bourgeoisie as it accepted that they had to improve themselves "for the sake of the tribe." It provided a measure of control over land in the rural areas on behalf of African migrant workers and over women who were left to work on the land in the rural areas. Once the African intellectuals and the general population began to describe reality in terms of "tribal" groups, political unity among them was always threatened. This suited the colonial masters, who used divide-and-rule strategies. This has serious consequences on people's view of the modern African nation-state as an imagined community. In many ways the African nation-state has failed to attract full intellectual attention and emotional allegiance from the African imagination. Ethnicity remains the main object of fascination to the extent that even the modern African nation-state is understood in its terms. It has been used as a tool for struggling over constantly changing environments. At best, the modern African nation-state has been used as a cow to be milked but hardly fed or an elephant in the wild to be poached. It has proved to be a limited tool for social transformation and African liberation. AFCAST networks experiment with new solidarities and sensibilities, using CST to inspire them.

There have been attempts to reconstitute ethnicity and the role of the chief in African society by establishing one-party nation-states and declaring life-presidents. This has been disastrous, for it has meant choosing the myths and symbolic meanings of one ethnic group to represent the rest and to subordinate others. This has always resulted in conflict. For as long as there is no meaningful and genuine mediation, dialogue, and engagement of myths and symbolic meanings between ethnic and other communities brought together under African nation-states, peace will always be difficult to establish. Ethnic consciousness has restricted and impoverished the African imagination. This has, in turn, undermined the conceptualization of African liberation.

Imaginative Tools of African Liberation

African modernity is characterized by the predominance of politics over other realms and values. This is not surprising, given the fact that Africa has emerged from colonialism and apartheid. The fight for independence from colonialism has tried to inform and shape how Africans look at themselves, the world, and the personalities they could create in themselves. Anticolonial struggles were real opportunities for African peoples to transcend themselves and construct wider social imaginaries. While genuine strides have been made in these processes, many opportunities were also missed. The cultures and values formed by anti-colonial struggles also inform how the post-colonial challenges are being handled. Can the personalities, systems, and processes created by the liberation struggles lift us into true human development, justice, and peace? Can they help us respect God's creation?

Liberation struggles created ambivalences that have become challenges to the development of a universal culture of justice, peace, and respect for the life and dignity of every human person and the rest of creation. These chronic ambivalences show themselves in post-colonial nation-states. African people simultaneously love and hate modern African institutions, including the post-colonial state. African nation-states themselves are products of colonialism and, paradoxically, also of resistance to colonialism.

Rule of law is not the same as justice. Africans fully understand this because they suffered under the rule of law and institutional structures of colonial administration. It was through the rule of law that land was claimed from them. They suffered under Bantu Education or what was called African education. Hence their suspicion of these institutions, processes, and procedures even in the post-colonial period. Yet Africans have taken over responsibility for these nation-states, legal systems, and educational institutions, and even the church institutions. What mediated meanings do they bring to these institutions? When they reinterpret these institutions in terms of their own experiences, can they achieve what they are supposed to achieve? The church is caught up in these ambivalences. Questions of identity, intentions, and relevance are asked about church programs, institutions, and practices. To what extent, for example, are church organizations and programs African? Inevitably, Africans love and hate church institutions at the same time. To what extent, then, can the church be an adequate agent for Africa's social transformation, an agent that can help Africa transcend the paradoxes? These questions are at the heart of AFCAST's interest in CST as a tool for facilitating dialogue and genuine engagement.

Moral Nihilism

Presently, Africans and their leaders have not been able to deal adequately with these paradoxes. This has led to some form of moral nihilism that is, paradoxically, always accompanied by some moral justification. African peoples can simultaneously appeal to the values of modern institutions and yet withdraw to attack the same values and institutions on moral basis. They can appeal to modern principles and institutions of justice, freedom, democracy, accountability, and integrity, and yet systematically undermine them in the name of anti-colonial and anti-neocolonial struggles. This is the major challenge to fostering transformed personalities, transformed institutions, and processes.

Africans continually struggle with the question, Accountable to whom? This struggle has been demonstrated in Zimbabwe, where the government, in dealing with the land problem, has simultaneously used but also undermined its own laws and state institutions—all in the name of social justice. The question of accountability and rule of law has been interpreted as a political one. Many African leaders and peoples have generally been sympathetic to the interpretation. This is why many African leaders and people have refused to condemn Robert Mugabe's government. South Africa is presently facing the challenge of either following the rule of law and running the danger of becoming unpopular with the landless and marginalized or being forced to tamper with the existing laws. One can see this paradox being played out in the Mbeki-Zuma debate, wherein Mbeki has some respect for established systems and procedures and Zuma is more skeptical of them and threatens to undermine them in the manner of the Zimbabwe fast-track land reform program. African people and their leaders would like to be seen as accountable and to be recognized as people of integrity. Yet they do not feel that they have enough moral and social solidarity from the rest of the world. They do not feel that the issues of development in Africa are treated as universal challenges that give everyone the world over moral responsibility to deal with. They do not feel that they share the same social imaginaries. They feel as though the world is made up of ethnic groups, each fighting for its own interests. In this framework the common good is made irrelevant and universal solidarity ineffective. They look at how powerful governments and international organizations respond to events in Africa and compare the responses with how the same organizations and governments respond to similar events elsewhere. The result of that observation is that they are not fully convinced by the universality of concepts such as international community, united nations, rule of law, or even common good. Many Africans feel that international calls to follow "the rule of law" or indeed "good governance," in fact, tend to mean being subservient to international capital and Western political and cultural domination. Yet they cannot afford to abandon these concepts. They even justify their violence, corruption, and undemocratic actions using these same concepts. Unless this fact is appreciated and dealt with, international donors, church organizations, governments, civil society, and the private sectors will continue to be frustrated by the apparent lack of progress in the cultivation of integrity and accountability just as much as African peoples themselves and their leaders are also frustrated.

The best strategy for dealing with this challenge is to universalize/globalize these values and show social and political solidarity with the African people by dealing with development challenges in Africa as global challenges. This solidarity can be demonstrated in international institutions and processes. It can be demonstrated in rules guiding international trade, international peacekeeping and conflict management, and conflict transformation. It can also be reflected in the way African problems are described and understood. Church groups in collaboration with other civic organizations can network and form joint movements to teach skills for moral growth that will result in high-quality global multilateral cooperation with new moral responsibilities. AFCAST works toward this universalization of human solidarity.

Building Cultural Capital:
Starting with What Already Exists

The kind of universal solidarity that is required is one that demands social transformation. Social transformation is not intrinsically valuable. Neither are nation-states, economic institutions, social structures, and political organizations. Development programs, democratic processes, and poverty-alleviation initiatives are not intrinsically valuable. Indeed, political institutions and economic markets can be used as tools in poverty reduction, but it is human beings and all of God's creation that are intrinsically valuable. Authentic and integral development is about the growth and flourishing of human beings and their relationships to themselves and to the rest of creation. Poverty is a symptom of things gone wrong. Poverty-alleviation efforts are remedies to things gone wrong. But those efforts contribute to the building of a better world, better relationships, and better human beings.

While the story of development can be told without markets, it cannot be told without human beings and God's creation. We are lucky to have markets, but we should not be slaves of tools we have built. Yet we should be slaves to our humanity, our relationships to ourselves, to others, and to the rest of God's creation. We must build on what we already have to continue the building of conditions for authentic and integral development.

Some people have expressed this point with respect to building social capital:

> In essence, social capital refers to the "software" that can spur the development process: trust among people, standards of reciprocity and multiple networks of civic engagement. Where these features of social organization exist, collective action for mutual benefit is more likely to occur and those in power will tend to be more responsible and accountable to citizens. If standards of reciprocity and networks of civic engagements are weak, a situation characterized by ineffective government, lawlessness, clientelism and economic stagnation generally prevails.[29]

The building up of social capital must start with building good people and sustainable communities. This includes habits of thought and the general social imagination. Development cannot happen without good people and good communities with a wide imagination, which calls for cultivating virtues in people and in institutions. But the virtues and the people need to be sustained by appropriate institutions, systems, and processes. All of this entails the need for social and cultural transformation that builds into regional and international networks. However, this building cannot ignore people's constructed social knowledge. It must build on it. This is what AFCAST tries to do.

Starting with the African Social Imagination

This building up must start with what already exists and then strengthen, deepen, and expand what already exists rather than create new things. To deal with African spiritual, moral, and cultural experience is to deal with African traditional religious and ethnic experiences. It was a mistake for Christian evangelization to attempt to suppress African religious experiences. That mistake clearly shows itself in the ways Christian faith has on many occasions failed to inspire people to avoid evil, as in the

Rwandan genocide. The suppression of African traditional religions by opposing them to Christianity and Islam means that little space was provided for the religions to grow and grapple with new challenges. One area in which religions were not allowed to develop was in dealing with the stranger—not just one stranger but many. The forced construction of African nation-states by colonial powers placed different peoples into artificial and rigid boundaries. Urbanization of the African, effected mostly through forced labor and labor migration, did not leave a good impression on the mind of the African. Responding with fear and anger, there was a tendency to revert to traditional imaginaries that had been left conceptually underdeveloped, emotionally narrow, and politically provincial.

Aylward Shorter points out, however, that Christian faith has inspired individuals to fight for their fellow humans. This point is confirmed by Rutagambwa, who writes:

> Although the Church hierarchy has miserably failed to address the genocide, it is important to note that small numbers of individuals have shown admirable devotion to Christian morals and virtues. There were Christians—Catholic and Protestant, priests, nuns, and laity—who risked their lives for the sake of their fellow human beings. Some members betrayed the Church's mission, but others acted with true faith and commitment to the Gospel. It is in this small measure of true faith and commitment to Christian values and morals that we see evidence of hope for reconciliation. The faith and commitment of the heroes and heroines provides a foundation upon which to build and work toward the Church's renewal.[30]

But is Christianity adequate for this task? Is it anything more than another form of ethnicity, with its myths, rituals, and symbolic meanings? Can the church provide an imagination wide enough to accommodate and deep enough to attract the various African imaginaries? I argue below that CST can be a fantastic facility for inspiring the necessary transformation in Africa. But in arguing for this position, we should never lose sight of the fact that CST itself is not static. It is constantly growing through new social challenges and demands. Neither does it provide cookbook solutions to problems.

Catholic Social Teaching and African Social Transformation

CST inspires social transformation. It brings together people of the same faith and encourages them to live their faith in this world. However, it does so by encouraging people of the same faith to collaborate with others—normally referred to as "all people of good will." Catholic faith and Christian faith generally demand transformation of individuals, communities, and social structures, processes, and systems. But it is social transformation that is inspired by African experiences and made clear through the categories, values, and principles of the social teachings. AFCAST begins with these assumptions. It has brought together African practitioners who have worked for a long time in the area of CST. These are people who are both deeply African and deeply Catholic. They are people with a passion to make a difference on the continent—people who are also strategically placed in powerful and influential Catholic institutions such as the Catholic Parliamentary Liaison Office in South Africa, the Jesuit Center for Theological Reflection in Zambia, the Catholic Commission for Justice and Peace in Zimbabwe, Hakimani Peace Center in Kenya, and the Episcopal Conference in Tanzania and Uganda. These institutions are at the cutting edge of thinking about and implementing the social teaching. These strategic and influential people bring their experiences to AFCAST as members of the AFCAST Working Group. They help to create contacts and solidarity with individuals and organizations in the respective countries. When they share experiences with others in AFCAST, they also bring new strategies and support systems for social transformation to their countries and local church.

What Is Social Transformation?

The concept of social transformation means nothing until it is specified what is to change and what is to remain the same. Change, especially social change, can never be total. Even the most comprehensive revolutions do not sweep away everything of the previous regime. The attractive idea of starting afresh is, in this sense, misleading.

Social change might include a change of personnel or a social group as when a social group (say middle-class black people) replaces another (say middle-class white people) in a residential area (as happened in Harare in the late 1970s and 1980s, in places like Marbelreign, Marlborough, and Bluff Hill). Or one class can replace another. Or change can occur when leadership changes; powerful individuals replace other powerful individuals, whether in office or residential areas. In this kind of change the classes themselves or the residential places remain intact; the change is in who occupies them.

Another kind of change can occur with alteration of policies and procedures. Personnel may remain the same, but rules regarding how to proceed in social interaction are changed. This is what happened when apartheid was abolished. We had, on the whole, the same people, the same society, but new public policies and procedures, for example, in the distribution of resources like land, education, healthcare, social services, housing, citizenship, private property, and so forth. A system that uses an unbridled capitalist market to produce and distribute its resources is different from one that is dominated by a public control system. In a society, social transformation can mean that the people affected remain the same, and yet the legal, cultural, political, and economic procedures for production, distribution, and consumption of social goods can change.

In yet another scenario of social change, the people and procedures may remain the same while people's ideas and emotive responses change. For example, people may respond more positively to a black government than a settler regime, even though the system of government generally remains the same. Or it could be the institutions and social organizational structures that change.

In real life, though, social wisdom tells us that usually certain cultural ideas influence the organizational structures of society and their cultural actions and behaviors—that people who have certain cultural ideas will tend to organize their society in certain ways. Another way of understanding this is to say that cultures with oppressive tendencies will have difficulty working in democratic structures. Those oppressive structures do not allow human beings to be free to think and express themselves. Therefore, in conceptualizing social transformation we need to consider the following:

1. What values and cultural ideas explain the meaning and nature of the human person and of society generally, and motivate human beings either as individuals or as groups to organize themselves in certain ways?
2. What, given these values and ideas, are the appropriate organizational and institutional structures and procedural rules to be put in place in order to realize certain values and cultural ideas?
3. What social processes are appropriate to capture the realizations of specific values and institutions?

The popular phrase *regime change* is, like the phrase *social transformation*, an empty concept until it is specified what exactly is to change and what is to be retained. The *Concise English Dictionary* explains *regime* as "mode, conduct, or prevailing system of government or management: the prevailing social system or general state of things." When one looks at the situation in Africa, there is general agreement with the phrase "things cannot go on like this." We generally agree that the prevailing social system of corruption, poverty, and inequality needs to be transformed. When the government talks about economic turnaround, it expresses a desire to change the mode or manner of economic management. But this sense of regime change needs to be understood by all. We may all want some form of social transformation but may differ on what that means and find ourselves with a contested concept.

Some want a total revolution that sweeps the prevailing personnel, social structures, procedures and policies, and dominant ideas aside to bring about a new regime. A successful revolution seeks to be comprehensive in what it changes. Other kinds of social transformation are less ambitious and are usually referred to as reforms. Such reforms may focus on the economic regime (economic reform), or the political regime (political reform), or the social and cultural regime (cultural reform). In a reform the same people may be kept in position, but with their ideas and ways of thinking transformed through education, training, and developing skills. However, when it is thought that the people in position cannot be trained or improved, then calls are made for their total removal from office or positions of influence. So it is with institutions and social processes—they can either be reformed or replaced.

Catholic Social Teaching

CST includes the criteria to use in order to identify the kinds of social transformations that are desirable. It offers a values framework for characterizing the good society, one that facilitates the growth and fulfillment of human life and the rest of creation. CST is a translation of the values and principles of the gospel into, as Pope Paul VI stated in *A Call to Action on the Eightieth Anniversary of Rerum Novarum* (1971), "principles for reflection, criteria for judgment and guidelines for action" (no. 4). In *On the Hundredth Anniversary of Rerum Novarum* (1999), Pope John Paul II described CST as a "corpus which enables the church to analyze social realities, to make judgments about them and to indicate directions to be taken for the just resolution of the problems involved" (no. 5).

In order for Christian Social Teaching to achieve a "just resolution of social problems," it must contain the following things:

1. A close *understanding of social reality*, based on adequate information, a nuanced history, and analysis of the issues involved. In this sense CST demands a free social environment wherein information can be gathered, discussed, and analyzed. It demands the ability to listen to facts and to the feelings of people, especially the marginalized, voiceless, and impoverished.

2. A *values framework* for deciding what is good, life-giving, and fulfilling. Values are ideals we strive for. They help us envision life possibilities and help us imagine alternatives to the life we live. Moral principles give us guidelines for attaining practical goals, helping us to realize our visions. The values framework encourages realizing specific values on the one hand and denouncing and combating all that degrades and destroys the human person, human relationships, and relationships with the rest of God's creation. As Pope John Paul II wrote in *Ecclesia in Africa*, "The condemnation of evils and injustices is also part of that ministry of evangelization in the social field which is an aspect of the church's prophetic role" (no. 70).

3. *Planning for action* as a response to address issues of social justice. This planning must consider the capabilities of the church and society with respect to the knowledge, skills, and emotional capacity of personnel as well as institutional relevance and facility, taking advantage of social solidarity with the structures of the universal church, and other regional and continental bodies.

Therefore CST itself demands social transformation. It demands that society be organized according to gospel values and the principles of peace and social justice. Identifying the focus for social transformation in Africa, Pope John Paul II pointed out in *Ecclesia in Africa* that "the greatest challenge for bringing about justice and peace in Africa consists in a good administration of public affairs in the two interrelated areas of politics and the economy. Certain problems have their roots outside the continent and therefore are not entirely under the control of those in power or of national leaders. But . . . many of the continent's problems are the result of a manner of governing often stained by corruption" (no. 109). *Ecclesia in Africa* describes how the church can contribute to social transformation by advising that "Christians who occupy positions of responsibility are to be carefully prepared for political, economic and social tasks by means of a solid formation in the church's social doctrine, so that in their places of work they will be faithful witnesses to the Gospel" (no. 90). We can ask ourselves how the church in Africa has prepared itself for such formation.

If part of what social transformation means is the transformation of social institutions, then the church itself cannot escape the process. We can look at the church in Africa and ask ourselves if it is appropriate and adequate at all the three levels identified above for implementing the social teaching. At the first level, we can ask the following questions: Is the church in touch with the true facts about the African reality? Is it in touch with the feelings of its people, especially the marginalized and impoverished? Is the church able to gather relevant information and to analyze African realities? Above all, is the African social environment such that the true facts about the African reality and the feelings of the African people are being expressed and informing the church's understating of the situation?

At the second level we can ask the following questions: Has the church clarified its own values on the social in the African context? Has it committed itself to its own values? And has it taught its members these values? Is the church subordinating its mandate and vision to some other interests? Is there freedom in African countries to experiment with alternatives and possibilities? Is there sincere dialogue and discussion on values?

Third, is the church able to propose specific action, plan for it, and engage in action? Can capability be understood in terms of resources, personnel (knowledge, values, skills), and institutions (relevance, capacity, and values)?

Meaning of Social Transformation
in the Catholic Social Teaching

One way of understanding social transformation in the context of the church's social teaching is to look at Pope John Paul II's characterization of "structures of sin." Writing in *Sollicitudo Rei Socialis*, the pope explained that "structures of sin are rooted in personal sin, and thus always linked to the concrete acts of individuals who introduce these structures, consolidate them and make them difficult to remove. And thus they grow stronger, spread, and become the source of other sins, and so influence people's behavior" (no. 36).

This passage is critical not only to understanding how social ideas, behaviors, cultures, laws, institutions, structures, and systems are developed, but also how they can be transformed or dismantled. Any desire for social transformation, according to social teaching, should address the various levels through which structures of sin are built, from the ideas in people's heads, feelings in their hearts, their acts and behaviors based on their skills and capacities, to the relationships they build and the social structures and institutions that make their society. Given that no society is made up only of structures of sin, social transformation is usually about increasing and deepening the social ideas, behaviors, laws, and structures that enhance life while fighting the structures of sin that undermine life and diminish healthy human relationships. Social transformation is not a one-directional or one-dimensional process. It is a reflexive process wherein the personal affects the social and the other way round. Ideas build people and institutions just as those institutions help to stimulate ideas and to construct human characters.

Personal Transformation

CST provides guidance to individuals in their personal lives and how they relate to themselves, to others, and to the rest of the world. It influences individual consciousness and molds the conscience. It encourages individuals to make moral and just decisions on many issues, for example, about wages to pay; treatment of men, women, and children; and respect for the environment. As is pointed out in John Paul's *Ecclesia in Africa*, "Entrance into the kingdom of God demands a change of mentality *(metanoia)* and behavior and a life of witness in word and in deed, a life nourished in the church" (no. 87). In the context of social transformation CST guides individuals on how to think, that is, what to have in one's head (this involves the ability to engage in social analysis, for instance, asking questions such as, Why do things happen the way they do? and What concepts do we use to understand the world?).

We need to appreciate that concepts are the windows through which we look at the world. They facilitate our seeing the world the way we see it. But precisely because they do so, they also limit our world. As Wittgenstein pointed out, "The limits of my language are the limits of my world." Christians must therefore be very careful about what language they use. In Zimbabwe, especially after the liberation struggle, many Christians were evangelized by politicians and have since failed to go beyond the language of the liberation struggle, even though they have the social teaching available to them. Such teaching encourages the Christian to reinterpret the liberation struggle in Christian terms and reflect on it theologically and understand its meaning in Christian categories. If we continue to speak in borrowed language, as we do, it will not be surprising if we claim to be Christians but act in very unchristian ways. The social teaching of the church gives us relevant language, values, and principles that can help us analyze the world and shape the emotional responses of the Christians and others in the church and society.

Transformation of the Church

CST is also supposed to shape the responses of the church to issues such as social and economic justice, governance, racial and tribal attitudes, political involvement, and care for those made poor by our social, political, and economic systems. In this sense it demands the transformation of the church itself. As an example of the situation that demands the transformation of the church in response to social reality, Pope John XXIII explained in *Ad Petri Cathedram* (1959) that

> all the evils which poison men and nations and trouble so many hearts have a single cause and a single source: ignorance of the truth—and at times even more than ignorance, a contempt for truth and a reckless rejection of it. Thus arise all manner of errors, which enter the recesses of men's hearts and the bloodstream of human society as would a plague. These errors turn everything upside down: the menace individuals and society itself. (no. 6)

This is another way of describing the growth of the structures of sin. Describing the relevant response to this situation Pope John XXIII explains that "the peace which we seek, which we must strive to achieve with all the means at our disposal, must make no concessions to error, must compromise in no way with proponents of falsehood; it must make no concessions to vice; it must discourage all discord. Those who adhere to this peace must be ready to renounce their own interests and advantages for the sake of truth and justice, according to the words: 'Seek first the kingdom of God and his justice'" (no. 95). He then gives details on how the church could fight the culture of spreading falsehood:

> We must fight immoral and false literature with literature that is wholesome and sincere. Radio broadcasts, motion pictures, and television shows which make error and vice attractive must be opposed by shows which defend truth and strive to preserve the integrity and safety of morals. Thus these new arts, which can work much evil, will be turned to the well-being and benefit of men,

and at the same time will supply worthwhile recreation. (no. 16)

We can imagine what kind of transformation the Church in Zimbabwe needs in order to deal with this one area of fighting falsehood. Even more, we can imagine what kind of transformation Zimbabwean society needs in order for the Church to help society get rid of error. As Pope John XXIII points out, "Those who support truth, justice, and the real interests of men and nations do not refuse liberty, do not extinguish it, do not suppress it. The just prosperity of their citizens can be achieved without violence and without oppressing minds and hearts" (no. 139).

The pope insists that in order for the church to be able to transform society, it needs to transform itself. Addressing members of the church he pleads, "But we ask Our beloved children for more than prayers; We wish to see a renewal of Christian life. This, far more than prayer, will win God's mercy for ourselves and our brethren" (no. 142). Confirming this point, Pope John Paul II wrote in *Ecclesia in Africa*, "The church must begin by being evangelized herself." She needs to meet the challenge raised by "this theme of the church which is evangelized by constant conversion and renewal, in order to evangelize the world with credibility" (no. 47). In his exhortation, he insists that "the whole (church) community needs to be trained, motivated and empowered for evangelization, each according to his or her specific role within the church" (no. 53). Then he asks a question that we need to ask ourselves today in Africa, "Has the church in Africa sufficiently formed the lay faithful, enabling them to assume competently their civic responsibilities and to consider socio-political problems in the light of the Gospel and of faith in God?" And he explains, "This is certainly a task belonging to Christians: to bring to bear upon the social fabric an influence aimed at changing not only ways of thinking [what is in the head] but also the very structures of society, so that they will better reflect God's plan for the human family" (no. 54).

Transformation of the Public Sphere

Hence Christian social teaching is meant to influence not only our thinking and our behaviors, but also the organization and activities of the public sector. It contributes, for example, to discussions on peace, decisions on war, economic policies, political organization, technological and cultural developments, international relations, and many more. The aim of transforming the public sphere is summarized by the following statement made by the Second Vatican Council in *Gaudium et Spes*:

> Human culture must evolve today in such a way that it can both develop the whole human person harmoniously and aid men in their duties to whose fulfillment all are called, especially Christians in one human family. (no. 56)

Building Solidarity: The Example of AFCAST

AFCAST is a regional forum for eastern and southern Africa that is based at Arrupe Jesuit College for Philosophy and Humanities. It aims at making more visible the social teaching of the Catholic Church. We popularize and contextualize CST by supporting and strengthening the capacity of those involved in developing and implementing the social teaching at all levels of the church and society in eastern and southern Africa.

We strive for the formation of "good citizens" inspired by faith. But we also collaborate with "people of good will." We network closely with regional church bodies; local bishops' conferences; commissions for justice and peace, and development; and other civic organizations. We share experiences, dialogue, and communicate the social teaching to other parts of Africa and to the rest of the world.

We work to commit professional or functional suicide, always undermining our status. We work to eliminate the need for AFCAST, whose ultimate goal is to help organizations realize our vision without us, helping impoverished and marginalized people stand on their own feet without the help of the elite; making church institutions and organizations infuse the social teaching within their day-to-day work; encouraging the presence of social teaching throughout the public sector, through existing institutions, and personnel. Hence, the success of AFCAST will be demonstrated when church institutions express themselves, and people of faith influence the public sector through the values and morality of the social teaching in the context of Africa. This is why in AFCAST we work closely with already existing institutions, individuals, and organizations. We try to avoid forming new organizations or new programs but focus instead on strengthening existing ones. AFCAST itself is not an organization but a group of selected people who meet at least twice a year to share experiences and strategize on how to make the social teaching more visible, how to lobby policymakers and how to help the church and civil society implement its values.

AFCAST itself is not a big, bureaucratic organization. Although active in seven African countries, it has a coordinating office of only two people—a coordinator and an administrator. Much of its work is carried out through other institutions, organizations, and bodies that collaborate with our Working Group members and other Catholic and non-Catholic collaborators.

In order to facilitate this work we

• Develop inventories of individuals, institutions, and organizations working on the social teaching. This works for networking and encouraging collaborations among people working in the same areas and for the same goals.
• Develop inventories of existing materials that can be accessed by strategic groups.
• Encourage the sharing of existing expertise, good practices, and technologies.
• Facilitate dialogue on the themes of the social teaching.

We respond, through the organizations with which we work, to the needs of various communities, giving local communities opportunities to articulate their needs from their own point of view. This is difficult, given that we are a think tank. The danger of elite groups is that they tend to rush toward prescriptions without listening enough to those who are affected by the policies they advocate. Inspired by what we might understand to be social solidarity with the impoverished and marginalized, we run the danger of undermining people's dignity by assuming that they do not understand the issues.

Challenges of Programming to Human Solidarity

AFCAST works hard to avoid these pitfalls. We avoid them by working though other organizations that are implementing agents of the values we stand for. We struggle against the temptation to focus more on the need for our name to be known or on the internal consistency of the programs we run than on responding to the needs of the communities. Funding cycles demand this. Programming and funding conditions are challenges that sometimes undermine our goal.

Programming seems to me to be some formal expression of the narrowing and shortening of the planning vision. Programs are getting shorter time frames and becoming more and more "focused." It is becoming difficult to get support for programs that run for more than five years and programs that look comprehensively at the needs of the community. Programs are short and narrow, whereas the demands of implementing the social teaching require dealing with concerns and abilities of full human beings in families and communities. Programming, with its demands for "target groups" and areas of focus, sometimes treats human life piecemeal.

If one compares the trend of modern programming to how the church works, one can see the difference. I am thinking more of the Catholic Church. When it is established, it looks at the whole life of the community—it gets involved in the education, health, faith, culture, and social activities of the community. Remember the old priest who walked so close to the community that he did not have time for himself? Now the new priest is being pushed more and more into focused programming. The church as a whole is being encouraged to adopt the programming approach that is easier to monitor and evaluate. But does it result in genuine development?

I understand programming to be part of the development culture of modernity, which defines itself in contrast to the traditional. In its self-definition, modernity presents itself as dynamic, enlightened, and civilized. The traditional is presented as modernity's binary opposite: static, ignorant, and primitive. African societies generally are considered traditional. This way of defining social reality creates obvious blind spots for modern development programs in Africa. They are unable to appreciate and respect the dynamism and capabilities of local communities, so modern programming tends not to recognize local problem-solving strategies so it can build on them.

The language of programming has the danger of burying human beings under the technical needs of program. Program goals, methodologies, strategies, and reporting procedures have sometimes become more important than human beings. Human beings, both those who run the program and those who are supposed to benefit from it, are turned into cogs in the programming machine. I suggest that programming is the thing that has to change in order to adapt to the needs of people. While I recognize that the existence of programs is a symptom of an unsatisfactory situation, I pray for a situation when there will be no need for programming—when human beings will be able to help themselves and one another without the need for formal programming.

As a modern concept, programming follows the modern processes of differentiation. It tends to separate aspects of life that shouldn't be separated. For example, programming chooses some aspect of life (such as HIV, AIDS, governance, human rights, poverty reduction) and deals with it separately from other aspects of life. AFCAST tries to create bridges and reconnect aspects of social life separated by modern programming. We dialogue on the needs of local communities through workshops, seminars, and publications. Workshops are held twice a year; we rotate the sites, moving to each of our member countries— Uganda, Kenya, Tanzania, Malawi, Zambia, Zimbabwe, and South Africa. Each topic is a response to the burning issues of the particular country. When a topic is identified, relevant individuals, organizations, and institutions are identified and invited to the workshop. An expert on the topic is invited to present an analysis of the issues. A member of AFCAST or an expert on the social teaching is identified to reflect on the issue from the perspective of the social teaching. Selected members of AFCAST are then identified to share the experiences, on the same issues, of their respective countries. Selection of participants is critical to make sure that people who know what the issues are and people working on the ground are brought together to reflect with experts and policymakers. Therefore, a holistic approach to issues is taken. Some of the issues we have discussed include elections and good governance, poverty and poverty-eradication strategies, the land issue in Africa, corruption, child defilement, the environment, violence against women, conflict transformation, constitution making, human dignity, faith, and good governance and the role of the church. The proceedings are published as booklets that are, in turn, used for lobbying and advocacy work. Documentation and production and distribution of other CST materials is done. AFCAST supports and encourages the teaching of CST in seminaries, formation houses, and Catholic institutions. Guidelines for teaching CST have been produced and distributed. As a regional network AFCAST has been encouraging regional and global integration and international solidarity.

AFCAST was formed for the following reasons:

- The need existed.
- We have experiences to share among ourselves and with the rest of the world and society.
- People, programs, institutions, and projects existed but were working in isolation. AFCAST has been able to link many

of them through workshops, seminars, publications, and direct communication.

* People in need—the voiceless, needy, and marginalized—sought our assistance.
* CST offers a moral framework, social vision, and motivation for needed social transformation.
* Some capacity to do this work exists in Catholic traditions, church institutions, and organizations. These should be taken advantage of.

Building Social Solidarity and Reflections about the Future

The social teachings suggest that social solidarity is both the fundamental virtue and moral principle that can help realize the common good more easily. In an important sense, solidarity is the other side of the common good.

Solidarity as a Moral Principle

We all belong to one human family because we were all created by God. It is this relatedness as children of God that gives us obligations toward one another. These obligations cut across communities and nations to encompass all humans as well as all other creations. We do have obligations not only toward other humans but also toward the environment, animals, the earth, planets, and the rest of creation. We are obliged to treat other creatures with respect and help create the conditions for their growth and fulfillment just as the rest of creation supports our lives. To understand solidarity as a moral principle is to use it as a criterion for judging right moral actions. We use it to judge the morality of individual actions, human behaviors, community actions, and social arrangements and processes. Social structures, institutions, processes, and behaviors known to encourage solidarity are seen as good, and those that undermine it are judged as wrong and immoral. Thus social processes and structures that estrange people or make them become enemies are morally wrong. Sexism, ageism, tribalism, racism, and other forms of discrimination are condemned. Arrangements that encourage exploitation, oppression, and other forms of cruelty toward other humans, animals, and the rest of the environment are also condemned in the light of the principle of solidarity.

Solidarity as a Moral Virtue

Solidarity can also be seen as a quality or characteristic to be cultivated in individual people as well as in communities and societies. Good people and good communities are those that exude this quality. This is why the Second Vatican Council asserted in *Gaudium et Spes* that a good Christian community is one imbued with this quality: "The joy and hope, the grief and anguish of the men of our time, especially of those who are poor or afflicted in any way, are the joy and hope, the grief and anguish of the followers of Christ as well. Nothing that is genuinely human fails to find an echo in their hearts" (no. 56). To be in solidarity with others is to recognize and respect their needs, desires, life plans, and goals. It is to be moved by their suffering and to be uplifted by their happiness. How many of us are moved by the happiness and suffering of animals, plants, and the future generations?

Solidarity as Part of the Common Good

Solidarity is also a constituent part of the common good. We can appreciate this when we look at solidarity as a social good that is needed and enjoyed by all people in common, not by individuals separately. While it is true that there are some things that individuals can, and indeed ought to pursue privately, there are others that ought to be pursued in common. In order for private lives to be possible, common life must be the foundation. Even a radically pluralist society pursues some goods shared in common. Solidarity is one of the most fundamental of such common goods. Applying this idea to a democratic republic, David Hollenbach has this to say:

> A democratic republic is a social good, not simply a summation of the goods of its individual citizens considered one at a time. From this social standpoint, tyrannies and authoritarian governments undermine the common good itself. It is obvious, of course, that tyranny harms the individuals who are oppressed by it. But Aristotle and Thomas Aquinas pointed out that a tyrant is a ruler who uses governmental power for the ruler's own private good or for the good of some faction, rather than for the good of all the members of the community being governed. Tyranny, like war, makes it impossible for many to share in the life of society in a way that actualizes their potential both as persons and as contributing members of the community. A tyrannical regime treats those it opposes as if they did not really belong to the society.[31]

Solidarity creates an atmosphere wherein everyone collaborates with everyone else, even when differences exist. It is what prevents common life from disintegrating into warring factions. The virtue of social solidarity is also recognition that while individual freedom is desirable, it does not mean being isolated and being completely self-sufficient. No individual or community can live in isolated self-sufficiency.

Conclusion

Social solidarity is a virtue for both individual persons and communities in Africa. Possession of such a virtue creates better people and better societies. We have been lucky that it is recognized in both African traditional cultures and the church's social teaching. AFCAST has taken advantage of this convergence to encourage the process of social transformation in Africa through

CST in dialogue with modern African social imaginaries. By attending to the African spiritual and moral condition, AFCAST hopes to help inspire Catholics in the grassroots communities and those in positions of power to use their sense of self to contribute to a better world. CST, especially the value of social solidarity, is an antidote to popular consumerist orientations of modern individualism and the chaotic rivalries created by tribalism, racism, sexism, and other common social evils. Therefore, social solidarity is transformative inasmuch as it demands new social arrangements, new moral responses, and new personalities. This transformation should result in justice and peace in local, regional, national, and international governance. It should deliver new and fair relationships in international trade and environmental management. With greater visibility of the values of the social teaching, we should begin to see the emergence of better leaders with more pleasant and moral personalities. With these developments our African cultures and social, political, and economic practices should rid themselves of oppression, exploitation, corruption, and disrespect toward the dignity of all forms of God's creation.

Notes

[1] Yvon C. Elenga, SJ, "The Congolese Church: Ecclesial Community within the Political Community," *The Catholic Church and the Nation-State: Comparative Perspectives*, ed. Paul Christopher Manuel et al. (Washington DC: Georgetown University Press, 2006), 247. Elenga points out that "this new dawn of the Africa 'nation-state' model proved illusory, in part because it was based on the Western European experience, which proved irrelevant to the realities of post colonial Africa."

[2] The results include ethnic conflicts, ethnic cleansing, and genocide. Most African politics are characterized by tribalism, nepotism, cruelty, violence, and cheating. The economic practices are rife with corruption.

[3] William Easterley, *The White Man's Burden: Why the West's Efforts to Aid the Rest Have Done So Much Ill and So Little Good* (London: Penguin Books, 2006). See also Carol Lancaster, *Aid to Africa: So Much to Do, So Little Done*, A Century Foundation Book (Chicago: The University of Chicago Press, 1999).

[4] Alexander de Waal, *Famine Crimes: Politics and the Disaster Relief Industry in Africa* (Bloomington: Indiana University Press, 1997), 66.

[5] Aylward Shorter, *Christianity and the African Imagination: After the African Synod Resources for Inculturation* (Nairobi, Kenya: Paulines Publications Africa, 1996), 11.

[6] The atrocities of this campaign are reported in *Breaking the Silence: Building True Peace–A Report on the Disturbances in Matabeleland and the Midlands 1980–1988*, Zimbabwe Catholic Commission for Justice and Peace and Legal Resources Foundation, April 1997.

[7] Joseph E. Stiglitz, *Making Globalization Work* (New York: W. W. Norton and Company, 2007); Jeffrey D. Sachs, *The End of Poverty: Economic Possibilities for Our Time* (London: Penguin Books, 2005); Muhammad Yunus, *Banker to the Poor: Micro-Lending and the Battle against World Poverty* (New York: Public Affairs, 1999).

[8] Several calls, however, have been made for the reform of these institutions. See Jonathan R. Pincus and Jeffrey A. Withers, *Reinventing the World Bank* (Ithaca, NY: Cornell University Press, 2002); Ngaire Woods, *The Globalizers: The IMF, the World Bank, and Their Borrowers* (Ithaca, NY: Cornell University Press, 2006).

[9] William Easterly, *The White Man's Burden* (London: Penguin Books, 2006), 9.

[10] Chris Landsberg and Shaun McKay, compilers, *Engaging the New Pan-Africanism: Strategies for Civil Society*, joint publication of ActionAid International-Southern Africa Partnership Programme and the Open Society Initiative for Southern Africa, in partnership with Center for Policy Studies, Mwelekeo wa NGO, Southern Africa Regional Poverty Network, World Alliance for Citizenship Participation, and Southern African Development Community—Council of Non-Governmental Organizations.

[11] Ibid.

[12] Ibid., 3.

[13] De Waal, *Famine Crimes*, 217.

[14] Lancaster, *Aid to Africa*, 75.

[15] This call has recently been made by Dambisa Moyo in her book *Dead Aid: Why Aid Is Not Working and How There Is Another Way for Africa* (London: Allen Lane, 2009).

[16] Terrence Ranger, *The Invention of Tribalism in Zimbabwe*, Mambo Occasional Papers, Socio-Economic Series no. 19 (Gweru: Mambo Press, 1985). See also Mahmood Mamdani, *Citizen and Subject: Contemporary Africa and the Legacy of Late Colonialism* (Princeton, NJ: Princeton University Press, 1996).

[17] Shorter, *Christianity and the African Imagination*, 7.

[18] Ibid.

[19] Ibid.

[20] Ibid., 8.

[21] Peter L. Berger and Thomas Luckmann, *The Social Construction of Reality: A Treatise in Sociology of Knowledge* (New York: Anchor Books, 1966), 1.

[22] Peter Berger, *The Sacred Canopy: Elements of a Sociological Theory of Religion* (New York: Anchor Books, 1967), 4.

[23] Ibid.

[24] Ibid., 19.

[25] Joseph A. Komonchak, *Foundations in Ecclesiology*, Supplementary Issue of the *Lonergan Workshop Journal*, vol. 11, ed. Fred Lawrence (1995): 33.

[26] Ibid., 33–34.

[27] Many examples demonstrate the persistence of such phenomenon among modern Africans, including political, economic, religious, and social leaders. There is a story about Zimbabwean cabinet ministers who were duped by a female traditional healer who claimed to be able to produce processed diesel from a rock. Myths have been reported that make it difficult to deal with HIV and AIDS. Ritual murders, rape of children, and cruelty to animals are negative aspects based on traditional myths. Myths, however, are not necessarily evil.

[28] Genocide, tribal cleansing, and political violence are examples. Some African governments are known to have used state structures to persecute some ethnic groups and deny them development opportunities. Struggles for power in many African political parties are waged on ethnic grounds.

[29] European Centre for Development Policy Management (ECDPM), InfoCotonou No. 5: *Building Social Capital* (Maastricht: ECDPM, 2004).

[30] Elisee Rutagambwa, SJ, "The Rwandan Church: The Challenge of Reconciliation," in Manuel et al., *The Catholic Church and the Nation-State*, 181.

[31] David Hollenbach, SJ, *The Common Good and Christian Ethics* (Cambridge, UK: Cambridge University Press, 2002), 68.

3.

Connecting Catholic Social Teaching to Contemporary Australia

Sandie Cornish and David Freeman

Introduction

This chapter introduces the reader to contemporary efforts to connect CST to Australians' mind and soul, to generate concerted social action from that interaction, and to thereby exercise moral traction within Australian private and public life. While the "take home message" of this chapter is to identify initiatives that possess either *current* cultural resonance or *future* promise, each is inexplicable without reference to the contextualizing pre-history of recent decades.

The Catholic social justice tradition within Australia finds itself in a situation of rich paradox. It is simultaneously prone to immense success and underachievement. CST is today largely uncontested as constitutive of the faith, enjoys surprising levels of intermittent traction within public policy debates, and is the fortunate recipient of intense commitment and creativity by many. Yet it probably remains the case that few Australian Catholics could tell you what CST's core precepts are, other than an ethical urging to "care about the underdog and do something practical to help." Moreover, in practice it is often discretionary whether a parish priest or Catholic schoolteacher engages more deeply than this.

The chapter moves through six parts: demographic context, pre–Vatican II approaches, the post–Vatican II period, the work of pertinent official national agencies, a snapshot of local, diocesan, lay, and congregational initiatives of recent decades, and an attempt to identify key challenges for CST. Just as politics, work places, and international and community development differentiate the national from the local, and the "top-down" from the "bottom-up," so this chapter affirms the distinctive contribution of each of these within an overall mosaic that comprises CST's impact within Australia. Hence Part 4 focuses upon national efforts and official church agencies and initiatives of the Australian Catholic Bishops' Conference, while Part 5 provides multiple snapshots over the past two decades of efforts, especially at local and diocesan level by lay organizations, religious congregations, church offices, and others. Part 6 suggests some of the most significant challenges that will need resolution if CST is to realize its vast potential for creative dialogue with the Australian public, and its ultimate end game of "a civilization based upon love."

Part 1: Demographic Context

Australia is an ancient continent—probably the most ancient—at the axis of the Asia and Pacific regions. Its original inhabitants—the Aboriginal and Torres Strait Islander peoples—are proud to claim their two hundred language groups and cultures as, collectively, the world's oldest continuous living culture. Anthropologists date Aboriginal arrival from between sixty-five thousand and eighty thousand years ago. Notwithstanding several earlier explorations by French and Portuguese adventurers, the first Europeans arrived from Britain to establish a new penal colony in 1788. Six discrete colonies became the Commonwealth of

Australia on January 1, 1901. The story since 1788 has been extensively told elsewhere. Suffice it to say here that the modern Australian nation is deeply marked by its history as a former British colony, established without the consent of the Aboriginal and Torres Strait Islander peoples, and without treaty or compensation. Reconciliation, justice, and opportunities for Aboriginal and Torres Strait Islander peoples remain major social issues. At a minimum, 2.6 percent of Australians belong to these peoples.

It is only in recent decades that Australian society is beginning to feel at home in its regional neighborhood. Australia's cultural identification with the United Kingdom, and with countries such as New Zealand, Canada, and the United States of America that have similar colonial pasts, began to weaken significantly with the end of the infamous "White Australia" immigration policy from the early 1970s. Successive waves of migration have made Australia one of the most multicultural countries in the world. The 2006 national census found that 24 percent of Australia's total population was born overseas.[1]

Australia is an independent, secular state with no official religion. The 2006 Census reported religious affiliations as 26 percent Catholic, 19 percent Anglican, 19 percent other Christian denominations, and 6 percent non-Christian religions. Thirty percent of respondents indicated either no religion or a response not amenable to classification. The fastest growing religious groups are Buddhism, Islam, and Hinduism (at 2.1 percent, 1.7 percent, and 0.7 percent of the population respectively); these are largely associated with immigration.[2] Religiosity among Aboriginal Australia remains high, spread across traditional practices, devout Christianity, and syncretic formations that simultaneously integrate tradition with Catholicism, evangelical Christianity, and very recently, Islam.

Generalizations about Australia as a godless state and polity, as spiritually as it is meteorologically arid, underestimate the spirituality of past and present Australians. The Great Southern Land has always been and remains a unique locus of God's ongoing revelation.

Part 2: Pre–Vatican II Approaches
to Catholic Social Teaching in Australia

For nearly as long as its modern origins within *Rerum Novarum* (1891), CST has had surprising levels of intellectual influence within Australian public policy and debate, albeit usually informally and unacknowledged. The Australian industrial-relations system of arbitration and conciliation—the oldest such system in the industrial world—was influenced by CST's emphasis on conciliating class interests. Australia's landmark 1907 *Harvester* judgment by High Court Justice Higgins prescribed that the minimum wage must be sufficient to "support a workman and his family." The consensus among labor historians is that Higgins's judgment was almost certainly influenced by his reading of *Rerum Novarum*. *Harvester* generated probably the best working conditions of the day for laborers anywhere, albeit valorizing a gendered understanding of work-place entitlement. Between 1910 and 1920, social scientists from Europe and the United States visited Australia to ascertain whether there was substance to rumors of a "workingman's paradise" in Australia.

Australian Catholicism has been, and remains, well regarded within Australian society for insisting that its members exercise practical charity and compassion in daily life. Yet it has always been far less straightforward to prosecute the distinction between charity and justice, and to require a commitment to structural change despite the powerful evidence of socially structured inequities in the national and global systems.

Part 3: The Post–Vatican II Period—
Aggiornamento and Revival

Vatican II brought CST in from the cold, paradoxically during the Cold War. It followed that to be a "social justice Catholic," or to question social structures within one's own society, was now to be accused of being in bed with Marxism and effectively a "fifth columnist" intent upon "white-anting" the national interest.[3]

The post-1989 near-global collapse of communism removed apprehensions that to criticize one's society, or make inquiries about, say, transnational capital or the CIA, was effectively to provide aid and comfort to international communism. Supporting CST and its works of justice moved toward becoming mainstream "common sense" within Australian Catholicism. New challenges were afoot just as the intellectual challenge of mainstreaming CST was won. The most productive incubator of CST among the Australian laity since the 1940s has been the Jocist movements with their methodology of regular cell-group meetings and the see-judge-act stages that form the Review of Life.[4] This methodology has been regularly endorsed within papal encyclicals commencing with John XXIII's 1961 encyclical *Mater et Magistra*, in which he described see-judge-act as a method for the "reduction of social principles into practice"—and by the Australian Catholic Bishops.[5] Some formation models, such as the Pastoral Spiral, which may today be more familiar in some dioceses, build on the Review of Life.

Yet by the beginning of the 1980s, the Jocist movements in Australia were declining in size, as were other university undergraduate student groups. By the late 1990s student activity on campus was more focused on individuals and their worship and devotional faith practices, rather than upon social commitment or the integration of these two pillars of a vibrant faith. Formation methodologies dependent upon group membership and regular meeting attendance were faltering in quantity of recruits, albeit not in efficacy or "quality" of formation. This was echoed within Jocist movements throughout the Western world, and within broader Australian Catholic developments in which regular mass attendance was somewhat in decline. This was replicated within the wider Australian society insofar as numerous community service and other civil-society organizations, along with political parties, struggled to recruit or retain members.

By the time that John Paul II led a revival of the social encyclical tradition, the groups that had previously received, disseminated, studied, and sought to apply such documents in the local context were no longer strong. New ways of passing on the tradition, receiving new teaching, and contributing to the development of the teachings from local experience were needed—and continue to frame the ongoing challenges that this chapter seeks to capture.

Efforts to inculturate CST in Australia during the 1980s and 1990s included the establishment of new official agencies of the Bishops' Conference with specific documents in the areas of justice, development, and peace; experimentation with the "American model" of preparing justice statements in a consultative manner; educational materials and processes including exposure/immersion experiences; and festivals or peak events.

Part 4: Official National Agencies

The Catholic Commission for Justice and Peace

The Pontifical Commission for Justice and Peace had been established in the upbeat, post-conciliar mood of 1967. The Australian bishops responded—as did most other national Bishops' Conferences—to the Holy See's encouragement to create a national justice and peace commission. A national commission was established in 1969, within the international aid and development agency Australian Catholic Relief (now known as Caritas Australia). In 1972 this commission became an independent body, and by 1976 it was known as the Catholic Commission for Justice and Peace (CCJP).[6]

The staff and membership of the CCJP were composed predominantly of laypeople who brought to the task a range of experience and expertise in areas such as law, community development, and politics. The CCJP was given responsibility for the revived tradition of annual "Social Justice Sunday Statements," the first series of which had ended in 1966.[7] A number of these "Social Justice Sunday Statements" were produced ecumenically during the CCJP period. The CCJP published an extensive range of educational materials and was involved in lobbying and advocacy on such social justice issues as land rights for Aboriginal and Torres Strait Islander peoples, youth unemployment, women's rights, peace, uranium mining, and international development. As well as working with Catholic parish and diocesan staff and organizations, the CCJP built links with Aboriginal organizations, trade unions, the peace movement, and other Christian churches.

The CCJP sought to bring the theology of Vatican II to bear on the interpretation of and response to social issues in Australia. It took up themes of liberation, development, and an option for the poor from the social teachings of Paul VI. John Paul II's *Laborem Exercens* was enthusiastically received by the CCJP, which used it to ground its later work on economic issues.

Following a review of the bishops' initiatives in education for justice, development, and peace, which was conducted for the Bishops' Conference by Monsignor James Nestor, the Australian bishops decided in 1987 not to renew the CCJP's mandate. They replaced the CCJP with a new structure, the Australian Catholic Social Justice Council (ACSJC). The Episcopal Committee for Development and Peace was replaced with a larger Bishops' Committee for Justice, Development and Peace (BCJDP). Both the ACSJC and Australian Catholic Relief (ACR) were to be responsible to the Bishops' Conference through the BCJDP, which, unlike other committees of the Bishops' Conference, was given its own Secretariat.

Why did this come about? One of the difficulties experienced by a predominantly lay commission of the Bishops' Conference was that the status of the commission's statements and positions was often questioned, particularly by those opposed to their content. For example, the annual "Social Justice Sunday Statement" had been issued with the approval of the bishops but in the name of the CCJP.[8] Were they "bishops' statements" in the same sense as the earlier series? Did the commission speak for the bishops? Did the commission's view represent the church in Australia? Indeed, who could speak for the Catholic Church? Could multiple voices have validity?

Some, including Catholics prominent in politics and business, challenged the CCJP's legitimacy on such grounds as being allegedly unrepresentative of the views of the Catholic community on such public issues as Aboriginal land rights, unemployment, and peace.[9] Others asserted that the CCJP had no authority to speak for the church.

Opinion among the Australian bishops on these matters varied, and not all bishops publicly backed their agency.

The Nestor report considered these questions and presented nuanced conclusions. Nestor acknowledged that there was "an assumption by the church itself, and society at large, that the voice of the church at national and local levels is most authentically presented by the bishop."[10] His caveat was that this may not be so in the future, as it was a time of change in which Catholics in Australia were still receiving and seeking to implement the insights of Vatican II and to "understand the requirements of being church in the public forum." Nestor felt that in a time of transition the role of the bishops would be especially important. He suggested that, consistent with other areas of church life, the role of the bishops should include:

Full endorsement of the criteria for the selection of any persons who assume a full-time role in the social transformation activity of the church; Full appointing power to any committee appointed for the task; and Full approval power over the manner in which such a committee carries out its functions.[11]

By implication, Nestor had suggested that the bishops should exercise responsibility for any national justice and peace structure that they established, rather than seeking to distance themselves from its words and actions on inherently politicized and hence controversial matters.

The Nestor report repudiated the view that the church should not be involved in "political" matters or social transformation and should confine itself to charitable or welfare responses. Nestor based this repudiation on the documents of Vatican II and the papal social teachings. The report also received allegations that Australian Catholic Relief funds were finding their way "into the hands of Marxist guerrillas and Communist United Front agencies."[12] This allegation provided a platform to question the legitimacy of deploying modest ACR funds for social justice education and advocacy work within Australia (reasoning that the rich world is the home of decisions that affect the poor world). Nestor concluded that "the Australian Catholic community need not entertain further fears on this matter," and that education and advocacy efforts undertaken with appropriate episcopal supervision "can and should be funded by money contributed by the Australian Catholic community to ACR."[13]

Many, including some critics of the CCJP and ACR, expressed a desire for deeper participation by the whole church in the broad project of justice, development, and peace. One challenge with which the CCJP's small staff struggled was to provide education on social issues and formation in the CST tradition across twenty-eight dioceses of the vast Australian continent. In the majority of dioceses there was no diocesan justice and peace commission with which to collaborate. The main strategy was the dissemination of printed materials. Perennial challenges confronted by this approach were the limited promotion of these materials within Catholic parishes and schools, influenced in turn by the social dimension of the church's mission enjoying mixed levels of understanding among church personnel.

Nestor's vision was for a whole-church response in which action for social transformation "must be integrated closely with the rest of the life of the church," including education, welfare, worship, and spirituality.[14] National efforts would need to be more grounded in local efforts. While Nestor saw a role for a specialist national agency, he was skeptical about specialist diocesan justice agencies. At the same time he believed that every diocesan agency "should be pressed to incorporate the social transformation dimension into its current agenda, and not allow it to recede from continuous attention under the pressure of its regular tasks."[15]

The Australian Catholic Social Justice Council

The bishops explained the replacement of the CCJP by the ACSJC as stepping up to a more direct, visible, and supportive leadership role in the work for social justice and the oversight of their agencies, "in order to give a clear message to all members of the church that all who follow Christ are called to work for justice."[16] The replacement of the CCJP by the ACSJC was highly controversial, with many lay and religious CST supporters quite dubious. Some accepted that it signaled a more serious commitment to episcopal responsibility to utilize CST publicly to respond to local social issues, as Vatican II's *Christus Dominus* put it, "in a manner suited to the needs of the times" (no. 13). Others saw it as a withdrawal of delegated authority to, and trust of, the laity to pursue their vocation to incarnate the gospel in daily life, and/or a win for anti-CCJP agitators largely drawn from ultra-conservative Catholicism.

The newly established ACSJC was given responsibility for preparing the annual "Social Justice Sunday Statements," now to be issued in the name of the bishops.[17]

Nestor's vision of a whole-church approach that integrated social transformation into all areas of church life at the local level was ultimately dependent upon the action of each local bishop in his own diocese as well as the national Bishops' Conference. In truth, only the national element of the vision was acted upon systematically. This left the new national body with an even smaller secretariat than the previous body, and without a strong network of local justice and peace action coordinated through designated diocesan personnel. In a classic case of unintended consequences, Nestor's vision of the integration of social transformation into the mission of every diocesan body seemed more remote rather than closer.

Perhaps the greatest challenge for the ACSJC throughout the 1980s and 1990s—apart from the perennial question of resourcing—was role confusion between it and the secretariat of the Bishops' Committee for Justice, Development, and Peace. The ACSJC was largely an observer to the BCJDP's major projects that experimented with consultative means of producing local teachings, explained below. This made it difficult for the ACSJC to establish an identity as a significant mechanism through which the laity might contribute to the development of CST.

Caritas Australia

Caritas Australia's origins can be traced to 1964, when the Catholic Overseas Relief Committee was formed to administer the distribution of funds received from the United Nations' Freedom From Hunger Campaign. Lenten appeals for overseas relief were held in some dioceses that same year. In the following year the organizers encouraged the bishops to institute a national appeal. Project Compassion was born, and the coordinating organization became Australian Catholic Relief. In 1995 ACR changed its name to Caritas Australia, thereby emphasizing its membership in the Caritas Internationale network.

From the 1970s, and increasingly through the 1980s and 1990s, the agency's philosophy shifted from emergency relief to one of partnership and international social development. With this shift came a growing emphasis on education and awareness raising, and upon advocacy aimed at transforming the causes of poverty and injustice within Australia and abroad. A shared commitment to social justice education often generated collaboration between ACR/Caritas Australia and the CCJP/ACSJC. These collaborations sometimes led to tension, duplication, and at times open competition.

The post-Nestor restructure was intended to provide coordination and avoid duplication and competition between these agencies through their oversight by the BCJDP and, at the day-to-day level, by its executive secretary.

Experiments with the "American Model" of Public Consultation

One of the suggestions made in the Nestor report was that the Australian bishops consider a consultative process for the production of social justice statements. The exemplar was the United States Conference of Catholic Bishops and its pastoral letters on peace and the economy. Marist Brother Mark O'Connor was sent to the United States and Canada to gather information and, with the help of a working party including sociologists, management consultants, and theologians, submitted a report to the Australian Bishops' Conference. On December 3, 1987, the Australian bishops received the report and accepted its recommendation of such a process for the production of the next "Social Justice Sunday Statement."

The O'Connor report advocated a consultative and dialogical approach to the teaching function of bishops in relation to social issues as a way of expressing in practice the ecclesiology of Vatican II.[18] It suggested that a more collaborative approach to preparing statements would go some way toward achieving reconciliation within the church in the wake of the negative response to the bishops' May 1987 decisions, which included withdrawal of the CCJP's mandate.[19]

O'Connor identified broad similarities between the United States and Australia, namely, a perceived "moral vacuum in public life"; a widespread pluralism of society, in which Catholics were integrated; and the complexity of policy issues. These factors had led the US bishops to adopt a new way of teaching that involved public hearings, consultation on draft documents, and educational programs.[20] The report judged this new approach successful because the US Bishops' Conference gained

> the opportunity to consult the laity more broadly and effectively; the opportunity to hear and take account of all viewpoints, so that no one can accuse the process of being manipulated by factions or pressure groups; an assurance that close ecumenical contact will be achieved, because every effort is made to involve other churches in public hearings and in joint educational programs when the letter is being promoted; greater authority and impact as formers of public conscience; and greater coherence and unity.[21]

It was felt that the US process had achieved greater lay participation, greater participation of the bishops, and greater lay acceptance of the teaching thereby generated.[22]

The process proposed for Australia was intended to secure the role of the laity in the formulation of teaching on social issues by providing a place for the *sensus fidelium* to be heard. At the same time it would foster the role of bishops as teachers in the church and moral leaders in Australian society. The eighteen-month process was to include a preliminary commitment by the bishops, issue selection, a first consultation, clarification of gospel teaching and principles, a second consultation, compilation of the statement, proclamation of the statement, implementation, internal review, and evaluation. The centerpiece of the process was to be the two rounds of consultations by means of written submissions and national and diocesan hearings or "listening sessions."[23]

The Wealth Enquiry

In February 1988 the Australian Catholic Bishops' Enquiry into the Distribution of Wealth in Australia was launched. It was expected that the Wealth Enquiry would result in a pastoral statement within two years. Although a draft or progress report was published in October 1988, the process proved so extensive that the final statement was not released until four and a half years later, in September 1992.

The BCJDP and its secretariat, which had responsibility for the task, grossly underestimated the volume of written and oral submissions that would be made by the community and the consequent labor and skills that would be required to deal appropriately with the material.[24] The process was slower, more expensive, and more controversial than expected.

The open nature of the hearings attracted people and organizations expressing a broad range of passionately held views. Similarities with the Senate inquiries of the Australian Federal Parliament's Upper House possibly encouraged overtly political behavior in the lobbying of bishops and officials, and perhaps an expectation by some that the final statement would be swayed on the basis of majoritarian sentiments as reflected in the submissions. A number of prominent Catholics in business, or associated with conservative political parties, urged—publicly and privately—a focus upon wealth creation rather than its distribution. Some interpreted the bishops' questioning of neoliberal economics ("economic rationalism," in Australian parlance) as political support for the Australian Labor Party, then the Federal Government incumbent. Others reacted against the draft statement, "Common Wealth and Common Good,"[25] claiming it lacked a sufficiently prophetic edge at a time when executive salaries were rising and unemployment was nearing 11 percent. Some regarded the draft as defensive and failing to deal substantively with the church's own wealth.[26] All of this reprised the fixed positions aroused by the old CCJP.

The final statement, *Common Wealth for the Common Good*, ran to 198 pages and was launched at the National Press Club and debated in both Houses of the Federal Parliament.[27] The document carefully distinguished between principles and their application,[28] and its recommendations were hotly debated within the church and in the community. The statement was successful in contributing to public debate but did not establish a clear, unified Catholic voice on the issue in the public domain. The Wealth Enquiry had provided expanded opportunities for the laity to participate in the process of developing a teaching document. It probably engaged more bishops more directly in the process of drafting a "Social Justice Sunday Statement" than ever before. That the newly established ACSJC was largely an observer, with little role in the process, scarcely assisted it to establish itself as a significant body within the church through which the laity could contribute to social teaching and action. It was clear that the value of the consultation exercise would ultimately rest on effective dissemination of the statement and implementation of its recommendations, especially the recommendations that urged action by the church itself. The value of the consultative process per se was, widely, well regarded.[29]

A Consultation on Young People and the Future

Encouraged by the Wealth Enquiry, the Australian bishops decided in 1994 to adopt a similar process to produce a "Social Justice Sunday Statement" on young people and the future. The process was again placed in the hands of the BCJDP and its secretariat, rather than the ACSJC.

Initial conversations with young people and youth organizations confirmed the need to adjust the consultation process to suit the topic and engage this particular audience. Rather than consulting *about* young people, the first stage of the process would focus on *dialogue with and listening to* young people. Rather than written submissions and public hearings, an open-ended questionnaire, group discussions, and public forums were used. The bishops made special efforts to access and listen to young people at risk, young indigenous people, and young people from non-English-speaking backgrounds by meeting them in their own contexts. The next stage invited the whole community to reflect on the issues identified by the young people. Practical suggestions for action were invited and, in the final stage, the bishops drew upon the CST tradition to teach and to act.

"Young People and the Future" was published as the 1998 "Social Justice Sunday Statement." It included a vision statement, an open letter from the bishops to Australian youth, and suggestions for action on a range of issues. By then, the BCJDP was already deeply involved in its next project and relinquished responsibility for ongoing action to the Bishops' Committee for the Laity (as the latter already had regular liaison with youth movements and organizations).

Research on the Participation of Women in the Catholic Church in Australia

The next major project of the BCJDP was an ambitious piece of social research in partnership with Australian Catholic University and the Australian Conference of Leaders of Religious Institutes (now known as Catholic Religious Australia).

Topics around gender (sexism in the church, the role and status of women in Australia, and the contribution of women to the life of the church) were among suggestions for consultation. Widely differing views were evident; many claimed to speak on behalf of the majority of Catholic women. Taking advice from their secretariat, the bishops decided that data on the actual participation of women was needed as a basis for constructive dialogue, theological reflection, and pastoral planning.[30] In a situation in which claims and counterclaims were forthcoming about matters of fact, they concluded that something more objective than a consultation was needed.

The consequent involvement of academic researchers in the planning and management of the project was a significant departure, one experienced by some women's groups as disenfranchising. The Research Management Group adopted a research design with five major research approaches, including qualitative and quantitative methods. These were written submissions, the inclusion of pertinent questions in the Catholic Church Life Survey (which interrogated a statistically representative sample of mass attendees), public hearings, targeted groups (focus-group discussion with groups whose voices had not emerged through other research instruments), and a survey of Catholic Church organizations and theological institutes. Four key questions provided the unifying framework for each of these five research approaches:

1. What are the various ways in which women participate in the Catholic Church in Australia?
2. What assistance and support are currently offered to women to participate in the church?
3. What are barriers to women's participation in the church?
4. What are some ways in which women's participation in the church can be increased?

Planning for the research began in earnest in 1994. The project was launched in August 1996, and the final research report was submitted to the bishops in April 1999.

Again, community desire to participate was overwhelming. More than twenty-five hundred written submissions were received—more than any Australian Government enquiry had ever received—and thirty-two days of public hearings were conducted in twenty-three centers across Australia. A weight of expectation concerning the bishops' response was generated by these open, participatory processes. Unsurprisingly, the results revealed significant polarization between "those wishing to maintain the current participation of women in the church or even return to the position of the pre-Vatican II church, and those seeking an expanded role for women."[31]

The bishops published the research results in full, so that all concerned could access the data directly. This took the form of the 1999 book *Woman and Man: One in Christ Jesus*. This contributed to the goal of providing solid information as a basis for dialogue, theological reflection, and pastoral planning at various levels, and a check against claims of selective presentation or interpretation. The bishops also established a committee to consider their further response and agreed that such responses would be announced in the "Social Justice Sunday Statement" for 2000. The nine action commitments of the bishops that followed included the establishment of the Commission for Australian Catholic Women and a list of more than thirty possible actions at the diocesan level.[32]

This would be the last major project of the BCJDP. The scale and resource requirements of the "American model," and the action expectations generated, proved too much of a challenge for the smaller church in Australia.

As part of a restructuring of the apparatus of the Australian Catholic Bishops' Conference in 2006, the BCJDP and its secretariat ceased to exist. At least nineteen Bishops' committees were replaced with a much smaller number of Bishops' commissions. The subsidiary agencies of the BCJDP continued to function under the guidance of new Bishops' Commissions. Since 2006 the titles and scope of the commissions have been adjusted on at least two occasions, and now all of the subsidiary agencies of the former BCJDP are again responsible to the same episcopal body—the Bishops' Commission for Justice and Development.

Catholic Earthcare

As the ACSJC prepared the 2002 "Social Justice Sunday Statement" on the environment, the BCJDP was moving to establish a separate national Catholic agency to address environmental issues. The BCJDP's mandate had been adjusted by the Bishops' Conference in 2000 to include ecological and environmental matters. By May 2002, Catholic Earthcare Australia was founded, and the BCJDP was renamed the Bishops' Committee for Justice, Development, Ecology, and Peace (BCJDEP).

Initially, Catholic Earthcare Australia had twenty expert members, two bishop members, and an executive director. Among the membership were prominent members of political parties, leading, predictably, to accusations of party political bias because not all major parties were "represented." Today only members of the Bishops' Commission for Justice and Development (the successor to the BCJDEP) are eligible for membership in Catholic Earthcare Australia, while its secretariat is staffed by laypeople.

Following a similar trajectory to that of the CCJP, the mandate of Catholic Earthcare Australia is now substantially the same as that of the ACSJC, but with specific reference to the environment and ecology.[33] It advises the Bishops' Conference and undertakes research, education, networking, and advocacy. While specialized knowledge is clearly required for a substantial church response to environmental issues, some wondered whether establishing separate infrastructure would lead to missed opportunities for the integration of an ecological perspective across the full range of the church's justice and peace action.

Commission for Australian Catholic Women

The aforementioned nine action commitments of the Bishops' Conference for the participation of women included establishing a Commission for Australian Catholic Women. Its purpose was

- to act as a focal point for ongoing dialogue and integration of ideas pertaining to women and their participation in the Catholic Church in Australia, and
- to assist in the implementation of the decisions and recommendations arising from the Plenary Meeting of the Australian Catholic Bishops' Conference in May 2000 concerning the participation of women in the Catholic Church in Australia.[34]

Although the research had been initiated and conducted through the justice and peace agencies of the Bishops' Conference, the new commission was to be accountable to the Bishops' Committee for the Laity. This appeared to some women's groups as walking away from positioning the participation of women in the church as itself a social justice matter (gender justice), not merely a pastoral matter. Moreover, in the rough and tumble of Bishops' Conference politics, the Committee for the Laity was not considered a powerful actor.

Initially, the commission focused on developing a network of contacts in the dioceses and fostering dialogue with women therein. Later it initiated an interfaith fellowship to enable young women to undertake a period of study in interfaith relations. It was hoped that this would equip more women for participation in a field of growing size and importance in church life. Some, pointing to a lack of visible progress in the implementation of the other eight action commitments of the Bishops' Conference, saw this as a case of mission drift. Was this not the work of the Bishops' Committee for Ecumenism and Interfaith Relations?

In the 2006 restructuring of the apparatus of the Bishops' Conference, the commission was reconfigured as an advisory council to the Bishops' Commission for Church Ministry. It would no longer have its own executive and staff but, rather, would receive support from an Office for the Participation of Women (OPW) within the Bishops' Conference Secretariat. The director of the OPW would be accountable to the bishops' delegate for the participation of women, a member of the Bishops' Commission for Church Ministry, rather than take direction from the Council for Australian Catholic Women. In October 2009 the OPW and other Catholic women's groups held a national conference in Canberra to celebrate and revisit the decade since *Woman and Man: One in Christ Jesus* had been published, and to discern progress since. A sense of widespread disappointment, tinged with some grounds for optimism, was the predominant message that emerged from that conference.

Part 5: Recent Developments

We turn now to significant applications of CST inculturation during recent decades outside that of official national church agencies. While few organizations have the resources to work on all three dimensions simultaneously, virtually all agree that the CST tradition requires the mobilization and integration of "head, heart, and hand." The specific operational choices of each organization may straddle such axes as being action-focused through participation in social movements, advocacy or solidarity work; creating spaces to meet and live with the poor; providing formation through education, action, and/or their integration; providing countercultural witness irrespective of its apparent worldly efficacy; providing induction into a spirituality that does justice; and providing explicit education in CST.

The work of the national church agencies provides important support to these efforts and is among the primary sources of networking and quality social justice education resources customized to Australian culture, all provided on a complementary or subsidized basis to local church networks and individuals.

National Church Agencies

The **Australian Catholic Social Justice Council** supports local efforts through its range of educational materials. Various resources are promoted at varying levels of education or CST familiarity. A subscription ensures that multiple dimensions of each subscriber's ongoing formation are addressed.

The ACSJC also issues numerous media releases on matters of public concern, along with submissions to Cabinet and Government enquiries, variously provided in the name of its chairman, Bishop Christopher Saunders, or its executive officer, John Ferguson. In addition, the ACSJC provides an annual three-day formation event that brings together in a national forum the current and emerging diocesan leaders in social justice. **Caritas** is highly pertinent to localized efforts. It produces educational resources for schools and parishes, especially distinguishing itself in areas pertinent to the MDGs. Its free monthly e-magazine, *Oz Spirit*, also provides social justice education and spiritual resources. Caritas annually joins with AngliCORD, Act for Peace, Uniting World, and the Anglican Board of Mission Australia to celebrate Simply Sharing Wee, producing a resource kit for students, parents, and teachers. Further, Caritas is one of the world's—and Catholic Church's— great aid agencies in bridging charity and justice, aid and development, into a new, post-charity paradigm. Caritas also supports community-driven development projects within remote Aboriginal Australia. In addition, Caritas runs one of the most effective grassroots campaigns in the country that simultaneously raises funds and raises awareness. Its annual Lenten Project Compassion campaign has a presence in most Australian parishes and schools, raising some ten million Australian dollars from a population of about five million nominal Catholics. Finally, Caritas is now in the "formation business," providing annual Study Tours of developing nations, education officers (some stationed within diocesan Catholic Education Offices), and its Be More program, focused especially on youth.

Catholic Earthcare Australia has developed multimedia educational materials on stewardship and climate change, and tools for auditing the carbon footprint of schools, parishes, and church agencies. It also provides advocacy on such matters as rehabilitation of the Great Barrier Reef and the Murray-Darling Basin.

With sixty-six member organizations, **Catholic Social Services Australia** (a commission of the Australian Catholic Bishops'

Conference) is committed to contributing to a national climate that reflects and supports the dignity, equality, and participation of all people.[35] CSSA provides social services across the country, spanning aged care, migrant and refugee services, children's services, disability services, school, drought relief, financial and gambling counseling, drug and alcohol services, emergency relief, mental-health services, foster care, and youth services.[36] The policy interventions and values of these Catholic social services organizations often bear strong witness to CST, grounded in a grassroots pastoral and service presence.

We proceed now to initiatives beyond those of national church agencies.

Diocesan Action

Some dioceses have made social justice a priority. During much of the 1980s and 1990s the Archdiocese of Adelaide was a leading example. Adelaide's historically strong Jocist movements provided a self-regenerating pool of nationally and internationally prominent lay leaders supported by eminent priest and religious assistants. Adelaide Archbishop Gleeson and then Archbishop Faulkner supported an attempt to renew and evangelize parishes along the lines of Latin American basic ecclesial communities (BECs). BECs sought to integrate such dimensions of life as worship, social action, economic coops, and much else, almost imitative of the early apostles. Lay animators worked at the parish level, virtually synthesizing pastoral work, formation, and community-development work. If the BECs project has now considerably receded, some of its fruits remain, such as the current diocesan chancellor, Cathy Whewell, being one of the original BECs parish workers.

Today a number of dioceses have a justice and peace office, but these are strikingly under-resourced. Typically, the executive officer of a diocesan Catholic Justice and Peace Council is employed two days a week, either as a "part-timer" or wearing other "hats" on other days. While in a sense consistent with the Nestor report—to integrate rather than ghettoize justice work—

the de facto outcome is that social justice remains marginal within many dioceses, with everybody's business having become nobody's business. Executive officers are often expected to co-ordinate and provide a secretariat to their council of parish representatives, advise their bishop and draft statements on his behalf, provide training on request to church and Catholic school employees, make advocacy representations to decision-makers, establish relationships with leading-edge works with the marginalized, and network with other Catholic, ecumenical, and secular social justice actors. Better resourcing bears fruit in some of the quality online resources in such dioceses as Melbourne and Brisbane. The efforts of diocesan executive officers to build strong working partnerships with their counterparts in the Anglican Church, Uniting Church, and Council of Churches provide their personal support networks, exemplary ecumenism in action, and concerted Christian campaigns with the considerable weight of multi-church support. In Perth, for example, a coalition of executive officers, along with the Edmund Rice Institute for Social Justice, Fremantle, and Caritas, issued a strong joint statement in support of the National Apology to Indigenous Australians on February 13, 2008. This coalition has made several joint submissions to government subsequently, in conjunction with the Society of Friends (Quakers).[37]

Catholic Universities and Theological Institutes

The emergence over the past two decades of two Catholic universities—University of Notre Dame Australia (UNDA) and the Australian Catholic University (ACU)—has also created a new resource. Each is multi-campus, with UNDA in Fremantle, Broome, Sydney, and Melbourne, and ACU in Brisbane, Canberra, Sydney, Ballarat, and Melbourne.

UNDA requires all undergraduates to take at least two units in philosophy, ethics, or theology. UNDA encourages volunteerism and community service, and it works with Caritas and the Edmund Rice Institute for Social Justice, Fremantle, to create immersion and service-learning opportunities for students and staff. UNDA's Nilungu Centre for Indigenous Studies is based at its Broome campus. This campus—in the heart of the Kimberley region of North-West Australia—bridges local indigenous people into vocational and undergraduate studies, and provides a focal point for students at UNDA's other three campuses through which to engage with Aboriginal Australia. Providing students with month-long volunteering opportunities within several remote communities is a long-term commitment made by the university with Aboriginal settlements such as Umbulgarri. For those undertaking UNDA's social justice major, these activities are integrated with pertinent academic study in the social sciences.

In addition to the Catholic universities, tertiary institutes of theological and pastoral formation provide explicit CST teaching.

Experiential Learning

Education and awareness-raising in justice, development, and peace issues has used the "exposure tour" method since the 1970s, beginning with the work of the ecumenical Action for World Development organization. In the past twenty years this methodology has gradually deepened and broadened and has been taken up by many more Catholic organizations, especially schools and universities. Now, study tours, immersions, and service-learning integrated travel focus on intense periods of volunteering for several weeks or months, and extended preparation, debriefing in situ each evening, and ongoing follow-up. These programs address a desire for face-to-face encounters; living within community elsewhere; walking a mile in the shoes of the "other"; the bonding and camaraderie of an intense, connected experience; and the psychological satisfaction of knowing that one's presence might actually make a difference. There is an additional rationale in play: if many decisions affecting the poor world occur in the rich world, it is prudent to build a cohort of rich-world inhabitants who have seen the world through another set of eyes, however briefly. This can provide a real-world journey toward "critical cosmopolitanism[38] by challenging insularity and provincialism. All of this has resonated with pedagogical trends in education that valorize "experiential learning" as especially effective, not least due to high levels of participant engagement and "doing." Yet, immersions sometimes attract criticism on the grounds that they constitute "poverty tourism"; are self-indulgent when the host community might prefer the cash equivalent of participants' travel costs; are characterized by a feel-good, self-important, and patronizing edge among many participants, especially when the project is adopted by wealthy schools. The most skillful facilitators address these legitimate concerns carefully; they often find that enduring connections are made between their graduates and host communities.

Certainly, the provision of course credits at upper secondary and university levels dramatically increases student interest and commitment. But volunteering rates have surged in Australia during the past fifteen years, indicating a 50 percent increase in total hours volunteered, with the largest increase among eighteen to twenty-four year olds. If some of this is motivated by resume building, and some by the exoticism of it all, doubtless substantial parts emanate from genuinely altruistic sentiments. One of social justice's most powerful attractions—and forms of genuinely inculturated leverage—seems to be that the work can provide at least partial answers to the universal search for meaning and higher purpose.

The Movements

A strong revival is under way within the Jocist movements, and their see-judge-act Review of Life method. Young Christian Workers, Young Christian Students, and the graduate movement ACMICA (Australian Catholic Movement for Intellectual and Cultural Affairs) are all experiencing strong growth in particular dioceses. The national Cardijn Conference in Adelaide in October 2009 planned this revival. Former YCW National Secretary Stefan Gigacz's[39] efforts to communicate the timelessness of the formation method, and his vast twentieth-century scholarship into Jocism's history and pre-history, provide encouragement to new generations of student and worker leaders. It remains to be seen whether this revival can again generate the mass movements of the past or will be a smaller, more specialized operation for developing the next generation of lay leaders. Over the past five years the YCW and YCS have already made significant contributions to national policy debates.

Religious Congregations

The renewal of religious congregations in recent decades has provided a major fillip for the Australian inculturation of CST. While it took several years for Vatican II to influence many congregations' theology and formation methods, the leadership and much of the membership of most eventually came to commit substantively to CST. Most have undertaken a return to their founders and original charism, reevaluating their works in this light. For example, the religious orders historically ran the private Catholic hospitals, and today the Catholic health system has become a significant field of commitment to CST. This occurs both in the form of its peak organization, Catholic Health Australia (CHA), and individual provider groups such as St. John of God, St. Vincent's Health Australia, and MercyCare. Social justice typically features among the four or five core values and mission priorities of each such provider. They participate in CHA's executive leadership program, with a CST component, delivered as a certificate from the Australian Catholic University's Canberra campus. In 2007, CHA's scholar in residence produced a robust monograph summarizing the preferential option for the poor and its consequences for Catholic health providers.[40]

Many of the newer initiatives that follow have been initiated and funded by congregations. We now highlight a few contributions of each of three religious congregations that exercise a social justice leadership role in Australia: Jesuits, Christian Brothers, and Mercy congregations. We choose these examples only for the purpose of brevity. Inevitably, to do so neglects other significant initiatives such as the Columban Centre for Peace, Ecology and Justice in Sydney.

The Jesuits

The Australian Jesuits have been strongly influenced by the American, Filipino, and Latin American Jesuits' radical engagement with CST, along with their scholarly leadership in the field. With over one hundred staff and another hundred skilled volunteers, Jesuit Social Services[41] undertakes cutting-edge work with young people with complex needs and with communities experiencing compound disadvantage, and undertakes important work in research, policy, and advocacy. Jesuit Refugee Service Australia is part of an international organization that accompanies, serves, and advocates for forcibly displaced people. The Jesuits' e-magazine *Eureka Street* is one of Australia's premier sites for debating public issues through a values-oriented and theological prism. The Jesuits' monthly magazine for the faithful, *Australian Catholics*, is distributed to every parish; it emphasizes practical yet ambitious works of justice, with real-life profiles of those on the front lines. The Jesuits' Faith Doing Justice website is a more recent project aimed at building a critical mass of people with a thorough grasp of the CST tradition.

The Faith Doing Justice project was launched in November 2006 as a partnership between Church Resources and the Loyola Institute (an organization of the Australian Jesuits promoting Ignatian formation for mission) to resource the collection and development of materials dynamically integrating the theory and practice of social justice in ways that are accessible for nonspecialists. The materials focus on events, themes, or principles of CST, key documents of CST, and particular social justice issues. They are grounded in and addressed to the unique Australian context and complement the direct services and advocacy work being undertaken by other entities by providing formation in the Christian foundations of such activities.

The project attempts to make use of the potential of new media to communicate the Catholic justice tradition, especially to younger, IT-savvy generations who are beginning to assume leadership positions in church and society. It seeks to provide easy, approachable paths into a rich and sophisticated tradition without oversimplifying content, and to present material in bite-sized pieces for a largely post-book audience. Its three initial elements are a website, a free monthly electronic newsletter, and an email-based moderated forum.

The web-based approach has enabled a much broader, free distribution of educational and formation material than previous print-based strategies. It also offers greater flexibility in the organization of and access to material compared with a traditional print approach. The search function allows material to be accessed by CST themes as well as by issues, and a modular approach responds to the cyberspace reality of multiple points of entry. Because many of the resources already available from other sources focused either on issues, or on CST, while relatively few integrated the two, this dynamic of integration is a focus of many of the original resources produced for the project. Nonetheless, issues-based pathways and CST-based pathways are also offered through different sections of the website. It is hoped that in the future an online learning facility will be added to the website, facilitating the use of site resources in coherent sequences for particular learning objectives.

The initial partnership with Church Resources provided the project with access to an extremely broad range of contacts for the distribution of the newsletter. Church Resources combines the buying power of the churches and not-for-profits to achieve savings for ministry. Its databases include the parishes, schools, healthcare facilities, and social services of a number of Christian churches across the country, as well as a range of not-for-profits. When Church Resources withdrew from the partnership after two years, having played its role in facilitating the startup, subscription levels suffered without the support of regular updating of institutional contacts. Nonetheless, the readership remains at a level sufficient to place the *Faith Doing Justice* newsletter in the "large publications" category of the Australasian Catholic Press Association membership.

The project has continued as an activity of the Australian Province of the Society of Jesus and was "rebranded" as a Jesuit project with a program of workshops on the Jesuit justice tradition previously offered through the Loyola Institute now packaged as part of the Faith Doing Justice project.

The third initial element of the project, the forum, was the least successful. After several months of "seeding" the forum with stimulus material, with very little response, the editor terminated this aspect of the project. In late 2009 a Twitter account and Facebook fan page were established with a similar intention, and with rather more success. In early 2010 two-thirds of the Facebook page fans were under the age of thirty-five. The geographic spread of the Facebook page fans is broad, and there are more fans from Jakarta than Melbourne! By contrast, the readership of the email newsletter appears to be an older cohort with stronger links to church institutions, particularly in service delivery and education. A new challenge for Faith Doing Justice is imagining ways of making social networking spaces an arena for effective action by a geographically dispersed cyber community for social transformation.

The Faith Doing Justice project has been seen by some as a democratizing project, giving the people of the church ready access to their own justice tradition and challenging the perception of CST as a documentary tradition belonging to popes and bishops. It takes seriously Paul VI's exhortation in *Octogesima Adveniens* (1971) to the laity not to wait for pronouncements by bishops, but to analyze their own concrete contexts and draw on the teachings to inform action (no. 4).

The vast majority of resources on CST available in English in Australia originate from the United States. While Australian political culture is broadly similar to that of the United States, our political institutions are different. The ecclesial context is also different, particularly in the levels of staffing and resourcing of church organizations. The Faith Doing Justice project has sought to go beyond the easy habit of adapting American resources and processes in order to authentically inculturate the social teachings from the ground of Australian experience and sensibilities.

The Australian continent is unique in sitting at the axis of Asia and the Pacific. A challenge and a hope for the future is for Faith Doing Justice to promote greater exchange of local teachings and action grounded in the extraordinarily diverse experiences of the Asia Pacific region. The growing role of regional bodies in Jesuit governance and action, and a revitalization of the Jesuit Conference of East Asia and Oceania's social apostolate network, which is currently under way, may support such a venture.

A focus on chronological presentation of the formal teaching documents in the presentation of CST in Australia had fed a perception of the tradition as something male and clerical. The influence of women in the development of formal teaching documents has been neither extensive nor highly visible. By focusing more on principles and how they animate advocacy and action as well as teaching documents on particular issues, the Faith Doing Justice project enlarges the space for and visibility of women and laymen as practitioners of CST whose thought and action contribute to the development of the tradition.

Challenges for the future include mobilizing sufficient resources to enable the project to continue, and to make more effective use of multimedia; staying abreast of developments in new media and developing models of effective transformative action through their use; finding local collaborators in Asia Pacific countries to enable a more regional perspective to be presented; and succession planning to ensure that the next generation of leadership is equipped with an adequate grasp of the tradition to take the project forward.

The Christian Brothers

Edmund Rice founded the Christian Brothers in Ireland over two centuries ago. A desire to return to his radical, edgy ministry at the margins has led the Christian Brothers to embrace social justice as their premier focus. Edmund Rice International provides the international thrust for this, collaborating with Franciscans International in human rights advocacy among NGOs and the UN system in Geneva and New York. The congregation has dedicated social justice centers in Sydney, Auckland, and Fremantle, Western Australia. Many other Edmund Rice ministries also have social justice as their raison d'être. Since 1996 Edmund Rice Centre (ERC) Sydney has distinguished itself with its landmark *Deported to Danger* reports (2005 and 2006), its 2006 award from the Australian Human Rights and Equal Opportunity Commission, and a 2007 documentary on SBS television (*A Well Founded Fear*) about the fatal return to Afghanistan of failed applicants for asylum in Australia.[42] With its "awareness–advocacy–action" focus, the ERC concentrates on three major areas of operation: indigenous issues and reconciliation, refugees and asylum seekers, and eco-justice. The ERC is a leading actor in, for example, the Pacific Calling Partnership, which publicizes the plight of low-lying Pacific islands due to climate change. Other activities include immersions to Aboriginal Australia and Latin America, regular media commentary and newsletters on public issues, business ethics breakfasts, and the promotion of fair trade products.

The Edmund Rice Institute for Social Justice, Fremantle (ERISJ) is based in a coastal suburb of Western Australia's capital city, Perth, home to 1.6 million people. The purpose of the ERISJ is to build community commitment, skills, and action for social justice. Like many other social justice centers and institutes worldwide, ERISJ engages in advocacy, research, and social action, seeking to find new methods of formation suited to the times and to deliver social justice education and training capable of rectifying deficits in hope, skills, insight, and resilience among supporters. It also seeks to be equally present to people "of all faiths and none," and similarly to those of all education levels. The "end game" is to form a critical mass of social justice supporters capable of genuinely influencing public policymaking.

The Sisters of Mercy

In November 2009 the Institute of the Australian Sisters of Mercy held an inaugural Mercy Justice Conference. Intended to be annual, the national conference seeks to network and encourage initiatives emanating from Catholic social justice. The four areas of Mercy commitment are asylum seekers and refugees, eco-justice, indigenous concerns, and women and poverty. The Sisters of Mercy have started a national youth movement across their network, seeking to recruit girls within Mercy schools and maintaining membership into adulthood. The sisters provide leadership programs for early and mid-career Catholic women with leadership potential, including a strong justice focus. They also collaborate in their works of charity and justice in the Asia-Pacific region.

Part 6: Future Challenges

It has taken a long time for CST to attain its current status as theologically uncontroversial. As the 1971 Synod of Bishops' *Justice in the World* statement put it, work for justice is constitutive of the faith. Today this is widely accepted by most Australian Catholic leadership. Some of the laity also embrace this understanding, but many others either do not concur or are unaware of the issues.

Several phenomena on the near horizon contain both promise and threat for the ongoing inculturation of CST. These include the role of laypeople, the availability of adequate resources for the work, and the search for formation methods that best suit the times.

Resources

In large measure for financial reasons, two highly effective CST-inspired centers closed during the past four years. This is representative of the severe financial constraints upon CST work in

Australia. The Global Financial Crisis has added to the burden. Additionally, CST ministries frequently face questions from the public about various child-abuse cases that occurred in the past at the hands of congregation members and the clergy. Nevertheless, the congregations tend to be asset rich even when cash poor. Perhaps the next challenge will be for cash-strapped congregations to establish joint CST centers in capital cities, possibly also housing the diocesan CST office in conjunction with the bishop. One such congregation—or the diocese—might donate a large former novitiate, presbytery, or other building as an equity contribution, while others contribute cash and/or staff. A large building could be ecumenically based, housing also the Uniting, Anglican, and Council of Churches social justice offices within that diocese. The different strengths and charisms of multiple congregations, and even denominations, could each have a home.

Unlike the congregations and the clergy—with their declining numbers, and their financial responsibilities to abuse claimants, and their own aging membership—Catholic health providers and universities are in growth phases. All of this may render their substantial resources—human, income, land, and buildings—available in principle to support CST work even more fully than the Catholic universities and health providers currently do.

The Laity

The laity is challenged to be the leaven in the bread of the world, and thereby to bring CST to fruition (a civilization of love). This chapter has been justifiably celebratory about the contribution of religious, priests, and bishops to CST's inculturation within Australia. It does not diminish any of this to observe simultaneously that we are yet to see Vatican II's invitation to all the faithful to assume their place as priest, prophet, servant, and king.

Yet progress has been made. Recalling the development of the national justice and peace organizations of the church in

Australia we observed a tension between the desire for strong episcopal leadership and official status and the desire for lay participation in authentic leadership. More than ever laypeople are finding their own performative space—often with the support of the religious congregations—and their own voice, rather than looking to the bishops. The credibility of this voice in public debate is often grounded in research, community engagement, and experience in service delivery rather than formal authority within the church.

Absence of a Critical Mass with CST Familiarity

Debates within Australian Federal Parliament of the past decade and a half were sometimes clearly influenced by concepts grounded in CST. Debates regarding Australia's participation in the Gulf wars were influenced by just-war theory. Campaigns to promote the interests of Aboriginal Australians seeking native title land rights, of asylum seekers to access fair processing within Australia, and criticism of legislation to curtail workers' rights also mobilized concepts originating within CST. In the work-place-reform debate, the Australian Catholic Council for Employment Relations played an important role in articulating classic CST underpinnings about fair employment and worker dignity. Yet not enough laypeople in the country actually know CST well enough to understand the intellectual markers in play, even when criticizing the government from a putative CST stance.

Given the important role of the congregations, drawing out the typically strong affinities between their charisms and contemporary CST becomes a significant formation objective. Much of what is most impressive about these founders could be simultaneously expressed as a prophetic prescience about the shape that CST would take centuries later. This would ensure that the congregations propagate among the faithful both an understanding of their founding charism and founder and of CST.

A Concluding Tribute

We have sought here to provide a preliminary account of various efforts of the past thirty or so years to connect CST to the Australian church. We have fixed our gaze here upon organizations and structures. That is worthwhile, because for CST to be more than aspirational, it needs institutions that incarnate it and carry it forward. Yet it is fitting to pay tribute here—by way of closing—to the daily unheralded and undocumented heroism of so many individuals and informal collaborations that truly live the CST call to a faith that does justice.

Notes

[1] The main countries of birth reported in the 2006 Australian census were—in descending order—United Kingdom, New Zealand, Italy, China (excluding Taiwan and the Special Administrative Regions), Vietnam, India, Philippines, Greece, South Africa, Germany, Malaysia, Netherlands, Lebanon, and the Hong Kong SAR. In June 2008, Australia was home to immigrants from over two hundred countries, and in 2007–8 migration contributed 59 percent of population growth for the year. Statistics available on the www.abs.gov.au website.

[2] Ibid.

[3] "White-anting" is an Australian term that refers to the action of termites in undermining a foundation from within.

[4] JOC is the French-language acronym for Young Christian Workers; the descriptor Jocist or Jocism denotes the YCW, Young Christian Students (YCS), Tertiary Young Christian Students, and graduate organizations affiliated with ICMICA, the International Catholic Movement for Intellectual and Cultural Affairs.

[5] See Bishop Leonard Faulkner's 1979 public statement as chair of the Bishops' Committee for the Laity.

[6] Michael Hogan, *Australian Catholics: The Social Justice Tradition* (North Blackburn: Collins Dove, 1993), 95.

[7] The first series of "Social Justice Sunday Statements" are reproduced in full, together with commentaries, in Michael Hogan, ed., *Justice Now! Social Justice Statements of the Australian Catholic Bishops 1940–1966* (Sydney: Department of Government and Public Administration University of

Sydney, 1990); the second series, for which the CCJP was responsible, are reproduced, together with commentaries, in Michael Hogan, ed., *Option for the Poor: Annual Social Justice Statements of the Australian Catholic Commission for Justice and Peace 1973–1987* (Sydney: Department of Government and Public Administration University of Sydney, 1992).

[8] Michael Costigan, "Social Justice and the Australian Catholic Bishops," *Voices: Quarterly Essays on Religion in Australia* 2, no. 1 (Mulgrave, Victoria: John Garratt Publishing, 2009): 14.

[9] The "Social Justice Sunday Statements" of 1979 (*Beyond Unemployment*), 1983 (*Changing Australia*), and 1985 (*Work for a Just Peace*) were the most controversial of the CCJP's statements.

[10] J. Nestor, "Report of Review of Episcopal Initiatives for the Promotion of Education for Justice, Peace, and Development" (Surry Hills: Bishops' Secretariat for Justice and Peace, 1986), 4.

[11] Ibid., 5.

[12] Ibid., 6.

[13] Ibid.

[14] Ibid., 4.

[15] Ibid.

[16] Australian Catholic Bishops' Conference, *media release*, May 7, 1987.

[17] Dr. Michael Costigan, the only person ever to serve as the executive secretary of the BCJDP during its nineteen-year history, suggests that "an issue never fully resolved during the lifetime of the Bishops' Committee was the division of responsibilities between it and the ACSJC. On the one hand, the ACBC wished the bishops in this area to have a higher profile and a more 'hands on' role than their predecessors on the Episcopal Committee for Development and Peace. On the other hand, the ACSJC was constructed along similar lines to the CCJP and was expected to have a similar role, spreading the social justice message, making public comments whenever matters requiring intervention came to light in the community, assisting in the drafting of annual statements and giving advice to the bishops. If anything, there was a little more emphasis on the ACSJC's advisory role than on the kind of initiating, assertive role assumed by the CCJP. It was understood that the BCJDP or the ACBC itself would deal with issues of great importance, with appropriate advice from the Council, although no formula existed to aid assessment of degrees of importance" (Costigan, "Social Justice and the Australian Catholic Bishops," 21–22).

[18] Mark O'Connor et al., "A Report on the USA Bishops' Model of Preparing Pastoral Letters on Justice and Peace" (Sydney: 1987), 4.

[19] Ibid., 9.

[20] Ibid., 6.

[21] Ibid., 7.

[22] Ibid., 8.

[23] Ibid., 11–12.

[24] Costigan, "Social Justice and the Australian Catholic Bishops," 24–27.

[25] BCJDP, "Common Wealth and Common Good" (Victoria: Blackburn, 1991).

[26] Ibid.

[27] Australian Catholic Bishops' Conference, *Common Wealth for the Common Good* (Victoria: Blackburn, 1992).

[28] Chapter 3 of the document deals with this issue but offers no commitment to act, saying only that "issues raised in numerous submissions deserve attention and may well prompt church authorities to review the matter in whole or in part" (39).

[29] Professor Muredach Dynan's evaluation report on the Wealth Enquiry process, quoted in Costgan, "Social Justice and the Australian Catholic Bishops," 30.

[30] Marie Macdonald et al., *Woman and Man: One in Christ Jesus* (Sydney: Harper Collins, 1999), 2.

[31] Ibid., 373.

[32] See the www.socialjustice.catholic.org.au website.

[33] See www.catholicearthcare.org.au.

[34] See www.socialjustice.catholic.org.au.

[35] Marie T. Farrell, *Mercy and Justice Embrace: Towards an Australian Mosaic*, draft prepared for the Catholic Social Justice monograph series (Sydney: ACSJC, forthcoming).

[36] For a list of member organizations and the 2008–9 annual report, see www.catholicsocialservices.org.au.

[37] Some of these submissions may be viewed on the www.erisj.org.au website.

[38] Fuyuki Kurasawa, *The Work of Global Justice: Human Rights as Practices* (New York: Cambridge University Press, 2007).

[39] See Stefan Gigacz, "'See, Judge, Act' More Than Truth by Consensus," *Eureka Street* 17, no. 12 (June 28, 2007). Available on the www.eurekastreet.com.au website.

[40] Gerald A. Arbuckle, *A "Preferential Option for the Poor": Application to Catholic Health and Aged Care Ministries in Australia* (Deakin West: Catholic Health Australia, 2007).

[41] See "Reports and Highlights" on www.jsc.org.au.

[42] Available from the Edmund Rice Centre, erc@erc.org.au, PO Box 2219, Homebush West, NSW, 2104.

4.

East Asian Discourses on Harmony

A Mediation for Catholic Social Teaching

Agnes M. Brazal

Christianity in Asia has largely been viewed as a foreign religion, a religion of the colonizers. The call of the Federation of Asian Bishops' Conferences (FABC) to give Christianity an Asian face[1] is a challenge as well to CST and its principles. The mediation of Asian philosophical-religious world views is necessary if CST is to make an impact both on Asian Christians and peoples of other faiths.[2] In addition, since Christians are a minority in Asia, the task of promoting justice and peace requires all the more collaboration with peoples of other faiths. The principles of CST must therefore find resonance in the ethos of other religious/cultural communities. In lieu of this, it can be asked: On the one hand, how are the principles of CST in line with local cultural world views? Can they be rearticulated in vernacular[3] idioms? On the other hand, how can the local cultural narratives challenge and enrich CST and vice versa?

This essay elaborates in particular on East Asian philosophical-religious[4] discourses on harmony. East Asia is a subregion of Asia bounded roughly by the Indian subcontinent on the west, the Pacific Ocean on the east, Australia on the south, and the

Arctic Ocean on the north. Oftentimes the term *East Asia* is used to refer to the countries with significant Chinese influence (e.g. The People's Republic of China, Taiwan, Korea, and so forth), which are also called the Northeast Asian countries. In other contexts *East Asia* is employed to likewise encompass what are designated as Southeast Asian countries (for example, Vietnam, the Philippines, Malaysia, Indonesia, Thailand) that have a significant Chinese population and cultural influence as well as vibrant Hindu and Islamic communities. It is in the latter, broader sense that we are using the term *East Asia*.

Globalization and Cultural Hybridity and Fragmentation

Before proceeding further, it may be useful to clarify in what sense we understand culture and thus can speak of an East Asian cultural mediation. For this, we shall make use of the thoughts of the post-colonial theorist Stuart Hall. Culture, posits Hall, is primarily concerned with the practice of "the production and exchange of meanings—the 'giving and taking of meaning'— between the members of a society or group."[5] His definition focuses on culture first as a verb or praxis that entails a process of exchange of meanings, even before it becomes a noun (a way of life).

Hall rejects the static view of culture in culturalist models wherein society is understood as a homogenous and unified totality corresponding to a particular experience: a set of particular political interests, roles, and actions, as well as a set of what is considered authentic cultural practice and/or position in the economic sphere and so on.[6] In line with the thoughts of the Italian neo-Marxist philosopher Antonio Gramsci (1891–1973), and in critical dialogue with structuralist and post-structuralist thoughts, Hall stresses the heterogeneity and complexity of societies.[7] Many systems and currents of philosophical thought can thus exist in a given society.[8] Hall also recognizes how globalization has brought about the pluralization of cultural codes and fragmentation of identities. Due to external cultural influences it has become more difficult for national identities to remain "intact." Through media and other communication systems, we are bombarded by a variety of identities appealing to different parts of ourselves from which it seems possible to choose.[9] Even as identities get fragmented in a global society, identity remains important, according to Hall, because it defines a place or space from which people speak. Identities, nevertheless, should no longer be understood in the sense of a unified stable core. Cultural identity is not the "collective or true self hiding inside the many other, more superficial or artificially imposed 'selves' which a people with a shared history and ancestry hold in common."[10]

Hall instead links identity with identification viewed as a construction, an articulation, and a continuous process. He adopted the term *suturing* to describe this process of identification. Identification is our "suturing" into the story; by this means our identities arise (for example, myths of ancestry), thus operating partly in the realm of the symbolic and the imaginary and always partially constructed.[11] Thus, identities are "points of temporary attachment to the subject positions which discursive practices construct for us. They are the result of a successful articulation or chaining of the subject into the flow of discourse."[12]

Identities remain important vis-à-vis the question of agency and politics: "Identities are about questions of using the resources of history, language and culture in the process of becoming rather than being: not 'who we are' nor 'where we came from' so much as what we might become, how we have been represented and how that bears on how we might represent ourselves."[13] Consequently, Hall speaks of the need to shift from what has been referred to as "identity politics," which espouses an essentialist notion of identity, to a "politics of representation." A politics of representation moves from either/or binaries to deconstruct the binaries of stereotyping themselves (for example, East versus West), by focusing on the different forms of representations in their complexities and ambivalences.[14] It is within such a framework that we speak of the mediation of East Asian cultures. East Asia is an invented category, produced by a certain articulation. While there is no essential East Asian culture, it remains important to express or employ the resources of history, language, and culture in East Asia in translating or articulating CST in this part of the world so as to make it more intelligible to both Christians and peoples of other faiths. This should not be construed as a return to nativism but simply a consideration of the cultural habitus of a people—the "place" from which people speak and understand the world. As a construction it risks exclusion of other discourses, but as Hall rightly notes, there is simply no other way to speak:

> Meaning is in that sense a wager. You take a bet. Not a bet on truth, but a bet on saying something. You have to be positioned somewhere in order to speak. Even if you are positioned in order to unposition yourself, even if you want to take it back, you have to come into language to get out of it. There is no other way. That is the paradox of meaning.[15]

Harmony as a Key Element in the East Asian World View

According to the report on the assembly of the first Bishops' Institute for Interreligious Affairs on the Theology of Dialogue (BIRA IV/1, no. 13), "*Harmony* seems to constitute in a certain sense the intellectual and affective, religious and artistic, personal and societal soul of both persons and institutions in Asia. Hence the imperative of a study in depth of the theology of harmony in the Asian context."[16] To speak of the "soul" of a culture may sound culturalist, distinguishing between the "kernel" (soul) and the "husk" (body) of a culture. In our post-colonial framework we have moved beyond this concept of culture. Nevertheless, it remains important to note the centrality of the category *harmony* for East Asians.

Harmony was first employed from a theological perspective at the BIRA IV/1 conference held in Thailand in 1984. The need for such a theological reflection emerged from concrete situations of disharmony that can be observed in Asia: economic exploitation and poverty, oppressive forms of government and social control; religious, cultural, and communal conflicts; ecological and environmental crises; abuse of science and technology; the burden of Christian prejudice and divisions.[17]

BIRA IV/10 and BIRA IV/11, held in Indonesia in 1988, were both on the theology of harmony. Summarizing the BIRA IV series, the BIRA IV/12 report notes, "It has been suggested that Asia can contribute a theology of harmony. But the potential contribution goes further than this. It lies precisely in the interconnectedness of these issues of harmony (which is the fruit of dialogue), of the search for a more human society, of inculturation, of spirituality" (BIRA IV/12, no. 52).[18] The BIRA V series that followed continued to focus on developing a theology of harmony in dialogue with other religions.[19] In 1995 the Theological Advisory Commission (TAC) to the FABC also produced a more in-depth and systematic reflection entitled "Asian Christian Perspectives on Harmony."[20]

The significance of harmony as a vision and a value[21] goes beyond the sphere of interreligious relations. It is also at the heart of the search for a more human society, which is the concern of CST. The Asian churches have hoped that a theology of harmony could be among its special contributions to the universal church. The *Compendium of the Social Doctrine of the Church* maintains that "the whole of the Church community priests, religious and laity participates in the *formulation* of this social doctrine, each according to the different tasks, charisms and ministries found within her" (no. 79, italics added).[22] The analytical index of the *Compendium of the Social Doctrine of the Church*, however, does not even have a reference to the important Asian vision of harmony. Is this because it basically synthesized only the papal social encyclicals? This brings us to question whether CST (in the limited sense of papal social encyclicals) reflects in a large part simply the theological reflections, discourse, or constructs in Europe and Northern America. It also shows a lack of interreligious dimension in CST.

To proceed with the task of rereading some principles of CST through the lens of East Asian concepts of harmony, it is important to first conduct a cursory survey of some discourses on harmony in East Asia. We have noted that in a politics of representation, it is necessary to be aware of different forms of representations in their complexities and ambivalences. There is no essential concept of harmony in Asia or even a common language to express it. It is not the goal of this essay to be exhaustive in its survey of the representations of harmony in various East Asian cultures. The aim is simply to provide the broad outlines to begin a dialogue with CST and show how some of its principles can be expressed through East Asian constructs of harmony. In the dialogue with the Christian tradition we shall employ from a standpoint shaped by the effective history of the gospel both a hermeneutics of appreciation and a suspicion to the various discourses. A hermeneutics of appreciation retrieves or reinvents the ways in which a particular discourse can be employed in life-giving or humanizing ways. A hermeneutics of (ideological) suspicion critiques the manner in which a discourse has been used to promote the interest of dominant groups and thus serves to marginalize others.

This process can be more aptly called interculturality, which not only refers to a "creative communication between cultures using the available living symbols,"[23] but also emphasizes that the gospel and culture are not two monolithic and closed meaning systems and that the dialogue is occurring between multiple cultural orientations.[24] The term *inter* implies mutuality and reciprocity in the relationship with the other. Interculturality is engaged in the politics of constituting unities-in-difference. It is a stance characterized by otherness and engagement. This means respecting particularities as well as facilitating dialogue among different cultural communities and the interanimation of ideas. Interculturality involves a politics not of either-or but in-between and in-beyond.

East Asian Discourses on Harmony

There have been various ways in which harmony has been represented in East Asian discourses. A discourse, according to Michel Foucault, refers to several statements that provide a language to talk about a topic at a particular historical conjuncture. It is a way of representing knowledge through language. Discourse prescribes what can be talked about and in what way it can be talked about, as well as rules out ways of speaking or constructing knowledge on the topic.[25] When discourses have a similar object and style and support a common institutional, administrative, or political strategy, then they belong to the same discursive formation. In this section we outline the discourses on harmony linked to some of the major religions/philosophies as well as popular religiosities/beliefs in East Asia.

Harmony through Wu-wei (Daoism)

In Daoism, harmony is the central goal to be achieved. The Dao (Tao), oftentimes translated as "way" or "path," is itself perfect harmony. Spiritual cultivation is the means toward harmony. In philosophical Daoism a person needs to be philosophically awakened to the virtue of wu-wei (non-action or non-striving). To live harmoniously with the natural world, one should never go against its rhythms, never fight with one's emotions and desires. Practically speaking, when a philosophical Taoist reaches the state of wu-wei, the person is emancipated from all human-made fixations of language, concepts, and prejudices, which are the main causes of disharmony. At this stage every action the person takes follows the way of Nature, and a perfect harmony of life is achieved (BIRA V/4, no. 3). Combined with the traditional Chinese emphasis on politeness, wu-wei has been interpreted as or identified with passivity.

Religious Daoism, on the other hand, seeks harmony through interior practices that refine one's bodily Qi (Ch'i).[26] Qi is the "source of vitality, harmony, creativity, and moral courage." Qi seems to be parallel to the Japanese notion of ki and the Indian prana (divine breath on which everything depends for health and life). In attaining the purity of the original Qi, Daoists also gain the philosophical enlightenment of wu-wei. Daoists, whether philosophical or religious, bring about social harmony "not by interfering with mundane affairs, but by remaining in silence." An alternative representation of wu-wei, however, would not identify it with sheer passivity. Daoism, like stoicism, stresses the need to respect and flow with the rhythms of nature. But unlike stoicism, the *Daodejing*[27] does not foster withdrawal from the world: "One continues to look at the world through hooded eyes; and the focus is not merely on the dynamics of the world, but also on what one is to do."[28] Thus, harmony is not achieved through passivity but through "active waiting" or a "wait and see" stance. Joel Kupperman asserts that "indeed, the *Daodejing* cannot be appreciated unless we realize that the continuous assumption is that a good Daoist is, and will continue to be, an independent agent and not a conformist or a doormat."[29] He or she can steer the course of events quietly and inconspicuously. Direct confrontations are avoided, and the opposition is given a space to maneuver.[30]

Harmony as Achieved in "Balance"

In many East Asian cultures harmony is believed to be the fruit of a balance of the elements. In Daoism, the Dao (Tao) is usually represented in the form of Tai Chi, which symbolizes the two generative forces in the universe—yin and yang. The notion of yin originates from the image of a shadow, whereas that of yang comes from brightness.[31] They represent bipolar forces of the universe—a duality that is interconnected and interdependent. Neither yin nor yang can exist without the other. These forces continually interact, thus symbolizing harmony within creative tension; that reality is in a process of constant transformation.

The imbalance of yin and yang can affect the flow of Qi and produce chaos. An earthquake occurring in 780 BCE was explained in terms of the domination of the yin by the yang:

> Chou is about to perish, for the fluid (Ch'i) of Heaven and Earth do not, of themselves, lose their proper order, and if they transgress this order it is because the people have put them into confusion. When the yang is concealed and cannot come forth, and when the yin is repressed and cannot issue out, then there are earthquakes. At the present time these three rivers have suffered from an earthquake, which is because the yang has lost its proper place and dominated the yin. The yang having lost its place and occupying that of yin, rivers and streams must necessarily be obstructed.[32]

Many alternative healing methods also are based on the balancing of the universal life force (Qi). Illness in the Chinese culture is believed to be rooted in a blocked Qi. Therapies like acupuncture and acupressure allow the life force to flow freely. Health occurs in the harmonious balancing of yin and yang. For example, sleep is associated with darkness, and therefore yin is balanced by wakefulness, identified with brightness, which is yang. In other discourses the yin-yang symbolism has been extended to include oppositions considered hierarchical: yin is female and subordinate to yang, which is male; yin is young and subordinate to yang, which is old. Social hierarchies based on gender and age have been linked to a perceived natural subordination of yin to yang.[33]

Other narratives opt to stress the nondualistic harmonious nature of yin-yang. In Java, Indonesia, the ability to contain opposites in balance is interpreted as a sign of power. This is classically symbolized by the juxtaposition in the *ardhanari* image of male and female characteristics (the left side of the statue is physiologically female and the right side male). According to Benedict Anderson, "The essential characteristic of this combination of opposites is . . . their dynamic simultaneous incorporation within a single entity. . . . He is at once masculine and feminine, containing both conflicting elements within himself and holding them in a tense electric balance."[34]

Harmony through Benevolence, Wisdom, and Compassion

Confucianism seeks a harmonious relationship among human beings and between heaven and the human. A person realizes this harmony through self-reflection and self-realization, for *jen* (benevolence) is believed to be at the inner core of a person. Through self-cultivation one's possession of a loving heart extends to other individuals and groups, embracing all. Harmony in Confucianism is understood in relation to the maintenance of social stability. Confucius has a well-defined code for duties of the ruler and subject, parents and children, husband and wife, elder sibling and younger, as well as duties among friends, also referred to as the Five Relationships (BIRA V/4, no. 2). Very important is the respect accorded to superiors, who in turn provide protection to the inferiors.[35]

In the Buddhist perspective, following the principle of Conditioned Arising, nothing exists independently; each being "depends on others to condition its arising and existence."[36] Thus everything is inconstant or devoid of a permanent essence. Disharmony occurs because of ignorance of this reality, resulting in cravings and attachments that in turn lead to suffering. A person attains harmony through contemplation and meditation, which lead him or her to wisdom and compassion (BIRA V/2, no. 41).

Harmony through the Respect for Dharma and for Plurality

Hinduism promotes harmony by upholding the order of dharma. Dharma, as the universal principle of all things, holds together the various parts of reality: cosmic, social, and individual. These are mutually interrelated, so that a disruption in the cosmic level, for instance, would likewise affect society and individuals. Popular Hinduism believes that respect for dharma (order, righteousness, and justice) brings about bountiful harvest, whereas its violation results in natural disasters and cataclysms.[37]

Harmony evolves when plurality is respected and its significance in relation to the whole is recognized (BIRA V/3, no. 6). The goal of dharma is reached by considering the good of all beings, not simply the good of specific groups.[38] Plurality, in the Hindu perception, is ultimately rooted in Brahman, the Absolute Being, who "constantly unfolds in the multiplicity of realities in which it is immanent and transcendent" (BIRA V/3, no. 4).

Dharma in practice, though, has been primarily and narrowly identified with the caste system, a social order with functions and duties determined by one's caste. The preservation of this order ensures social well-being and maintains harmony in the universe. Disharmony is the result of various types of alienation, such as ignorance, egoism, and attachment, which are accentuated in the current sociocultural and economic realities in Asia.[39]

In Islam, harmony amid differences is underlined in a passage in the Qur'an: "O humanity! Truly We created you from a male and a female, and made you into nations and tribes that you might know each other. Truly the most honoured of you in the sight of God is the most God-conscious of you. Truly God is knowing, Aware" (49:13). Addressed to humanity, not just to Muslims, the creation of nations and tribes is deemed a positive value. People are encouraged to go beyond their differences, and the best people are not necessarily Muslims but those who are God-conscious.[40] Religious plurality is recognized as well in the oft-quoted verse: "To you your religion and to me my religion" (Al-Kafirun, v. 6).[41] The Muslim practice of Shura, or deliberation by consensus, also ensures that the voice of the minority is heard: "In this common agreement, within the ideal of unity of the entire Muslim community, the opinion of the majority has to take into account that of the minority."[42]

The type of Islam that was first introduced in Indonesia, Malaysia, and the Philippines was Sufism, the mystical practice in Islam that blends well with popular beliefs. Many Muslims practice folk Islam. Folk Islam believes in the existence of spirits: God is not a personal being but the "aggregate of all supernatural forces immanent in creation."[43] In continuity with the folk both/and way of thinking, there is broad tolerance for other religions and customs in Malay East Asian Islam.[44] The Muslims follow *adat*, the local customary law, and "the people see no conflict with Islam when they follow adat even when it actually contradicts Islamic law."[45]

Harmony through Reciprocity
and Respect for Each Other's Space

Popular Daoism, Confucianism, Hinduism, Buddhism, and Islam are built on the primal religious belief that we are inhabiting a spirit-filled or spirit-animated world. The aim is to live harmoniously with the spirits. In the Filipino primal religion and popular world view, the animals, plants, forests, rivers, and mountains are believed to be animated by environmental and ancestral spirits. The spirits own the land and the resources. The users consult and negotiate with the spirits regarding the use of these resources for house building, road construction, and so forth by means of rituals. Many architects, even today, in addition to following feng shui[46] guidelines, also perform the ritual of *padugo* (bloodletting), sacrificing an animal to ask permission and to appease the spirit inhabitant in the site of construction.

As in a human's relationship to other humans, reciprocity and propriety are morally expected in a human's relationship with the spirits. For instance, when humans encroached on an ancestral or environmental spirit's habitat or killed one of its pets, they made an offering to appease the spirit and to compensate for the offense.[47] Reciprocity and propriety here are actually related, because mutual consideration requires propriety. The notion of propriety in these beliefs communicates the understanding that each one's home and place have to be respected: "An attitude of respect is called for as proper and necessary in maintaining that each individual or social group (family, community), and likewise the symbolically identified spirits, can enjoy the privacy of their own place."[48]

The common practice of *pasintabi* (which literally means "please move aside" or "excuse me") when crossing a river, throwing water, "stems from the recognition of the presence of an invisible component of the topography."[49] It is the task of the shamans to mediate between humans and the spirits. Along this line, the Filipino social scientist Raul Pertierra notes that "the most distinctive feature of indigenous religion is the contractual character of the tie between humans and the spirit world. These relations stress the need for reciprocity on both parties, rather than the insistence on a fixed standard of behavior or a total trust in ultimate beneficence."[50]

Synthesis

To synthesize the discussions above, some of the noteworthy similarities in most of the East Asian discourses on harmony are the following: (1) reality is seen as an organic cosmic whole with a multiplicity of independent parts; (2) there is no dualism between nature and human; rather they are more like "chords in a universal symphony . . . maintained in unity through a universal rhyme *(Rta; Tao)* (BIRA IV/11, no. 6);[51] (3) there is unity in the person's organically interlinked sense, consciousness, and spirit; (4) since reality is basically in constant flux, among the main causes of disharmony are human-made fixations of language, concepts, and prejudices; (5) and following from this is "a logic that does not operate on the principle of contradiction and exclusion (either/or), but of identity and inclusion (both/and)."[52] Certain discourses, however, have narrowly identified harmony with the preservation of a hierarchical social order based on caste, gender, age, or religion, which has the effect of marginalizing certain social groups or muting their voices. Wu-wei has also been associated with passivity as the means to preserve harmony.

Catholic Social Teaching and Harmony

In the Christian tradition the ultimate source of diversity shaping cosmic and human reality is the Trinity, experienced as a unity in plurality (BIRA V/3, no. 5). The three Persons are unique but one same ousia, different hypostases or individualities whose harmony is nourished in perichoresis, which has brought forth creation. Creation reflects this harmonious relationship in the Trinity. In the beginning there was original harmony, original justice,[53] original shalom.[54] But sin brought about disharmony. God's saving history, which began as soon as sin came into the world, aims to restore harmony in creation. This finds its fulfillment in Jesus Christ. The church as a sacrament of harmony functions at the service of social and cosmic harmony. CST provides us with basic principles of justice and harmony.

Rearticulating Some Principles of Catholic Social Teaching

Common Good

Common good in East Asian categories is attained when the interdependence of various beings (humans, different social groups, and other earth beings) is acknowledged[55] and when each one's place is respected. This integrally includes the planetary common good[56] as the circle embraces not only the family, society, region, nation, and continent but the world and the universe (BIRA IV/11, no. 21). In its identification with the stability of a particular social order, however, harmony in the Confucian, Hindu, and Islamic perspective has reinforced a complementary and hierarchical relationship among groups that are considered superior and those that are regarded as inferior. In popular discourses what is considered as the place of each being has been fixed, which often results in imbalance and can lead to disharmony.

The discourse on common good in CST, like that on harmony, at times has been utilized to suppress the voices of others. The common good has been defined as the harmonious ordering of society in accordance with natural law. In practice, though, this harmonious ordering was identified in the past with the maintenance of the feudal order, thus restricting actions that would challenge this unjust system. In the encyclical *Gaudium et Spes* we note a shift in methodology toward a more inductive approach of discerning the common good. Common good is now defined as the "sum of those conditions of social life which allows social groups, and their individual members access to their own fulfillment" (no. 26). The actual conditions of people show whether they do indeed have access to the realization of their potential. This resonates more with the context-dependent East Asian moral tradition, in which an ethical theory is assessed pragmatically in the context of the circumstances, in contradistinction to an a priori use of absolute principles.[57]

Solidarity

In CST, society had been viewed as an organic unity—a body with different parts but still one. This reflects the church's rejection of individualism and constitutes the basis for the demand that those who have power and wealth should respect and care for the less-privileged sectors of society. In the principle of solidarity, according to John Paul II's *Sollicitudo Rei Socialis* (1988), we shifted to a notion that holds in dialectical tension "the good of all and of each individual" (no. 38). The concept of solidarity presupposes that society is a community of diverse elements where all are called to cooperate together for the common good. This call is based on the fact of our interdependence (ibid.) and our sharing a bond of common origin. Even as the elements are diverse, solidarity involves a deliberate, free choice to link together.[58] I remember that in one FABC meeting, some participants from Myanmar expressed their dislike of the term *solidarity* because, for them, it connotes an imposition by the government to be in union with the goals of the nation. Thus, "solidarity" is forced on them.

The East Asian concept of harmony likewise recognizes the existence of diverse elements in society that are interdependent and interrelated, albeit with a stronger sense of the unity of the one and the many. An imbalance in the yin-yang blocks the flow of Qi in the whole of creation. My mother used to say, "If you see ugly realities around you, even if you are not poor, you cannot really feel that happy."

Yet solidarity is a choice. It is important to stress the element of freedom in the act of solidarity. Solidarity can be understood as a free commitment actively to affirm this oneness with others, especially with those who are suffering.[59] In the Buddhist perspective this solidarity can be positively reinforced by the belief that without a person's knowing, other suffering humans and animals could be a relative or a loved one of theirs earlier, now transformed in reincarnation.[60] Compassion or delivering others from suffering also results in karmic fruitfulness or the accumulation of good karma.[61]

In Zen Buddhism, which developed in China and highlights the practice of seated meditation, a practitioner may initially be too focused on "studying the self but in the deepening of the practice . . . is able to forget the self" and realize that he or she is not separate from other beings in the universe.[62] Solidarity embraces this awareness through social engagement.

Justice

From an East Asian perspective, justice can be reframed in relation to the importance of balance between the yin and the yang. The yin-yang discourse, which stresses the superiority of yang over yin, can only reinforce the domination of some groups over others. But the alternative discourse, which focuses on balance between divergent forces, can function as an alternative way of explaining justice. When one force overpowers the other, the consequence is chaos. The domination of some social groups over others would result in poverty and social conflicts. During the protests against the Marcos dictatorship in the 1980s, one famous slogan was *Sobra na, tama na, palitan na* (This is excessive! This is enough! It's time for change!). It can be said that although the Filipino people endured the dictatorship for more than a decade, there was a limit to their patience when things become too excessive.

The FABC underlines that "social justice is integral to creating harmony" (BIRA IV/10, no. 11). Today, many East Asian countries are undergoing rapid economic development. The structures of global capitalism, however, are characterized by an imbalance between the developed North and the developing

South in trade exchange, exploitation of cheap labor, destruction of natural resources, and unfair prices, leading to massive poverty.[63] While the gross national product of East Asian economies is increasing, the widening gap between the rich and the poor in each country as well as among the developed and developing countries reflects an imbalance between the yin and the yang that needs to be addressed.

Democracy and the Culture of Dialogue and Negotiation

Rising out of colonialism/neo-colonialism and dictatorial regimes of the Right and the Left, East Asian countries are currently engaged in the task of nation building, and democratization should be at its core. Genuine participation by various social groups is essential in addressing the post-colonial problems of East Asia such as ethnonationalist/religious conflicts, gaps between the rich and poor, the city and country, the rapidly modernizing and traditional sectors, and the changing roles of women.

Such democratization, however, can be hampered by the cultural emphasis on harmony, leading to conflict avoidance instead of real conflict resolution. In "Engaging Virtue Ethics in the Philippines," James Keenan noted how he found it difficult to find expressions of anger among Filipinos.[64] He wonders how genuine reconciliation can be achieved when people are not able to express their anger. In the highly personalized cultures of East Asia, just the expression of a divergence in opinion from another or a critical remark can be seen as a personal affront. Many choose to remain silent or just ignore another person's position rather than express dissension. The stress on harmonious cooperation oftentimes leading to the avoidance of open conflict has been cited in one study as the "most important micro-level Confucian value for the study of democracy."[65] As John Paul II points out in *Centessimus Annus* (1991), participation is integral to a democracy (no. 46). This means, according to the *Compendium of the Social Doctrine of the Church*, that the different subjects of civil community at every level must be informed, listened to, and involved in the exercise of carried-out functions" (no. 190).

The East Asian culture of negotiation or dialogue can be a starting point toward developing democratic participation. Within the popular world view that each one has a place, a person cannot simply intrude or expropriate another's place without negotiation. Democracy also presupposes the practice of subsidiarity. The principle of subsidiarity ensures too that there is a proper place for the role of individuals, civil society, and state and international organizations. The yin-yang logic, furthermore, operates on the principle of opposition that may likewise be balanced through negotiation. Negotiation, oftentimes with a mediator, is a way to confront issues in a manner that allows parties room to maneuver. A traditional Malay custom for resolving community problems is called *mushawara-mufakat* (practiced in Indonesia and in the Maranao area of Southern Philippines), meaning discussion/consensus wherein everyone ideally ends up a winner. But the Asian church's promotion of dialogue as the main means to attain harmony must not be confined to cultural groups (intercultural). Dialogue among various groups within a culture (intracultural or intrareligious), including inside the Catholic Church itself, should be fostered.

BIRA IV/12 proposes an image of the church as a community of dialogue. Here dialogue is "more than a conversation of experts" but "an attitude and a practice of every Christian." For Christians to be able to shift to this dialogical way of life, the church itself should be the primary witness:

> This change of consciousness is likely to happen only in a Church which is dialogical in its internal life and structures. At present, the life of some Church communities is characterized by monologue. In particular, young people, women and the poor remain often voiceless within the Church. Unless these people, who constitute the majority of humankind, can find their true voice, dialogue beyond the Church's boundaries will remain deeply flawed. (BIRA V/12, no. 54)[66]

Indeed, dialogue must not be only intercultural; it must also be intracultural or intrareligious. Outright censure by Catholic

fundamentalists or individuals or groups that propose alternative views geared toward the development of church doctrine
seems to run counter to the Asian church's stress on dialogue
and the cultural value for negotiation. BIRA IV/11, no. 15 rightly
states that "harmony in Asian societies . . . would require recognition of legitimate pluralism and respect for all the groups.
Diversity is not something to be regretted and abolished, but to
be rejoiced over and promoted, since it represents richness and
strength. . . . The test of true harmony lies in the acceptance of
diversity as richness." This insight can guide the church too in
dealing with the diversity of opinions among the faithful.

Challenge of East Asian Discourses on Harmony

In this section, we identify at least two main challenges of East
Asian discourses on harmony to CST: cosmic view and care for
the earth; and achieving harmony through the balance of fluid
dualities.

Cosmic View and Care for the Earth

Care for the earth in CST is inscribed within a traditional hu-
manistic or homocentric framework. We need to care for the
earth for the sake of humans and the future generation of humans. Only relatively recently has CST, in *Sollicitudo Rei Socialis*,
for example, gradually moved beyond homocentrism in its recognition of the need "to respect the integrity and the cycles of
nature" (no. 26) and to take into consideration "the nature of
each being and of its mutual connection in an ordered system"
(no. 34). CST, nevertheless, continues to uphold a hierarchical
anthropology wherein only humans are viewed as *imago Dei*.

East Asian philosophical-religious perspectives clearly reflect
a more nature-sensitive cosmic world view, stressing the interdependence among human beings, other earth beings, and the
whole cosmic order. Everything is bound up with everything
else in an integral whole. The Asian bishops, as a result of the
dialogue with East Asian world views, have begun to speak
more of this intrinsic connection to the earth we come from.

"Harmony and peace call for respect for the earth. She is the mother of whose dust we are made and to whose womb we shall all return. The usurpation of the fruit of the earth by some and deprivation of others of the same results in the rupture of harmony among peoples" (BIRA IV/11, no. 13).

Furthermore, BIRA IV/12, nos. 33–34 underlines the belief in the sacredness of nature in Asian religious traditions and the belief that it is an urgent responsibility of all believers from all faiths "to open themselves once again to the voice of nature and its mystery, to return to their primordial attachment to and respect for nature, to grow in a creation-centred spirituality."

Harmony in the Balance of Fluid Dualities

Plurality in East Asian discourses is deeply rooted in the concept of balance between polarities, viewed not in a dualistic fashion but as a fluid duality. The yin-yang, wherein the yin and the yang constantly interact and reshape the other, symbolizes this harmony. We have noted that one finds other representations of this in Southeast Asia, such as in the Indonesian *ardhanari* image, which has one side male and the other female, and both sides must be kept in balance. In the Philippines, the creation myth narrates the first humans (Power/Beauty-Male/Female) coming out simultaneously from a bamboo. A person, male or female, who is considered powerful would possess both qualities of power/inner strength and beauty/gracious goodness.[67]

In contrast, in CST the masculine and the feminine have been regarded as a dualism, with certain roles limited to each. This dualistic anthropology unwittingly becomes the very ideology that is used to justify the negative differential treatment of women in contrast to men in the field of labor (lower pay for the same work, double burden of women, and so forth). The pluralism that is exalted in the context of interreligious dialogue should also be applied with reference to CST's theological anthropology. A multi-nature anthropology where gender differentiation is fluid[68] rather than rigid can lead to a better balance between the yin and the yang.[69]

The Challenge of Catholic Social Teaching

Prophetic Dimension of Christianity

While the East Asian value of preserving harmony through negotiation and dialogue is very important, when all negotiation
breaks down, true harmony, the FABC declares, is promoted by
a "courageous condemnation of evil in its various forms, and an
active tolerance, if not a charitable acceptance, of the other in
his or her otherness."

In the name of preserving harmony, of not destabilizing the
social order, some may opt not to speak up further against an
injustice. The bishops warn "against idyllic peace or sinful coun-
terfeit harmony in society" that simply serves "vested interests
and egoistic goals" (BIRA IV/11, no. 14). It is the poor and the
excluded who bear the cost of this kind of harmony. The well-
being of the poor and the marginalized will "depend upon peace
and harmony nourished by justice."[70]

The prophetic dimension in Christianity, which stresses the
counter-cultural and critical role of religion vis-à-vis structures
of oppression, is an important complement to the "active waiting" or "wait and see" stance of East Asians. Prophets or
truthtellers who disturb us promote genuine harmony in the
long run. It may be necessary, at times, to pass through a phase
of conflict in order to attain a more just and fair society. The
bishops recognize that "conflict is often a necessary means to
attain true dialogue with people in authority. The poor do not
achieve this until they have shown they are no longer servile
and afraid" (BISA IV, no. 9).[71]

Preferential Option for the Poor

The Christian option for the poor can likewise be an important
enrichment to East Asian views on harmony. BIRA IV, no. 15
asserts that harmony entails "that the believers of all religions
take up the cause of the least: the oppressed, the exploited, and

the discriminated minority." Benevolence should be primarily practiced toward those who are oppressed or excluded in society. A central preoccupation of Buddhism is the overcoming of suffering in oneself and in others. Helping the poor will benefit not only the other but also one's self. The flow of Qi is blocked when groups of people who are suffering remain. By siding with those who have no voice, one not only provides them with a place where they can flourish but also helps balance the forces in society.

Integral to the preferential option for the poor is not only sharing one's excess but transformation toward social justice. Opting for the poor is opting for social justice. In cases of conflicts a preferential option for the poor does not exclude taking a class stance. This preferential option for the poor, according to the Second Plenary Council of the Philippines, is embodied in the "Church of the Poor," where "pastors and members of the Church will courageously defend the rights of the poor and the oppressed, *even when doing so will mean alienation or persecution from the rich and powerful.*"[72]

A Mutual Challenge: The Personal and the Structural

The Asian stress on interiority, meditation, and contemplation as means toward developing wisdom, benevolence, and compassion challenges Christians to recapture the link between justice and contemplation in order to promote harmony in our families, societies, and planet. "In the Asian vision of reality, there is an intimate correspondence between the exterior world and in the inner world of the self; one reflects the other" (BIRA IV/11, nos. 17–18). East Asian religions are strong in the development of interiority as a means toward social and cosmic harmony. The Asian bishops describe the spirituality of harmony as involving harmony within the self (body-mind), with others, with the cosmos, and with God. To develop interiority, meditation, and contemplation, they recommend the following: (1) that centers be created where Christians and people of other faiths can "spend time in deep silence and meditation"; (2) that Christians learn the manner of meditation and interiorization in other Asian religions like zen, yoga, vipasana, Samadhi, and so on; and (3) that mature Christians also make use of ashrams and centers of contemplation of peoples of other faiths.

CST teaches that personal conversion is not enough.[73] To bring about social transformation, structural changes are needed. The second "Instruction on Christian Freedom and Liberation" acknowledges the existence of "structures marked by sin" (no. 74) and encourages "structural changes in society so as to secure conditions of life worthy of the human person."[74] Personal conversion through interiority, meditation, and contemplation, on the one hand, and structural changes, on the other, can be regarded as a pair of chopsticks that should always go together to bring about harmony.

Conclusion

Christians are a minority in Asia. The social teaching of the church should increasingly draw from other Asian religious cultural resources so that Asians, Christians or not, can resonate more and be challenged by these teachings. In this essay we surveyed East Asian discourses on harmony and attempted to rearticulate some principles of CST based on the symbols and categories of East Asian philosophical-religious narratives. We have also identified how these traditions can challenge or enrich each other's perspectives on harmony. Our theoretical exploration, nonetheless, is just a minor part of the process of intercultural theological reflection on CST. The major task of interculturality happens in basic Christian/human communities, faith-based NGOs, political parties, and bishop-ulama forums where, faced with concrete struggles, Christians and neighbors from other religions reflect on their situation in the light of their faiths.[75] These communities are the ultimate agents of interculturality. It is they who can ensure that CST does not remain just a "dead letter" but becomes truly life-giving in Asia.

Notes

[1] The Asian bishops note that "the Fathers of the Church were well acquainted with their Graeco-Roman traditions." Like them "we dream of an Asian Church which feels at home in her own culture. . . . The local Churches should be entrusted to announce the message of the gospel in their own social and cultural idioms" for the purpose of promoting what is "authentically human" in these cultures, in the context of modernization and development in Asia. FABC Office of Evangelization, "Church Issues in Asia in the Context of Evangelization, Dialogue, and Proclamation: Conclusions of the Theological Consultation" (1991), no. 20, in *For All the Peoples of Asia: Federation of Asian Bishops' Conference: Documents from 1970 to 1991*, vol. 1, ed. Gaudencio Rosales, DD, and C. G. Arevalo, SJ (Quezon City: Claretian Publications, 1992); and Asian Bishops' Meeting (1970), no. 13, in ibid., 9.

[2] A mediation is a lens through which one understands, analyzes, receives, or even produces a cultural text/artifact.

[3] What can be considered vernacular is relative and movable, depending on who is using what and against whom. For instance, in medieval times, Latin was the language of learning and English was the vernacular. In many contexts local languages/idioms can be considered the vernacular as opposed to English. R. S. Sugirtharajah, *The Bible and the Third World: Precolonial, Colonial, and Postcolonial Encounters* (Cambridge, UK: Cambridge University Press, 2001), 178–81.

[4] In the Asian context, the philosophical and the religious usually interface.

[5] Stuart Hall, "Introduction," in *Representation: Cultural and Signifying Practices*, ed. Stuart Hall (London: Sage, 1997).

[6] Stuart Hall, "Cultural Studies: Two Paradigms," *Media Culture and Society* 2, no. 1 (January 1980).

[7] Paul du Gay, Stuart Hall, Linda Janes, Hugh Mackay, and Keith Negus, *Doing Cultural Studies: The Story of the Sony Walkman* (Keynes: The Open University, 1997), 12. Society is to be analyzed as a differentiated and complex totality with multiple and contradictory determinations that are historically particular. Each level of articulation or special form of practice (economic, political, ideological, and so forth) has its own relative autonomy.

[8] Hall rejects the "dominant ideology thesis," which posits that one unified wholistic ideology exists, which permeates everyone. The dominant ideology thesis is announced in Marx and Engel's *Communist Manifesto* (1848): "The ruling ideas of each age have ever been the ideas of its ruling class" (VI, 503).

[9] Globalization processes are producing hybrid identities not only in the centers of the global system but even in the peripheries. While identity choices are more extensive in the West, the pluralizing effects of globalization are felt also in the peripheries, albeit at a slower pace and a more uneven manner.

[10] Stuart Hall, "Cultural Identity and Diaspora," in *Identity: Community, Culture, Difference,* ed. Jonathan Rutherford (London: Lawrence and Wishart, 1990).

[11] For an elaboration of how the meaning of *suture* as employed in film theory is derived from Jacques Lacan's psychoanalytic theory, see Peter Brooker, *A Glossary of Cultural Theory,* 2nd ed. (London: Oxford University Press, 2002), 245–46.

[12] Stuart Hall, "Introduction: Who Needs Identity," in *Questions of Cultural Identity,* ed. Stuart Hall and Paul du Gay (London: Sage, 1996), 6.

[13] Ibid., 4.

[14] A politics of representation should also be sensitive to the negative consequences of such positionality to those who are excluded by its discourse.

[15] Stuart Hall, "Old and New Identities: Old and New Ethnicities," in *Culture, Globalization, and the World System,* ed. Anthony D. King (London: Macmillan, 1991), 51.

[16] "BIRA IV/1, 1984: Brief Report on the Assembly," in Rosales and Arevalo, *For All the Peoples of Asia,* 1:249.

[17] Theological Advisory Commission (TAC), FABC, "Asian Christian Perspectives on Harmony," in *For All the Peoples of Asia: Federation of Asian Bishops' Conferences Documents from 1992–1996,* vol. 2, ed. Franz-Josef Eilers, SVD (Quezon City: Claretian Publications, 1997), 233–41.

[18] Final Statement of the Twelfth Bishops' Institute for Interreligious Affairs on the Theology of Dialogue (1991), in Eilers, *For All the Peoples of Asia,* 2:133.

[19] The following are the themes of the BIRA V series: BIRA V/1 (1992): Working Together for Harmony in God's World: A Christian Muslim Dialogue; BIRA V/2 (1994): A Call to Harmony: Buddhists and Christians in Dialogue; BIRA V/3 (1995): Working for Harmony in the Contemporary World: A Hindu-Christian Dialogue; BIRA V/4 (1996): Taoist and Confucian Contributions to Harmony in East Asia: Final Statement (Eilers, *For All the Peoples of Asia,* 2:143–48, 2:149–54, 2:155–60, and 2:161–66, respectively.

[20] TAC (FABC), "Asian Christian Perspectives on Harmony," 229–98.

[21] BIRA V/2, "A Call to Harmony: Buddhists and Christians in Dialogue," and TAC (FABC), "Asian Christian Perspectives on Harmony," speak of harmony as a vision of an ideal society. It has also been referred to as a value. See Felix Wilfred in "Asia and the Social Teaching of the Church: Some Basic Reflections," *Info on Human Development* 33, nos.

1–3 (January–March 2007): 11; and Lode Wostyn, "Vatican II and the Asian Theology of Harmony," *Religious Life Asia* (July-September 2007): 10.

[22] Pontifical Council for Justice and Peace, *Compendium of the Social Doctrine of the Church* (Vatican: Libreria Editrice Vaticana, 2004), 48.

[23] This is how the Asian bishops define *interculturation*, FABC Office of Evangelization, "Church Issues in Asia in the Context of Evangelization, Dialogue, and Proclamation," no. 21, in Rosales and Arevalo, *For All the Peoples of Asia*, 1:336–38.

[24] Frans Wijsen, "Intercultural Theology and the Mission of the Church." Available on the www.sedos.org website.

[25] Hall, *Representation*, 44.

[26] The Chinese notion of Qi was developed in the period between the sixth and fourth centuries BCE by philosophers like Lao Ki, Kong Zu Fi (Confucius), and Men Zi (Mencius).

[27] *Daodejing* is the classic Chinese text central to Daoism and Chinese Buddhism.

[28] Joel Kupperman, *Classic Asian Philosophy: A Guide to the Essential Texts* (New York: Oxford University Press, 2007), 125.

[29] Ibid.

[30] Ibid., 124.

[31] Jung Young Lee, "The Yin-Yang Way of Thinking," in *What Asian Christians Are Thinking: A Theological Source Book*, ed. Douglas Elwood (Quezon City: New Day Publishers, 1976).

[32] Quoted in Kupperman, *Classic Asian Philosophy*, 343.

[33] Stephen F. Teiser, "Religions of China in Practice," in *Asian Religions in Practice: An Introduction*, ed. Donald S. Lopez, Jr. (Princeton: NJ: Princeton University Press, 1999), 118.

[34] Benedict Anderson, "The Idea of Power in Javanese Culture," in *Culture and Politics in Indonesia*, ed. Claire Holt with the assistance of Benedict R. O'G. Anderson and James Siegel (Ithaca, NY: Cornell University, 1972), 14.

[35] Stelmo Nauman, Jr., *Dictionary of Asian Philosophies* (London: Routledge and Kegan Paul, 1979), 67.

[36] Peter Harvey, *An Introduction to Buddhist Ethics* (Cambridge, UK: Cambridge University Press, 2000), 153.

[37] TAC (FABC), "Asian Christian Perspectives on Harmony," 259.

[38] Anantanand Rambachan, "Hinduism," in *The Hope of Liberation in World Religions*, ed. Miguel A. De la Torre (Waco, TX: Baylor University Press, 2008), 122.

[39] TAC (FABC), "Asian Christian Perspectives on Harmony," 259–60.

[40] Amir Hussain, "Muslims, Pluralism, and Interfaith Dialogue," in *Progressive Muslims: On Justice, Gender and Pluralism*, ed. Omid Safi, 251–69 (Oxford: Oneworld Publications, 2003), 255.

[41] Quoted in TAC (FABC), "Asian Christian Perspectives on Harmony," 261.

[42] Ibid.

[43] Robert Day McAmis, *Malay Muslims: The History and Challenge of Resurgent Islam in Southeast Asia* (Grand Rapids, MI: Eerdmans, 2002), 68.

[44] Ibid., 44, 48.

[45] Ibid., 63.

[46] Feng shui is the art of placement and arrangement of space in one's home or workplace so that there is free movement of Qi and thus harmony between humans and the environment. Yeow-Beng Mah, "Living in Harmony with One's Environment: A Christian Response to Feng Shui," *Asia Journal of Theology* 18, no. 2 (October 2004): 341.

[47] Raul Pertierra, *Religion, Politics, and Rationality in a Philippine Community* (Quezon City: Ateneo de Manila University Press, 1988), 131–32. Pertierra studied the moral values and the spirit world of the residents of Zamora, Ilocos.

[48] Edmundo Pacifico Guzman, "Creation as God's Kaloob: Towards an Ecological Theology of Creation in the Lowland Filipino Sociocultural Context" (PhD diss., Catholic University of Louvain, 1995), 337.

[49] Leonardo Mercado, "Pasintabi: The Seen and the Unseen," in *Filipino Popular Devotions: The Interior Dialogue between Traditional Religion and Christianity*, ed. Leonardo Mercado (Manila: Logos Publications, 2000), 27.

[50] Pertierra, *Religion, Politics, and Rationality in a Philippine Community*, 139.

[51] "Eleventh Bishops' Institute for Interreligious Affairs on the Theology of Dialogue," 1988, in Rosales and Arevalo, *For All the Peoples of Asia*, 1:321.

[52] Michael Amaladoss, cited by Jonathan Tan, "Theology of Harmony," in *Dialogue? Resource Manual for Catholics in Asia*, ed. Edmund Chia (Bangkok: FABC-OEIA, 2001): 118. The TAC (FABC) notes too that "the Asian way is one of integration and inclusion. Rather than saying 'A is true, so B must be false,' the Asian tends to say 'A is true, and B is also true in some sense.' This is not to say that truth is relative. There is but one Truth, but Truth is a Mystery which we approach reverently while we try to seek to understand its various aspects and dimension" ("Methodology: Asian Christian Theology," 2000, in *For All the Peoples of Asia*, vol. 3, ed. Franz-Josef Eilers, SVD [Quezon City: Claretian Publications, 2002], 331). For an elaboration on the difference between pluralism and relativism, see ibid., 332–38.

[53] See also *Catechism of the Catholic Church*, no. 400, definitive ed. (Manila: Word and Life Publications, CBCP/ECCE, 1994), 114; and *Catechism for Filipino Catholics*, no. 373. new ed. with expanded Subject Index and Primer (Manila: ECCE Word and Life Publications, 2004), 106.

[54] *Shalom* seems to be the closest biblical term for "harmony." TAC (FABC), "Asian Christian Perspectives on Harmony," 266, 272–73.

[55] For an analysis of common good using Confucian categories, see James T. Bretzke, SJ, "The Common Good in a Cross-Cultural Perspective: Insights from the Confucian Moral Community," in *Religion, Ethics, and the Common Good*, ed. James Donahue and M. Theresa Moiser, RSCJ, The Annual Publication of the College Theology Society, vol. 41 (Mystic, CT: Twenty-Third Publications, 1996), 83–105. In Hinduism, the Bhagavadgita (3:20) affirms those who act for the common good or concern for the world's well-being. It teaches that the basic goal of life—*artha* (wealth, power, success, social prestige), *kama* (pleasure), dharma (virtue, duty), and *moksha* (liberation) should be accessible to all. Anantanand Rambachan, "Hinduism," in De la Torre, *The Hope of Liberation in World Religions*, 123.

[56] US Catholic Bishops, *Renewing the Earth: An Invitation to Reflection and Action on Environment in Light of Catholic Social Teaching*, A Pastoral Statement of the United States Catholic Conference, November 14, 1991. Available on the www.usccb.org website.

[57] James T. Bretzke, "Moral Theology out of East Asia," *Theological Studies* 61 (2000): 113.

[58] See *Sollicitudo Rei Socialis*, no. 33: "In order to be genuine, development must be achieved within the framework of solidarity and freedom, without ever sacrificing either of them under whatever pretext."

[59] See the discussion on solidarity as *pakikiisa* (being-one-with-the-other) in Agnes M. Brazal, "Harnessing Political and Cultural Resources toward Solidarity," *MST Review* (forthcoming).

[60] "It is not easy, monks, to find a being who has not in the past been one's mother, or one's father, brother, sister, son or daughter' (S.II.189–90)." Quoted in Harvey, *An Introduction to Buddhist Ethics*, 35.

[61] Ibid., 125.

[62] Ruben L. F. Habito, "Zen Buddhism," in De la Torre, *The Hope of Liberation in World Religions*, 173.

[63] FABC, "Appendix: Conclusions of the Theological Consultation," 1991, no. 4, in Rosales and Arevalo, *For All the Peoples of Asia*, 1:336.

[64] James F. Keenan, "Engaging Virtue Ethics in the Philippines," *Landas* 15, no. 1 (2001). For similarities between Confucian virtues and Filipino family values, see R. Rafael L. Dolor, "Confucianism and Its Relevance to the Filipino Family"; available on the www.geocities.com website.

[65] "Chapter 7: Confucianism and East Asian Political Culture"; available on the www.dflorig.com website.

[66] "Twelfth Bishops' Institute for Interreligious Affairs on the Theology of Dialogue," 1991, in Rosales and Arevalo, *For All the Peoples of Asia*, 1:333.

[67] For a further discussion on this topic, see Agnes M. Brazal, "Mission and Power," in *The Mission to Proclaim and to Celebrate Christian Existence*,

146 Agnes M. Brazal

ed. Peter de Mey, Jacques Haers, and Josef Lamberts (Leuven: Peeters, 2005). In pre-colonial Southeast Asia, women had relatively equal status with men, unlike their Northeast Asian counterparts.

⁶⁸ In the document "On the Collaboration of Men and Women in the Church and in the World" (2004) by the Congregation for the Doctrine of the Faith (CDF), Ratzinger seems to be moving toward a more fluid understanding of gender when he expressed that femininity as the capacity for the other is not just a female trait. By implication, masculinity is also not just a trait of the male. "It is appropriate however to recall that the feminine values mentioned here are above all human values. . . . It is only because women are more immediately attuned to these values that they are the reminder and the privileged sign of such values. But, in the final analysis, every human being, man or woman, is destined to be 'for the other.' In this perspective, that which is called 'femininity' is more than simply an attribute of the female sex. The word designates indeed the fundamental human capacity to live for the other and because of the other" (no. 14). Available on the www.vatican.va website.

⁶⁹ For a rereading of the yin-yang symbol from a feminist perspective, see Young Lee Herzig, "The Asian-American Alternative to Feminism: A Yinist Paradigm," *Missiology* 226, no. 1 (January 1998): 15–22.

⁷⁰ Wilfred, "Asia and the Social Teachings of the Church," 11.

⁷¹ "Fourth Bishops' Institute for Social Action," in Rosales and Arevalo, *For All the Peoples of Asia*, 1:213.

⁷² *Acts and Decrees of the Second Plenary Council of the Philippines* (Manila: CBCP, 1991), nos. 122–36.

⁷³ The Chinese religions (Confucianism, Daoism, and Zen Buddhism) tend to stress self-cultivation of mind and body more than social awareness and social justice. See Wan-Ki-Ho, "Confucianism and Daoism," and Habito, "Zen Buddhism," in De la Torre, *The Hope of Liberation in World Religions*, 196 and 173, respectively.

⁷⁴ CDF, "Instruction on Christian Freedom and Liberation" (1986), nos. 74, 68. Available on the www.vatican.va website.

⁷⁵ For a concrete example of two faith-based communities that have successfully made use of vernacular idioms/indigenous practices in their promotion of housing for the poor and ancestral land claims, see Agnes M. Brazal, "Harnessing Cultural Resources toward Solidarity."

5.

Catholic Social Teaching and the European Project

From Applying Principles to Scrutinizing the Signs of the Times in the Light of the Gospel

Johan Verstraeten

> *[The European project] will not and may not remain an economic and technical enterprise: it needs a soul, the consciousness of its historical affinities and of its present and future responsibilities, a political will at the service of the same human ideal.*
>
> —ROBERT SCHUMAN[1]

Until the transition from a liberal agenda to a third-world agenda[2] during Vatican II, official CST was mainly deductive and Eurocentric. European think tanks, movements, and authors had an almost exclusive impact on social encyclicals and their ghost writers. In turn, these encyclicals influenced European society. In this essay I point out the impact of official CST on Europe and how, after Vatican II, European bishops and movements as subjects of Catholic social thought in the broad sense have participated in the church's efforts to scrutinize the signs of the times. Finally, I ask how the church can contribute to the transformation of European civil society today.

Principles Put Forward by the Popes and Their Influence on the Rhineland Model of Capitalism

There is no such thing as capitalism; there are different sorts of capitalisms. One of them is the European "Rhineland" model, which combines free-market economy with a social security system. This social-market model is in some respects the result of the historical influence of official CST, which, through the mediation of Catholic social movements, has had a real impact on the European political and social agenda.

Reflecting the discussions among various representative authors and groups that constituted nineteenth-century social Catholicism, the socio-ethical framework proposed by *Rerum Novarum* (1891) had immediate consequences for the development of a social-market economy, such as the recognition of workers' unions; a person-oriented moral justification of the criteria for a just wage (against the argument based on supply and demand); and the rejection of the laissez-faire state, which paved the way to social legislation. But the Magna Carta of social Catholicism did not sufficiently grasp the meaning of economic growth. It was only after the "crash" of 1929 and the subsequent economic crisis that a more realistic approach was introduced by Oswald von Nell Breuning, SJ, ghost writer of *Quadragesimo Anno* (1931) and expert in the morality of stock markets.

Reflecting on the increasing gap between rich and poor, and criticizing managerial captalism in extraordinarily sharp words, *Quadragesimo Anno* introduced the principle of social justice as sine qua non for the realization of the common good. The underlying idea was simple: a society cannot be just as long as the results of the economic growth are accumulated by a small group at the cost of the economic development of the entire population. The common good can only be realized in a society in which the fruits of work—defined as the results of the combined activity of labor, management, and capital investment—are distributed justly, and when citizens become full participants in a society interpreted as an organic whole. Social justice refers simultaneously to the duty of the citizens to serve the common good and to the duty of the state to enable the citizens to fulfill their duty. This enabling function is the basis of the European model of social security.

According to *Quadragesimo Anno*, it is not just the task of the state to redistribute the wealth created by economic growth. Crucial in this regard is the principle of subsidiarity. Literally, it means that the state has the duty to "help" subordinated spheres and groups to do what they must do in order to contribute to the common good. The state must provide its citizens with the basic conditions for their full development as persons.[3] Despite this positive meaning, *Quadragesimo Anno* refers predominantly to the negative meaning of subsidiarity: the state has no right to intervene in matters that belong to the sphere of subordinate groups.

In the further development of official CST there has always been tension between the positive and the negative meanings of the principle. This tension had an immediate impact on the church's official attitude regarding the European social security systems. Pope John XXIII referred positively to them in the context of his acknowledgment of the process of socialization. Despite his formal reference to the meaning of subsidiarity in *Quadragesimo Anno*, he interprets it mainly as an argument in favor of greater intervention of the state for the protection of social rights. Together with the "see, judge, act" method of the Christian Workers movement, *Mater et Magistra* (1961) became a sort of official recognition of the European social-market economy, and Pope John XXIII even proposed it as a solution for the development of the whole world.[4]

This positive attitude changed drastically in the fifth chapter of the 1991 encyclical *Centesimus Annus (CA)*, where Pope John Paul II refers to the principle of subsidiarity as a tool to criticize the social-market economy in its form as a "social assistance" state. The critique was not based on an adequate understanding of the complexities of the European social-market system, but together with the praise of voluntary work as an alternative strategy and the balanced approval of the free market and profit, it reflected more (and sometimes literally) the pro-capitalism and "anti-state intervention" ideology of a group of business-minded American Catholic intellectuals—the same group that had rejected the first draft of the American bishops' letter *Economic Justice for All.*

Despite this rather important shift, the socially corrected market economy remained one of the cornerstones of the European project, as reflected in the Charter of the Fundamental Rights of the European Union proclaimed in Nice on December 7, 2000, and incorporated in the Treaty of Lisbon. Several articles are devoted to solidarity in general and to social security, social assistance, and the right to healthcare in particular.

At the same time the negative aspect of subsidiarity remained an important moral criterion in the European Union. It was officially adopted by the Treaty of Maastricht as the moral basis for the relationship between the union and its member states, in accordance with the definition presented by Jacques Delors in his address to the European College at Bruges in 1989 as "the decentralised organisation of responsibilities, in such a way that one never assigns to a greater unity what can be better done by a smaller one."[5] The reference to subsidiarity in the Treaty of Maastricht is not unproblematic. As far as it is reduced to a principle governing the relationship between the European Union and its member states, it risks, if it were to be detached from the principles of social justice and solidarity, becoming an argument that in fact weakens the social dimension of the Union in the name of the rights of the sovereign states to determine their own social policy, even when such policy constitutes a neoliberal rejection of the social market (which was, in fact, the attitude of the UK for a time).

Moreover, if subsidiarity is reduced to a hierarchical relationship between the Union and its member states, it might lead to an underestimation of the role of European civil society, which is, as much as the states, a "middle field" between the Union's bureaucracies and the citizens. For the Catholic social tradition, this is crucial. And the fact that the Union has committed itself to an institutionalized dialogue with partners from civil society, including the religions and churches, is an important guarantee against misunderstanding. Apart from social justice, subsidiarity, and solidarity, the European Union also takes cognizance of another principle that plays a crucial role in CST; in fact, an entire paragraph of the Charter of the Fundamental Rights of the European Union testifies to its importance: All the fundamental rights of the European Union are based on human dignity, described as "inviolable" and a basic value that "must be respected and protected."

With regard to the influence on Europe of the principles of official CST, we can also refer to an underlying idea that was very dear to the *magisterium* until Vatican II: the harmony model of an "organic society" in which social problems are not directly resolved by the state, or by conflict, but through negotiations among the leaders of the different social groups (workers, employers, middle class, farmers) who focus on the common good.

Before World War II this idea was, moreover, framed as a "third way" model, according to which politicians and economists, under the moral guidance of the church, would create a particular "catholic" society as an alternative to both Marxist socialism and liberal capitalism. This model has gradually been abandoned, not only because it has been contaminated by fascist regimes in Italy, Spain, and Portugal, but also because of the disestablishment of the Catholic Church and the autonomy of the new Christian Democrat parties after the Second World War (the social ideas of these parties were more often mediated by the personalist philosophy of Maritain and Mounier than by applying Catholic social principles). Despite the new developments and the reality of social conflicts, it is not incorrect to say that the Catholic spirit of a "harmonious cooperation of the Industries and Professions" continued to have some influence on the development of a European "social-market economy." They are echoed in, among other things, the German idea of "Mitbestimmung."

From Applying Principles to "Scrutinizing the Signs of the Times in the Light of the Gospel"

Since the inductive method (see, judge, act) of the Catholic Workers' movement was adopted by Pope John XXIII in *Mater et Magistra* (no. 236), and particularly since Vatican II, it is generally accepted that CST is more than a matter of applying abstract principles to political and economic realities. It also requires an analysis of the signs of the times in the light of the gospel.

Vatican II's *Gaudium et Spes (GS)*, proposes a new approach based on the concept "i segni dei tempi" or "signa temporum"[6] (signs of the times): "The Church has always had the duty of *scrutinizing the signs of the times* and of *interpreting them in the light of the Gospel.*"

Scrutinizing and understanding the signs of the times starts neither from an abstract or apparently neutral perspective, nor from a church that posits itself in opposition to the world, but from a social discernment rooted in the commitment of the church to be "linked with humankind and its history by the deepest of bonds" (*GS*, no. 1) and called to contribute to the humanization of the world by way of participating in it. This task is, however, not easy, since it confronts the church with the real ambivalence of history—a history characterized by both positive trends and destructive developments, by a tension between life-giving forces and tendencies that lead to a culture of death. Such positive developments can be confirmed and articulated in the history of salvation as signs of the times that anticipate the kingdom of God, which is on earth "already present in mystery" (*GS*, no. 48). But what does such an interpretation of particular tendencies as signs of the times mean? The first task is negative and critical, since negative tendencies must be unmasked (see below). The second task is positive, since developments that contribute to the flourishing of humanity can be interpreted as significant indicators of the coming of the kingdom of God. In both cases theological interpretation must be mediated by careful analysis and ethical reflection. Judgments on the world cannot be merely made on the basis of faith alone.[7] Indeed, as a continuing process of learning (Nell Breuning), social discernment requires both social analysis and an interpretation of the facts "in the light of the gospel." Without the perspective of faith, social analysis either lacks depth or runs the risk of being disturbed by ideological biases (*GS*, nos. 38–40). This is as important as acknowledging that without social analysis the faith perspective either loses touch with reality or leads to the construction of a world of pious ideas, which is more an expression of social alienation than a solution to it. Indeed, "a vision must track the contours of reality; it has to have accuracy, and not simply imagination or appeal,"[8] but it must remain a vision.

One of the most significant articulations of the role of social analysis is in *Octogesima Adveniens*, in which Pope Paul VI acknowledges the impossibility of expressing a unified message as pope in which he would propose a solution that (as the text literally says) would be "in congruity with all local situations" ("qua solutio, omnibus locus congruens, proponatur"). His response to the problem is clear:

> It is up to the Christian communities [a clear reference to the integral ecclesiology of *Lumen Gentium*,, chap. II] to analyze with objectivity the situation which is proper to their own country, to shed on it the light of the Gospel's unalterable words and for action from the social teaching of the Church. . . . It is up to these Christian communities [in other words, it is not the task only of the magisterium or of bishops' conferences, although it is in communion

with them], with the help of the Holy Spirit, in communion with the bishops who hold responsibility and in dialogue with other Christian brethren and all men of goodwill, to discern the options and commitments which are called for in order to bring about the social, political and economic changes seen in many cases to be urgently needed. (no. 4)

The last sentence reaffirms how much Catholic social thought is practical. It is not a self-referential theory but a method responding to real needs and aiming at real historical change. In the sections of this chapter that follow, we describe how European Catholic movements and bishops' conferences have made use of CST.

But, as already mentioned, analysis in itself is not sufficient. As much as social analysis is required to complete judgments made in faith, so a faith perspective is needed to complete social analysis. What does an interpretation in the light of the gospel mean in this regard? Biblical stories, and particularly the gospel, are more than just a reservoir of citations that can be used to illustrate moral insights. They are also more than texts that constitute a sort of historical testimony of Christian thinking in the first stage of its development, as MacIntyre suggests.[9] On the contrary, Christian social movements as well as Catholic social thought have a living, hermeneutic relationship with biblical texts. Their commitment is rooted in a continuing remembrance of the biblical narratives in liturgy and memorializing celebration. One of the implications of such a living, hermeneutic relationship to the texts of the Bible in general, and to the gospel in particular, was pointed out by Pope John Paul II in *Sollicitudo Rei Socialis*, where he not only reiterated the necessity of analysis and of condemning actual injustices, but also contended that it is the duty of the church to proclaim a meaningful new future (no. 42).

Indeed, something new is announced, a vision that opens our closed hermeneutic horizon, a vision that stimulates our imagination and allows us to discover new and unexpected possibilities for change. This is not simply from our own perspective, but from the perspective of God. To put it in the words of one of the martyrs of our time, Bishop Oscar Romero, "We are prophets of a future that is not our own."[10] This visionary aspect does not mean (as Elsbernd and Bieringer rightly contend) that the church proposes something completely foreign to human experience. On the contrary, the vision is "already present in human longings, desires, and hopes."[11] In a pre-reflexive way, it is suggested by negative contrast experiences. These are experiences in which the negativity implicitly suggests something of the dream of what is or ought to be human.

But this requires a further articulation in a more substantial vision, as well as an understanding according to which the vision is not just a confirmation of what we already know about ourselves. It also produces something new. There is semantic innovation. The dialectic of the "already known" and "not yet known" is particularly present in the biblical metaphors (also in their predicative form of stories), which not only express what people experience but also suggest new meanings and new perspectives on reality.[12] The biblical narratives offer "generative metaphors" that contribute to a vision about the not yet.[13]

This vision reveals the paradoxical character of social discernment: the church functions as *sacramentum mundi*, as an inspiring and healing force in the concrete history of women and men, insofar as, on the one hand, it is fully connected with the world, and on the other hand, it marks a *difference* by way of *interrupting* time-bound hermeneutic schemes (particularly by way of proclaiming new life). To put it in the words of Elsbernd and Bieringer: "Vision is not an extension of present possibilities into the future, but rather the future reaching out to meet the present as an annunciation of something more or as a disjunction from what is."[14] One of the consequences of this is that there will always be an inevitable creative friction between vision (as a source of renewal) and reality. One could even say that, precisely because the Christian vision (although not alien to human experience) is different from merely secular interpretations of reality, it is capable of semantically enriching secular thinking.

In this regard Charles Curran's thesis about a dual audience in Catholic social thinking is not fully adequate. He makes a distinction between Christian communities and the secular world: the community of Christians can express its own distinctiveness and refer to the Gospels; when addressing the secular world, a more general and rational language can and must be used.[15] While not wishing to deny the utility and necessity of a universal language, or of one or other form of natural law thinking (including a human rights discourse), one cannot deny that such a dualism makes it impossible to assess the particular challenge that Christian thinking, as a source of semantic and practical innovation, can be for a secular society. Insights that are "universal," and hence valid for all, are not ahistorical, as if they were merely a matter of abstract and "thin" principles. The universal gets continuous meaning from particular traditions that provide the thin categories with meaning. What today is not yet considered universal can become universally acknowledged as reasonable under the influence of an enriched understanding of our own humanity through the semantic and practical innovation stimulated by our hermeneutic relation to narrative texts. From this perspective it is precisely through the distinctiveness of its social vision that the church realizes its universality.

This distinctiveness is one of the characteristics of the social action undertaken by new movements, while the focus on the victims of history becomes a genuine concern in the texts written by European bishops' conferences and social movements. They understand, moreover, that an interpretation of the signs of the times in the light of the gospel necessitates a semantic vigilance vis-à-vis the biases of our time. The story of the suffering of Christ inspires them to see with new eyes and to look at the achievements of markets or political powers from the perspective of the victims of history. It enables them to acknowledge, as the French bishops wrote, that "society has the face of its victims" and this face is real. In this regard the option for the poor, understood as a particular commitment of the church to see things from the side of the poor and to assess lifestyles, policies, and social institutions in terms of their impact on the poor, gets universal meaning: it opens the eyes of the world to a forgotten dimension of human life; and it contributes to a more universal consciousness of what it means to be humane.

Catholic Movements and Their Participation in the Transformation of European Society

As pointed out in the previous section, the church is not merely a distant teaching authority delivering messages to the world, but first and foremost a community of communities that is challenged by "the joys and the hopes, the griefs and anxieties of the men [people] of this age, especially those who are poor or in any way afflicted" (*GS*, no. 1). The response to this challenge is mediated by social movements, which are at the forefront of the transformative presence of the church in the world. The General Synod of Bishops on Justice (1971) has interpreted this radically in terms of "action on behalf of justice and participation in the transformation of the world;" it is a "constitutive dimension of the preaching of the Gospel or, in other words, of the Church's mission for the redemption of the human race and its liberation from every oppressive situation."[16] Even Pope John Paul II implicitly acknowledged this when he wrote, "The Church is aware that her social message will gain credibility more immediately from the witness of actions than as a result of its internal logic and consistency." This awareness, he continues, "is a source of her preferential option for the poor" (*CA*, no. 57).

Consequently, any project aimed at understanding the role of Catholic social thought in European society must start from the historical presence of Christians in the world operating through a cluster of social movements, charitable institutions, and actions for justice. One of the most striking characteristics of these movements is their amazing diversity. Particularly in Europe, Catholics are involved in at least five different sorts of movements:

Classical International Catholic Movements

The "classical" international Catholic movements such as the Christian workers' movement and its sub-movements, Catholic Farmers' leagues, Catholic organizations of employers, Caritas International, Justice and Peace commissions, and so on, are represented in the Vatican as "international Catholic movements."

Despite the fact that some of these social movements are quite secularized, they continue to work out a sort of middle-level thinking as a mediation between the socio-political reality and Christian inspiration. At a European level this is reflected, for example, in the organization of European Social Weeks, inspired by the still extant Semaines sociales de France. Members of the "classical" movements are sometimes connected with Christian Democratic political parties. Several members of these social movements have become members of the European parliament and other European institutions. They struggle with the tension between the requirements of using power and caring for their identity as Christians. This is not always easy to do. To the group of the classical movements also belong the local committees of Justice and Peace that contributed to new perspectives on Catholic social thought. Consider, for example, their influential documents, such as the document "Human Rights in the Church" published by the Flemish Justice and Peace Commission. Some of the "classical" social movements, such as Pax Christi, have succeeded, moreover, in mediating between Christian inspiration and political reality in a very effective way. Pax Christi not only offers its members a formation in Christian peacebuilding, but it also functions as a very effective advocate at the level of political lobbying. For example, it successfully mobilized support for the Mine Ban Treaty. Other "classical" social movements are very good at mobilizing funds for direct aid in case of disasters (such as Caritas International).

Movements in Religious Orders and Congregations

Movements operate in the context of religious orders and congregations, such as the Jesuit Refugee Service, the Dominican

Volunteers, the Vincentian Family, and many others. They constitute efficient networks that not only offer immediate help but are also very efficient in responding to specific needs. Moreover, they contribute to reflection and institutional change. They operate both in the spirit of the spirituality of the order or the congregation to which they are connected, and in the spirit of "scrutinizing the signs of the times."

Spirituality Movements

The *movimenti* or spirituality movements have become (perhaps too) prominent in the church since the Synod on the Laity in 1987. Despite their focus on spirituality and individual charity, many of these movements are engaged in social action. For example, the "economy of communion" in the Focolare movement (explicitly acknowledged in *Caritas in Veritate* by Pope Benedict XVI), the Movimento Populare in Comunione et Liberazione (which even played a direct political role in the former Italian Christian Democracy), and the many social initiatives by Sant'Egidio. The strength of the new *movimenti* is their concern for the orthodoxy of the Christian inspiration and their direct charity. They are excellent in raising funds, and they have representatives in the European parliament and the European Commission. They are well connected and are very good at networking with the church hierarchy (often not locally, but directly with the Vatican). Despite their genuine concern for the poor, they often lack a structural analysis or, at least, a critical analysis, while some (not all) lack focus on the structural and institutional dimensions of problems. Their strong point is what we described in section two as the "semantic and practical innovation" to which some movements have contributed, such as new forms of diplomacy that have resolved conflicts where traditional diplomacy had completely failed (for example, Sant'Egidio in Mozambique), or new economic practices such as the economy of community by the Focolare movement (which, according to Bruni, reconnects with the economic vision of the school of Genovesi).

Radical Christian Movements

The radical Christian movements such as Christians for Socialism, ATD Quard Monde (founded by a priest, but not a Catholic movement as such, the group engages in advocacy for the
rights of the Fourth World, the world of the urban sub-
proletariat), and the Movement of Missionary Commitment in
Flanders. These movements are not only active at the grassroots
level and among the poorest of the poor, but they also pay a
great deal of attention to a critical social analysis of the problems they try to resolve. The radical movements play a crucial
role in detecting new social problems and developing adequate
instruments for their analysis. These groups lobby for the rights
of undocumented people, refugees, and the urban poor, and they
often lie behind the origin of bishops' documents on such problems. They are the best guarantee against reducing the problems of the poor to no more than a problem of charity. They
combine their direct involvement in the struggle against poverty with an analysis in terms of justice.

Secular Social Movements

Some Christians actively participate in secular social movements,
such as Christian militants in secular unions and socialist parties, members of Amnesty International, Doctors Without Borders, Greenpeace, and so on. Members of these groups have to
cope with a tension between their "secular" commitments and a
sometimes disturbing lack of understanding by the church's hierarchy. Consider, for example, the case of Amnesty International,
which does great work for the protection of the rights and life of
political prisoners, but which is also criticized by the hierarchy
for its lack of concern for the conservative pro-life agenda.

Summary of Five Movements

This brief overview of the five sorts of movements shows that
there is an amazing variety, going from those that are operating

on the basis of a critical analysis of society and the "established disorder," to movements that practice charity without social analysis. They play an important role in European civil society, particularly with regards to the poor. The living presence of these movements is a clear testimony to the fact that the Catholic social tradition is more than a collection of official documents and even more than a tradition of thought. It "includes the prophets and activists, thinkers and analysts who wrestled with the meaning of Christian faith amid turbulent social times."[17] Apart from the *movimenti*, this wrestling is seldom given due recognition in official social teaching.

The Contribution of European Bishops' Conferences to "Scrutinizing the Signs of the Times" in Europe

In recent decades the European bishops' conferences have responded in many ways to the signs of the times, even if they did not always refer explicitly to the text of *Gaudium et Spes* to justify their intervention. It is particularly relevant to note that most of these documents are much more than mere "applications" of papal documents.

The first concern is the construction of the European Union. Apart from the Apostolic Exhortation *Ecclesia in Europa* (June 28, 2003), the most explicit text on the European Union was written by the Commission of the Bishops' Conferences of the European Union (COMECE). In May 2005 it published *The Evolution of the European Union and the Responsibility of Catholics*. Part 1, in particular, is a most interesting text on Christian discernment in the European Union on the basis of a rereading of the declaration of Robert Schuman, one of the founding fathers of the Union.

An inspiring document titled *A Europe of Values: The Ethical Dimension of the European Union* was published in 2007 on the occasion of the fiftieth anniversary of the Treaties of Rome, with the participation of prominent leaders and intellectuals such as Michel Camdessus, former IMF director general; Pat Cox, former president of the European Parliament; Thomas Halik, adviser to Vaclav Havel; Jacques Santer, former president of the European Commission; and others. This document argues that Europe must be more than a bureaucratic and technocratic power, more even than a matter of politics and law: "We must recall to mind those things which we should not have forgotten in the first place: over and above policies and institutions, the European project rests first and foremost upon values, upon an ethical view of life and society. Any community based on law should also be based on values." The bishops acknowledge that those values are not exclusively Christian, although "they are deeply rooted in the Christian tradition."[18] The values mentioned are peace and freedom (including the "willing participation of people"), togetherness, responsibility, diversity, subsidiarity, differentiation, multilateralism, tolerance, solidarity within the Union and with the rest of the world.

This global perspective is not a minor detail. The COMECE bishops have more than once drawn attention to the fact that *European* cannot be understood independently of the reality of *globalization*. This awareness has resulted in several global governance assessment reports and other texts related to the same theme. This concern for global governance is also present in the more analytical and biblical approaches to globalization by the social commission of the French bishops and the well-articulated document of the commission *Gaudium et Spes* of the Belgian Bishops' Conference. The latter offers not only an insightful summary of the basic principles of Catholic social thought but also perspectives for a vision that enables people to find meaning in the process of globalization.[19] In this way this document is fully in accordance with the perspectives opened up by Vatican II's *Gaudium et Spes*. The COMECE also published documents on themes such as the role of religious institutions with regards to European integration, the Euro and the monetary union, the future of democracy, peace and reconciliation, contemporary culture, global development, Latin America, the problem of migration and borders, biomedical research, the search for a common European heritage, solidarity, and others.

Like the COMECE, national bishops' conferences have also been very actively "scrutinizing the signs of the times." In the 1980s, when millions were concerned about the consequences of the nuclear threat and the installation of a new generation of mid-range nuclear missiles, several national bishops' conferences (the Dutch, German, French, and Belgian, among others) wrote peace letters, and their voices played a significant role in the debate in a way comparable to that of the American bishops' *Challenge of Peace* letter. In addition, during the conflict in Bosnia, several bishops articulated their concerns.

Another very significant theme is unemployment and economic crisis. This is connected with the question of social welfare, and in this regard the German bishops made an original contribution by issuing a well-articulated ecumenical text in collaboration with the Council of the Evangelical (Protestant) churches in Germany: *Für eine Zukunft in Solidarität und Gerechtigkeit* [For a Future in Solidarity and Justice]. *Wort des Rates der Evangelischen Kirche in Deutschland und der Deutschen Bischofskonferenz zur wirtschaftlichen und sozialen Lage in Deutschland* (1997).[20] Starting from a profound analysis of a society in transition, in which unemployment, poverty, financial burdens, and the ecological crisis are seen as threats, the text proposes a values-based way out. The commandment of love, the option for the poor, justice, and solidarity with subsidiarity are described as the cornerstones of a new consensus, in which secular values such as human rights and democracy also contribute to an "ecological social-market economy" and a new social culture in which Europe does not forget its international responsibility. The document argues for a consolidation of the social security systems (a much more nuanced and adequate argument than that presented in *Centesimus Annus*), and reaffirms the church's task to be at the service of society in view of a future based on solidarity and justice (a theme that *Justice et Solidarité* shows is also dear to the French bishops).

Other themes treated by European bishops' conferences include Christians and politics (with an excellent document by the French bishops, *Politique: L'affaire de tous* (1991), on political participation), the concern for the common good (with a very lucid text on the common good and political responsibility written by the bishops of England and Wales), Marxism (French bishops), unemployment, education, the economic crisis, migration (again excellent contributions by the French bishops), the Jubilee year 2000, and the alleviation of the debt of highly indebted countries (with an important initiative by the Belgian bishops that invited the universities of Leuven and Louvain-la-Neuve to study the problem), corruption (a most interesting text by the Italian bishops), and the transition from communism to a post-communist era (important reflections by the Greek Catholic bishops of Ukraine). Although the documents mentioned are only a selection, they are a clear testimony of the commitment of the European bishops to take the signs of the times seriously and to analyze the problems of European society in the light of *Octogesima Adveniens*.

Unfortunately, almost nothing of the work of the bishops is reflected in the official social documents from the Vatican. Not only do the many papal encyclicals from John Paul II and Benedict XVI seem to be unaware of the work done, but the official *Compendium of the Social Doctrine of the Catholic Church*, published in 2004, even limits the role of the bishops to being merely the propagators of the Roman social "doctrine." Although the *Compendium* acknowledges that the bishops bear "the primary responsibility for the pastoral commitment to evangelize social realities" (no. 539), it contends that they *only* have the task of "*promoting* the teaching and *diffusion* of the church's social *doctrine*" (no. 539, italics added). This is a denial of the consensus reached during the 1993 conference at the University of Fribourg, organized on the occasion of the presentation of the *Répertoire des documents épiscopaux des cinq continents* (1891–1991).[21]

During that conference Cardinal Etchegaray, then president of the Pontifical Council for Justice and Peace, gave his explicit support for taking more seriously the bishops' "ministry" with regards to the social teaching. He criticized, in clear language, the unilateral focus on papal texts. He also declared that the social teaching of the bishops would be "more and more continental and regional," and he suggested the possibility of documents "by both the bishops of the North and the South." Moreover, he explicitly criticized the fact that the social discourse of the church was "still too much Western," and he proposed a new conference that would take cognizance of the texts of the laity. He even pleaded for more ecumenical initiatives in this regard. According to Cardinal Etchegaray, who spoke in the spirit of *Gaudium et Spes* and *Octogesima Adveniens*, "ecumenical declarations are not less from the church than a strict catholic declaration."[22]

The Transformative Presence of the Church in European Political and Civil Society: A Reflection beyond Political Liberalism

One question remains unanswered: How can the church become a transformative power in a secularized European society? One thing is clear: as a consequence of the separation of church and state and of the "disestablishment" of the Catholic Church, direct interventions by the church in the affairs of a state of the European Union are excluded (the only exception is the officially recognized conversation between the European Union and the religions, but this is not a powerful intervention in the political affairs of the Union). The exclusion of a direct political intervention, however, does not necessarily imply a privatization of faith or an exclusion of it from the public square.[23]

The privatization thesis is very strongly present in the influential Anglo-American type of political liberalism that not only tends erroneously to identify the separation of church and state with the privatization of religion, but also tends to adopt a methodological exclusion of religious ideas from the public debate on the basic principles of society: the so-called method of avoidance. John Rawls in *A Theory of Justice* describes this in a nuanced way, not as an exclusion but as an agnostic attitude, an attitude that he described elsewhere as follows: "We try, so far as we can, neither to assert nor to deny any religious, philosophical, or moral views, or their associated philosophical accounts of truth and the status of values."[24]

This agnostic attitude toward the contribution of religious traditions, which is not followed by the European Union, is explicitly present in the hypothesis of the veil of ignorance, which excludes references to particular religious or theological ideas about the "good" of society; that is, participants not only know nothing about their place in society, their class position, or their social status, but also nothing about their conception of the good.

This expresses one of the great concerns of the liberal tradition: the state (or in this case a super-national entity like the EU) must abstain from any particular vision of the good. For Rawls, this means that the principles of justice that are the basis of the legal order must be based on rational arguments that do not depend on a particular religious, philosophical, or ideological conviction. Only the enlightened self-interest of the citizens who decide "under the veil of ignorance" leads to real fairness. In his later work Rawls has nuanced his "method of avoidance." His arguments are a most interesting starting point for an investigation into the conditions for the political involvement of the church in Europe.

In *Political Liberalism* Rawls still maintains that the basic political principles "should be, as far as possible, independent of the opposing and conflicting philosophical and religious doctrines the citizens affirm."[25] He distinguishes sharply between "the public point of view" and "many non-public points of view," and between a "public basis of justification generally acceptable to citizens on fundamental political questions" and "the many non-public bases of justification belonging to the many comprehensive doctrines and acceptable to those who affirm them." He does not, however, deny that there is a public concept of the good, as long as ideas of the good as a political concept are *distinct* from those in the more extensive views. The same holds for the conception of persons as free and equal.[26] In a democratic society characterized by a "reasonable pluralism" such a distinction is, according to Rawls, crucial. At first it seems as if there is again no room for particular contributions by specific religious traditions, such as the Catholic tradition. However, Rawls's theory in *Political Liberalism* is more nuanced than that. First of all, Rawls acknowledges religions insofar as they present themselves not as fundamentalist organizations but as "comprehensive doctrines." They can become "producers" of "an overlapping consensus," on the condition that their religious, philosophical, or moral doctrines are reasonable.

Catholic social thinking is a good example of such a reasonable tradition, because it is not only based on faith but also on reason, and on mediation.[27] On the basis of the intuitions and principles of their social tradition, Catholics can participate in public debates using reasonable arguments. For their right to contribute to an overlapping consensus, however, they have to pay a price. According to Rawls, they have to "thin out" the conflicting thickness of their particular convictions. They have to, so to speak, "dilute" their specific content, which implies that they might give up the specific interpretation that is its source of meaning.

This is problematic. There is a real risk that in a pluralistic society the level of "politics," and of its underlying principles and rights, is reduced to more or less formal principles void of any content or meaning. In this context it is crucial to reiterate that CST plays a role as a provider of meaning, not only by proposing "principles" (as was typical during the pre–Vatican II era), but also in a more dynamic way in the form of new insights and new practices that are generated, as we have demonstrated, through the continuous reading of signs of the times in the light of the gospel. As such, together with what other churches and religions do, CST participates in the formation of what the European Charter of 2000 has officially acknowledged as the "spiritual and moral heritage" in which the fundamental rights of the citizens of the Union are rooted.

Referring to our spiritual and moral heritage has more profound implications than merely an overlapping consensus would make possible. Even when a set of moral principles or rights becomes sufficiently universal to be acknowledged by different traditions, it remains necessary continually to revitalize their meaning from the perspective of these traditions.

Europe needs a general moral framework for its politics, but as soon as this formal framework is disconnected from the original traditions, which are the original providers of its meaning, it ceases to stimulate the participation and civic sense of its citizens. Citizens, as well as decision-makers, are not only rational subjects whose commitment to the public good is based on obedience to a set of procedures or formal rights that constitute an "empty shrine." There is no political community without values, which are the expression of a vision of the good life or an idea of the common good. And that is quite different from an empty neutrality, which is, incidentally, not neutral, but is itself the expression of a particular interpretation of the good society, namely, a society based on principles abstracted from the idea of the good.

There is, moreover, no living political community without a moral commitment. Without educating people toward practicing the virtues of citizenship, no political culture of responsibility will ever be possible. This education, the locus of which is the world of particular moral communities, forms the basis of "social capital."

Second, Rawls does acknowledge a direct role of religious traditions, though he situates this outside the political sphere. According to Rawls, particular traditions, as well as religious or philosophical associations, function as a sort of cultural background to politics. This is the domain of civil society, not of politics: "Comprehensive doctrines of all kinds—religious, philosophical, and moral—belong to what we may call the background culture of civil society. This is the culture of the social, not of the political. It is the culture of daily life, of its many associations: churches and universities, learned and scientific societies, and clubs and teams to mention a few."[28]

Based on Rawls's perspective, not only is the church's hierarchy, as an institutional partner of the European Union, important, but the participation of millions of Catholics in European civil society through the social and political movements to which they belong is also important. What Rawls describes as the "the culture of the social" is the space where the Catholic Church meets society at its best, not as "preaching authority" but as participatory community, a community of movements that participates in the transformation of European civil society.

Conclusion

Europe is not only influenced by the principles that were introduced by the Catholic social "doctrine" before Vatican II, but it has also been a space in which both movements and bishops' conferences have taken the responsibility to scrutinize the signs of the times in the spirit of *Gaudium et Spes* and of *Octogesima Adveniens*. This has resulted not only in a transformative presence in European civil society, but also in a rich heritage of inspiring texts and documents. On the one hand, this transformative presence and rich heritage have contributed to the search for a European soul. On the other hand, Europe should not forget that CST has above all a universal perspective and that the old continent is no longer the center of the world.

Notes

[1] Robert Shuman, *Pour l'Europe* (Paris: Ed. Nagel, 1964), 78. Translation by author.

[2] See Donal Dorr, *Option for the Poor: A Hundred Years of Catholic Social Teaching* (Maryknoll, NY: Orbis Books, 1992), 149–78.

[3] Oswald von Nell Breuning, SJ, *Soziale Sicherheit? Zur Grundfragen der Sozialordnung aus christlicher Verantwortung* (Freiburg: Herder, 1979), 177–78.

[4] Ibid., 113–48.

[5] Quoted in Johan Verstraeten, "Christian Social Teaching and Europe: A Reflection," in *A Critical Christian Inquiry into the Past, Present, and Future of European Integration*, ed. Jef Van Gerwen and John Sweeney (Kampen: Kok Pharos, 1996), 248–49.

[6] Pope John XXIII used this expression for the first time in his apostolic constitution *Humanae Salutis* announcing Vatican II on December

25, 1961 (see A.A.S. 54 [1962], 12). It was repeated as "signa temporum" in *Pacem in Terris*, no. 39.

[7] For a reflection on this problem, see Johan De Tavernier, "Eschatology and Social Ethics," in *Personalist Morals: Essays in Honor of Professor Louis Janssens*, ed. Louis Janssens, Joseph A. Selling, and Franz Böckle, 279–300 (Leuven: Peeters/University Press, 1988).

[8] See Ronald A. Heifetz, *Leadership without Easy Answers* (Cambridge, MA: Belknap Press, 1994), 24.

[9] Alasdair MacIntyre, *Whose Justice, Which Rationality* (Notre Dame, IN: University of Notre Dame Press, 1988), 354–55.

[10] Mary Elsbernd and Reimund Bieringer, *When Love Is Not Enough: A Theo-Ethic of Justice* (Collegeville, MN: Liturgical Press, 2002), 156n.20.

[11] Ibid., 155.

[12] Biblical stories do not simply tell us something about the past; they also open a new world of meaning and make a semantic and practical innovation possible. The metaphors play a particularly crucial role here. They not only function on the denominational level of words, but also on a level of predication in the broader context of sentence or text. As such, biblical narratives function as metaphors. Together with extravagant and eccentric elements, they create a metaphoric tension between everyday life and the extravagant world of the narrative (cf. Paul Ricoeur). See Johan Verstraeten, "Re-thinking Catholic Social Thought as Tradition," in *Catholic Social Thought: Twilight or Renaissance?* ed. J. S. Boswell, F. P. McHugh, and J. Verstraeten, Bibiliotheca Ephemeridum Theologicarum Lovaniensium (BETL) 157 (Leuven: University Press/Peeters, 2000), 72–74. My interpretation of Paul Ricoeur is mainly influenced by Alain Thomasset, *Paul Ricoeur, Une poétique de la morale* (Leuven: Peeters/University Press, 1996).

[13] In order to understand stories and metaphors, particularly the biblical ones, Christians need to be initiated into reading the Bible as well as reading texts in general. In order to learn how to discover new meaning, one must learn to interpret and disclose texts, which is a matter not of memorizing facts about texts or their authors, but of initiation into the art of reading. Therefore, courses on literature and on how to interpret reality and enrich our imagination are, as Martha Nussbaum has demonstrated in *Poetic Justice*, more necessary than ever. Without initiation into literature, the closing of the mind becomes a real danger in a world in which language, in general, becomes so impoverished by instrumental rationality and utility criteria that life itself loses meaning, since we are language animals.

[14] Elsbernd and Bieringer, *When Love Is Not Enough*, 156.

[15] Charles E. Curran, *Catholic Social Teaching 1891–Present. A Historical, Theological, and Ethical Analysis* (Washington DC: Georgetown University Press, 2002), 49.

[16] Synod of Catholic Bishops, *Justice in the World* (1971), sect. 6. Misunderstandings about these words have led to a reinterpretation of the link between action for justice in terms of "profound links" in *Evangelii Nuntiandi*. The misunderstanding was, however, not caused by the original text but by its translation in German and Dutch, in which *constitutive* was interpreted as "essential."

[17] Marvin L. Krier Mich, *Catholic Social Teaching and Movements* (Mystic, CT: Twenty-Third Publications, 2000), 1.

[18] COMECE, *A Europe of Values: The Ethical Dimension of the European Union* (2007), 6–7.

[19] The COMECE bishops have issued several global governance reports (2001–6), and the Belgian and French bishops have also paid attention to globalization.

[20] This is not the only common text of Catholic and Protestant churches in Germany. Eight other texts have preceded this document on themes such as organ transplantation, the economic situation in Germany, the relationship between church and state in Europe, church monuments in the new "Bundesländer" after the fall of the Berlin Wall and the Unification of Germany, end of life questions, and a document for the consultation process in view of the document on the social security system.

[21] The Fribourg conference took place April 1–3, 1993. The proceedings were published by R. Berthouzoz and R. Papini, eds., *Ethique, économie et développement: L'enseignement des évêques des cinq continents (1891–1991)*, Etudes d'éthique chrétienne, vol. 62 (Fribourg: Editions Universitaires; Paris: Le Cerf, 1995). The conference was organized on the occasion of a project that was later published as R. Berthouzoz, R. Papini, C. J. Pino de Olivera, and R. Sugranyes de Franch, eds., *Economie et développement: Répertoire des documents épiscopaux des cinq continents (1891–1991)*, Etudes d'éthique chrétienne, vol. 69 (Fribourg: Editions Universitaires; Paris: Le Cerf, 1997).

[22] Berthouzoz et al., *Economie et développement*, 257, 258, 259.

[23] See José Casanova, *Public Religions in the Modern World* (Chicago: University of Chicago Press, 1994).

[24] John Rawls, "The Idea of an Overlapping Consensus," *Oxford Journal of Legal Studies* 7, no. 1 (1987): 13.

[25] John Rawls, *Political Liberalism* (New York: Columbia University Press, 1993), 9.

[26] Ibid., xix.

[27] On the issue of mediation, see several articles in Boswell et al., *Catholic Social Thought*.

[28] Rawls, *Political Liberalism*, 14.

6.

Catholic Social Teaching and Its Application in Rural India

Joseph (Jeewendra) Jadhav, SJ

Introduction

When we look at the social teaching of the Catholic Church, we discover that one of the major themes running through these documents is the promotion and development of human dignity. The church interprets its social teaching in different historical contexts in order to promote and defend human dignity, which requires a comprehensive development of the human person. This complete development consists in achieving the overall well-being of each and every human being. To bring this about, social evil and other obstacles that stand in the way must be eliminated. As Pope Paul VI pointed out in *Populorum Progressio* (1967), people need to be helped to exercise their personal freedom to do more, have more, be more, so that they can increase their sense of personal worth (no. 6). The church wants to help people fulfill the vocation to which they are called by God, that is, their fulfillment and all-around development as children of God. This requires the development of certain rights and duties that flow from being a human person. Rights and duties are two sides of the same coin. The moment we demand our rights, we undertake the obligation of accompanying duties.

For example, as Pope John XXIII stated in *Pacem in Terris* (1963), the right to live is correlated to our duty to preserve life, and the right to a decent standard of living is correlated to our duty to live properly (no. 28).

Social Teaching of the Church and Comprehensive Development of the Person

The human person is not an island. We live in community, and it is in this community that we develop ourselves and in which our rights are realized. In our modern and globalized society we recognize that human life is tied to the lives of our fellow human beings; our own personal well-being is always connected with that of the other. In a well-ordered human society people recognize their mutual rights and duties, requiring from each a generous contribution to the establishment of "a civic order in which rights and duties are progressively and effectively acknowledged and fulfilled."[1]

Just as a mother is always interested in and works for the well-being of her children, so is the church interested in the all-around well-being of its members, for the goal of human life is not only to attain heaven but also to experience happiness in this life.[2] The church is far from looking on religion as a purely private affair. From the church's religious mission comes a function, a light, and an energy that can serve to structure and consolidate the human community according to the divine law. Therefore the church has addressed the world on questions of public morality such as social justice, the development of peoples, human rights, war and peace, and racism.[3]

According to divine revelation, God did not create humankind in isolation but for the formation of a social union in a society where human and social progress hinge on each other.[4] Viewed from this perspective, the human race is interdependent for its survival; it shares the same natural resources the Creator has fashioned for all. All have a right to use these natural resources for their survival and fulfillment of their needs. It follows that no individual or group should appropriate any of these for exclusive personal use at the cost of other human beings. Some nations exploit and appropriate these resources, and this often affects poorer nations and their populations. As *Populorum Progressio* puts it, When the hungry nations call and cry to the well-to-do nations for help, the church states that their cry should be answered. It is a matter of international justice to contribute to the development of poorer nations in order to bring about the complete development of the human race (see nos. 2–3, 5, 6).

Pope Benedict XVI's Peace Day Message for the year 2010 focused on the degradation of the environment, which is creating a grave moral problem and endangering the peaceful coexistence of the human race and human life itself.[5] He says that we cannot remain indifferent to what is happening around us, for the deterioration of any one part of the planet affects us all. He continued, saying that the policies of governments, the activities of multinational corporations, the negative effects of pollution, environmental exploitation, and present lifestyles have an impact on the environment. We cannot remain indifferent to climate change, desertification, the deterioration and loss of productivity in vast agricultural areas, the pollution of rivers and aquifers, the loss of biodiversity, the increase of natural catastrophes, and the deforestation of equatorial and tropical regions. The pope further stated that people are forced by the deprivation of their natural habitat to migrate in search of food, water, and unpolluted air. It is evident that the issue of environmental degradation challenges all of us to examine our lifestyles and the prevailing models of consumption and production, which are often unsustainable from a social, environmental, and even economic point of view (no. 1).

In the same message Benedict XVI warned of the actual and potential conflicts involving access to natural resources. Protecting the natural environment in order to build a world of peace is a duty incumbent upon each and every person. It is an urgent challenge and should be engaged with renewed and concerted commitment; it is also a providential opportunity to hand down to the coming generations the prospect of a better future for all (no. 14). Acknowledging the suffering and hardships which environmental destruction is already causing and the devastation it will wreak in the future, the pope said that "humanity needs a profound cultural renewal; it needs to rediscover those values which can serve as the solid basis for building a brighter future for all" (no. 5). Our present economic, environmental, and social crises are ultimately interrelated moral crises. Resolving these crises will require people to work together and to take responsibility for their individual actions. Specifically, a solution will require "a lifestyle marked by sobriety and solidarity, with new rules and forms of engagement, one which focuses confidently and courageously on strategies that actually work, while decisively rejecting those that have failed" (no. 5).

When the Bible said that the Creator made man and woman in God's own image and gave them dominion over the earth, this meant that God called them to be the stewards of creation, drawing from the earth what they needed and safeguarding its riches for future generations. "Sad to say, it is all too evident that large numbers of people in different countries and areas of our planet are experiencing increased hardship because of the negligence or refusal of many others to exercise responsible stewardship over the environment" (no. 7). The pope added that because the environmental crisis is global, it must be met with a universal sense of responsibility and solidarity toward people living in other parts of the world as well as toward generations who have not yet been born. The church's commitment to environmental protection flows from a religious duty "to protect earth, water, and air as gifts of God the Creator meant for everyone, and above all to save mankind from the danger of self-destruction" (no. 12).

By telling us again and again about our role in the world, Benedict XVI is telling us that our development should be based on the conservation and judicious use and protection of the environment.

The Actual Situation of the World Today

The Copenhagen climate summit discussed the alarming topic of climate change and how this is affecting the earth and its temperature as detrimental to our existence. On December 7, 2009, world environment ministers and officials met in Copenhagen for the United Nations climate conference to create a successor document to the Kyoto protocol in order to arrive at a solution to climate change by agreeing to limits for emissions and providing a remedy to climate change.

This meeting is certain to have its impact on India. Asian mega deltas, such as the Ganga-Brahmaputra delta, are at risk because of large populations and high exposure to rising sea levels, storm surge, and river flooding. Also, should the Himalayan glaciers melt, then flooding, rock avalanches, and disruption of water sources will follow. In tropical areas crop yield is projected to decrease, even with relatively modest rises of 1–2 degrees Centigrade in local temperatures, thereby increasing the risk of hunger and starvation. The changes in health will be most felt by those least able to adapt, such as the poor, the very young, and the elderly. India is doing its part with the National Action Plan on Climate Change (NAPCC), which includes eight missions: solar power, enhanced energy efficiency, sustainable habitat, water, sustaining the Himalayan ecosystem, green India, sustainable agriculture, and strategic knowledge for climate change. India has also reportedly offered to cut energy intensity of its emissions by 20–25 percent following similar moves from the United States and China. Energy intensity is defined as energy used per unit of income or output. This means that emissions still will increase, but more slowly. Emission intensity is the average emission rate of a given pollutant from a given source relative to the intensity of a specific activity. India's intensity of carbon dioxide (CO_2) use is among the lowest in the world (and equal to that of Europe in 2007), while China's is among the highest.[6]

We have just seen what Benedict XVI says about the preservation, protection, and judicial use of the natural resources in keeping with CST. "As regard the ecological question the Social Doctrine of the church reminds us that the goods of the earth were created by God to be used wisely by all. They must be shared equitably in accordance with justice and charity."[7] From the Copenhagen summit on climate change we find that the whole world is concerned about the drastic climatic changes that are occurring and the credence being given to these new threats to human existence.

The church, too, is concerned about the problems that the human race is facing because it understands human nature well and it shares its joys as well its sorrows. When we analyze various problems of the world, we realize that they are connected with the way we live, with the way we use natural resources, and with how we deal with one another. To give an example: Poverty is caused by a complex set of variables. This problem can be resolved only on the basis of the principle of the universal destination of goods, as is put forth by CST.[8] When we look at the present environmental crisis, we realize that it affects the poorest of the poor in a special way, wherever they may be. Many of them live in lands that are prone to erosion and desertification, many of them are forced to live in polluted areas of large cities,[9] and many of them are forced to migrate for the sake of survival.

The principle of a universal use of goods is also applied to water, an essential facet of human existence. Water is considered in the sacred scriptures as a symbol of purification (Jn 13:5–8) and also as a symbol of life (Jn 3:5). "[Water] is a gift from God, . . . a vital element essential to survival; thus everyone has a right to it. Satisfying the need of all, especially of those who live in poverty, must guide the use of water and the services connected with it."[10]

So, protection, promotion, and judicial use of the environment and of natural resources, gifts entrusted to us by God for our use, are essential. These gifts should be used on the basis of the principle of the universal destination of goods for the authentic development of humankind. To accomplish this we may need to change our lifestyles and our ideologies for the sake of the common good. Our lifestyle should be inspired with sobriety, temperance, and self-discipline—on both the individual and social levels. We must respect the order of creation by which basic human needs will be satisfied, by undertaking forms of industrial development and the new ways of undertaking agricultural development. We must become aware of our interdependence and make efforts to eliminate numerous causes of ecological disasters. Such cooperation could bring about the sense of solidarity, responsibility, and participation on the basis of democratic forms of decision-making for individual and community development.[11] In order to apply CST to the rural areas of Maharashtra, India, for authentic human development, I suggest replicating the comprehensive Watershed Development Programmes, where the principles of the common good, participation, and solidarity are applied, regeneration of natural resources is brought about, and their judicial use for the betterment of human life is advanced. In this program the development of the whole village is brought about by active participation, irrespective of caste and creed—Muslim, Hindu, Christian, and Buddhist. The people realize that in the watershed programs they are interdependent, and their own development depends on the development of their fellow villagers, for they share the same natural resources and the responsibility of looking after these natural resources for everyone in the village. This program also mitigates migration because the inhabitants of the watershed development area now find work in the village itself.[12]

Application of the Social Teachings of the Church in Ahmednagar District

The application of CST is based on its concept of the human person as created in the image of God and the resultant vision that the person is endowed with dignity. As Pope John Paul II wrote in *Centesimus Annus*, "Every individual . . . bears the image of God and therefore deserves respect" (no. 22).

The concern of the church is to protect and to promote human dignity, which is accomplished by bringing about the overall development of all individuals by supporting their human rights and corresponding duties. The church tells us time and again that to accomplish peaceful coexistence and real development we cannot forget the role of nature and natural resources. We will have to devise ways and means to help us to use creation and not to exploit and harm it. Following this line of reasoning, Paul VI, in *Octogesima Adveniens*, has suggested general guidelines for the well-being of workers (no. 14). It leaves it to the local churches to judge their situations in the light of the general guidelines it provides in its social teaching and to devise local methods and means to defend and promote human dignity. The famous method that the church suggests is expressed in John XXIII's *Mater and Magistra*: Observe, judge, and act (no. 236).

Applying this methodology of observe–judge–act, we always have to take into consideration the local situation where we are invited to apply CST. It is this idea of a local or situational application in which I propose to examine these teachings with a major concern for the judicious use, preservation, and regeneration of natural resources, keeping in mind future generations and our own survival, which are now at stake.

The application examines a rural setting of Maharashtra, India. The State of Maharashtra is highly industrialized, though agriculture continues to be the main occupation of these rural people. I do not necessarily propose this application to the whole of Maharashtra, nor to the whole of India since the situations are so different and need different parameters for application. But since I am considering a rural area of Maharashtra in the district of Maharashtra State called Ahmednagar, I need to point out that this is an underdeveloped area where much of the population depends on agriculture for its survival. Since this is the case in India as a whole, this methodology might be a valid one to consider for use in the wider Indian context.

Physical Aspects of Ahmednagar District

In the district of Ahmednagar the rhythm of life and the villagers' adaptation in the different parts of the district depend on the variations of the underlying soil, topography, the availability of water for irrigation purposes, and the amount of progress achieved by the farmers in implementing new methods of agriculture.[13] While there are variations within the district, the climate is normally dry and hot throughout the year, except during the monsoon season which begins the first week of June and continues until the end of September.

The Effect of the Climate on the District

Ahmednagar district is under the rain shadow zone of the Eastern Ghat. As the clouds approach Ahmednagar, they are practically empty, with whatever remains falling in the district. Significantly, more rain is realized in the western part of the district. The eastern side of the district is arid and receives very little moisture, and drought is regularly experienced.[14] Because of this climatic situation, the area has faced famines and diseases such as cholera and plagues.

The Comprehensive Watershed Development Programme

Following this snapshot of the area, we now look for a way of applying CST to this rural area in light of the pope's call to use the earth in a good and just way. What might be the best way to utilize the natural resources of the area while emphasizing conservation and regeneration? I suggest we look at a comprehensive approach to the area based on the Watershed Development Programme, a pioneering effort on the part of Jesuits in bringing an overall development of the people and building on the natural resources that they have. The Jesuits of the region have arrived at this program after many trials and errors, and they have succeeded and are still succeeding in these efforts to address the concerns and to encourage participation of the people in the area. This has been directly tied to the church's social teaching. Seeing the problems of drought for the farmers, we devised various methods to alleviate their sufferings and to bring about their comprehensive development. In the past, programs for the farmers failed because they did not take into consideration the judicial use of the natural resources. This caused us to rethink the programs and incorporate new strategies based on prudent use.

One of the most essential elements for farming is water, which, in this area, was not sufficient for the agricultural needs. To solve this problem we built over one hundred percolation tanks to store water for irrigation. When there was rain, this system worked. Unfortunately, when rain did arrive after drought, the water carried to these tanks was mingled with fertile soil that remained in the tanks. This caused two problems: the lifespan of the percolation tanks was diminished, and the fertile topsoil was carried away, thereby leaving the land unfit for farming. Since it rarely rained, the tanks remained empty for most of the year.

Energy went into various types of social work to help the people, but a real and sustainable solution to farming in this drought-prone area was not found. Drought played havoc in the area, and every solution was short lived, entailing lost monies and energy. This created an opportunity for us. Our center, called the Social Centre, started a process of rethinking and re-flecting on the actual situation. The people at the center discovered that in attempting to alleviate the problem, the process of digging wells led to compromising further the scarce natural resources of water and the land. This actually led to the deple-tion of the ground water levels, thereby creating desertification of the land. This, of course, was unintended, but in attempting to help, this added to the sufferings of small farms owned by the poor. As a result, their economic situation worsened, causing them to migrate to near or faraway urban industrial areas in search of gainful employment.[15]

The ongoing reflection at the Social Centre was effectively connected to several key variables. We realized that there were close links among the land, the depletion of natural resources, and poverty. The decision was made to change the approach from resource exploitation to resource mobilization, that is, conservation and judicial management of resources. At the same time we changed from sector interventions to comprehensive, integrated, area-based resource development. In the watershed there are two standardized points from which the water flows from the mountains to the drainage area. On this basis the Social Centre concluded that comprehensive development of the whole village community could be brought about by the regeneration of the natural resources of the village along the watershed line, involving active participation of the whole village community at all levels of the project—from the time of taking a collective decision to the implementation of the programs and its ongoing maintenance. The Social Centre decided to promote and support each village community through an approach entitled the People's Participatory Appraisal method, where the people themselves are actively involved in their own development and directly tied to the natural resources in their village.[16] This made people the protagonists of their own development through active participation at every stage of the program, putting into practice the principle of participation found in CST.

What Is a Watershed?

A watershed is a catchment area of a particular drainage line such as a stream, river, or other source that supplies water to the collection area. A watershed may consist of a few acres for a small stream or thousands of acres for a large river. The watershed, if used as part of a comprehensive program involving conservation, regeneration, and judicious utilization of the natural resources, seeks an optimum balance between the demand and use of the natural resources so that they remain sustainable over time.

For such a program one must take into account many factors: soil, farmland, wasteland, water, livestock, crop management, forest, pasture and fodder development, rural alternate-energy-generation management, and finally, the implementation of agro-based employment generation schemes to increase family income. In the most fundamental way community development is at the heart of this; without it, *no* development can take place. In 1999 the Social Centre issued a report on watershed development and discussed the impact on the land. To address community issues we conducted programs in community building and the building of self-confidence and self-reliance, and we held a variety of training programs and community meetings. To build awareness on the educational level, we organized tours to the Agricultural University of Rahuri and visits to other successfully developed watershed villages. Direct education was also provided through health camps, legal aid camps, and educational street plays.[17]

Special attention was paid to women in all the Watershed Development Programmes. We believed that the desired change could be brought about much more effectively through the development of women precisely because the women are constantly present in the villages, working in them, and in contact with their children (thus teaching them). Another important reason for paying special attention to women was the social patterns of the paternal society in the Ahmednagar District. There, discrimination and oppression of women followed the same path as that of the Dalits, the untouchables. Efforts were focused on women to make them more aware of their situation so that they might more actively participate in their own development.

Every watershed and village women's group was formed independently, and from each group two women were chosen as the representatives for a Comprehensive Women's Assembly. The objective of the assembly was to work for the development of women by mobilizing and forming self-help groups in the villages, coordinating different women's developmental activities, helping to develop necessary infrastructure for women's advancement, and executing and promoting awareness camps (for health education, gender issues, skills training, and income-generation activities).[18]

Conditions Required of the Watershed Inhabitants

Each village in the watershed area has to decide how to implement the program in the area and determine whether or not to participate actively in its implementation. Before such a decision is made, the villagers are prepared through regular visits by the social workers of the Social Centre, who hold formal and informal conversations with them about their problems with the drinking water, health, the drought situation and its causes, and so forth. The people are made aware that the solution to all these problems is in their hands. Should they implement the Watershed Development Programme, this will provide a long-term durable resolution to their problems.

It is not only in words but in deeds that the villagers have to prove that they are serious about participation in the plan. In the village, a test situation is established to examine the cooperation and active participation in a small watershed of about five hundred acres. This place previously has been identified by the villagers with the technical guidance of the Social Centre, and all the necessary soil and water conservation treatments are implemented. At this stage two youths from the village are chosen by the village membership and are trained on the site by the agro-technicians of the Social Centre, who offer supervision of the land management. The villagers themselves must provide free voluntary labor once a week for at least five weeks. If they are found earnest in their work, then the next steps are taken by the Social Centre. This test site serves as a demonstration to the villagers of effective land-management structures put in place to block the rain water flow. Rain water does not run off the land, as in the past, and this effectively shows the villagers how the system works to store water. Now the water can be stored in the nearby wells, which previously had been dry. This is a big surprise to the villagers.

Other than voluntary labor at this initial stage of launching the program, there are certain other conditions for a successful program. One member from every household has to do voluntary labor once a week during the implementation stage of the program. All family members, except for the landless laborers and those in single-parent households, are expected to participate in the work. Those family members who cannot work are asked to pay a day's wage to the watershed committee or send a substitute worker. The program implementation normally lasts for about five to ten years, depending on the total acres of the village.

First, voluntary work is a basic component of the package of the Watershed Development Programme. We discovered that people agreed to do voluntary labor only when they were convinced of the benefits of this development for their village. In the process of doing the work, a healthy give and take develops among the villagers, thus bringing about unity. They learn to take responsibility for the work done. They identify with this work as their own work, inculcating in them the sense of ownership of the labor that in the long run leads to the preservation and protection of the land management done by them.

Since the villagers profit from the very outset of the program, they are required to contribute 16 percent of the total cost of the program. Their voluntary labor is counted as a contribution toward the watershed development. Hence, they work for six days, but they are paid only for five days. This pay is kept aside for the maintenance of the work after the full implementation of the program.

The second condition is a ban on the free grazing of cattle. When free grazing is allowed, the cattle roam and their hooves loosen the soil, which is then washed away when the rain comes. This is the most fertile topsoil; when lost, the land becomes unproductive. Free grazing also destroys trees by loosening the soil. Further, cattle eat the roots of the grass, again loosening the soil. Cattle must be stall fed.

The third condition is that the villagers cannot fell trees; rather, they must plant more trees and protect those already present. Trees are needed for the maintenance of the environmental balance of the area because they control pollution and participate in drawing rainfall. They are needed for fruit, fodder, fuel, and firewood. They protect the soil by stopping erosion and thus prevent desertification.

The fourth condition is the cessation of alcohol intake in the village. Over time, the males have taken to drinking and this interferes with family life and positive work patterns. Their behavior hurts their families and creates cycles of dissolution and lack of family cohesion. This results in little to no income, children imitating the negative behaviors and personality disorders associated with drinking, and wives being left with family burdens. The social effect to the village is multiplied by problems connected with alcohol.

Active Participation of the Watershed Community

Every individual and every family of a village must be a beneficiary of the Watershed Development Programme. This requires individuals to achieve a certain level of self-reliance so that each individual can contribute labor, perspectives, knowledge, and skills to build up the community through participatory planning and in the implementation of the program for village development. The Social Centre has discovered that through this process an authentic village community may develop. Therefore, active participation of the villagers is a must at every stage of this program.[19]

The unified village ensures that, along with all-around development, the poorer sections of their village are attended to so that they can also build enough resources to accomplish an end to their poverty. Through an understanding and lived spirit of cooperation by all and for all, the community overcomes its difficulties. This was in sharp contrast to many government programs. Those programs, often using external agencies, targeted approaches for poor groups without considering the social, natural, and environmental contexts necessary for overcoming poverty. The difference in this program is that the Social Centre combines its own expertise along with the economic and social programs initiated by the government to help every villager. It is only when a whole village, utilizing a democratic process and taking full control of its development, is able to demand its rightful share in the national entitlements that true development of rural India can come about. It is this vision of decentralized planning that has made the Social Centre insist on the active participation of the whole village community; this finds its expression in the Village Watershed Development Committee and Village Forest Protection Committee.[20]

All these activities can be done only when there is cooperation and unity among the villagers. In this way the principle of participation of the people in their own development is put into practice as indicated in the application of CST. So, from the beginning of the project, community development is attended to with care. Every effort is made to bring about peaceful and harmonious relationships among the villagers by bringing about awareness among them that all are equal and that if they want to develop, the group must develop together because the natural resources belong to all of them. If they do not cooperate, no effective development can occur. They are also brought to realize that their political differences and affiliations to different political parties, if any, may hinder their progress. They are asked to make personal decisions to abandon these differences in order to embrace the common good of the village.

Impact of the Watershed Development Programme

Social and Community-based Changes

Wherever Watershed Development Programmes are implemented, the first issue with which the Social Centre has to deal is the various small castes and groups. This is a normal feature of all Indian societies. In every village of Maharashtra there exists a minority community that belongs to the low and oppressed castes called Dalits. Though a village forms one comprehensive unit, this does not indicate that it is based on equality, liberty, and justice. The caste and class prejudices often do not allow people to come together to form a unit. Further, in many of the environmentally impoverished villages where the project of a watershed development is undertaken, the villages tend toward more traditional beliefs about the purity and impurity of castes and religion. These more traditional villages actively practice untouchability. Anybody familiar with villages in India realizes that the caste system has done irreparable damage to human and social values. One cannot talk about a village community, for there is no community; a community exists only in terms of separated, opposed, and alienated groups.[21] To bring people together in these circumstances is a very difficult task. It can take several years of work by the Social Centre before the project can move ahead. This undertaking involves bringing a divided community together to form a single unit so that the villagers may deal with and communicate with one another, and then work together in collaboration so that they can share common space, touch one another, and drink water from a common source. The enormity of this can be seen when one considers that traditional views indicate that the Dalit will actually defile those of higher caste.

The initial work also involves learning to respect and listen to the viewpoints of those whose voices could not be heard before or who were belittled, ridiculed, and treated inhumanely. India has not provided this type of listening to other voices, so a comprehensive, action-oriented community development program is needed to accomplish attitudinal change in the villagers. A move away from the past to a desire to cooperate with one another and to deal with one another with justice, love, and mercy is the first order of business. To put this in the words of Mr. Bade, an upper-caste Maratha farmer who was the head of a village, "This program has brought us together and now we eat from one and the same plate."[22] Eating from one and the same plate means establishing a close relationship based on equality by sharing everything possible as brothers and sisters. Mr. Raqmzan Rasul Saysed says that the lifestyle in the village has changed. They do not practice the caste system in the village any more. All intermingle and attend one another's marriages and eat and drink together; these things were not possible before. Atmaram Satpute says that the Harijans (untouchables) were not allowed to come near the upper-caste people, but now they have all come together and they drink water from their jug. They are all united and have become one.[23]

The land management is visible, but there are hosts of other changes taking place in the community that are not so immediately obvious. The villagers now understand the effects of concerted efforts to work together and the benefits. People become aware of their rights and duties. For instance, in one village the people deputed one of their members to supervise the check dam being built for them. Previously, a contractor was given a contract by government officials without evaluative controls and accountability; this resulted in substandard work. Now, with the village supervisor around, the contractor has to do the work properly. People had become aware that the check dam was meant for them and that they were the primary beneficiaries of it; it was their right to have it. The government was not doing any "favor" by constructing an inadequate dam.[24] It does take some time for the villagers to understand their rights and duties, but in time they do. Unless the project begins properly with the training and collaboration necessary, the program will fail. The very concept of watershed takes root first of all in the minds of the people, and they see that it is an immense work. It cannot be done by one person; everyone in the village must come together with the others as community for the good of all.

People have become self-reliant and confident in their dealings with higher officials. They are able to look better after themselves and their legitimate interests.[25] They have become more confident that the future is in their hands, that it is their work to bring about their own development. They have even offered help to neighboring villagers. They visit villages and talk to the people about the progress they have made and how they have accomplished it. They encourage others to emulate their success. The evangelized have become evangelizers. The Village Watershed Development Committee members have visited other villagers to teach them how to implement a watershed project in their villages too, and many have listened to them and followed their example.[26]

When people begin to realize that their dream of prosperity is linked to transforming relationships among themselves, they slowly learn to put aside their differences and their individual self-interests in order to raise the resources of their entire community. The indicator of this process is that all the projects that are beneficiaries of the Watershed Development Programme have contributed 18 percent of the total cost of the project by their voluntary labor.[27]

Employment Generation

The first short-term benefit felt by the villagers is the availability of stable work in the village along with assured fair wages. This is true for both men and women, who are paid on the basis of their work and without pay disparity based on gender discrimination. The same continues after the land-development part of the program is finished. The quality of the irrigated land increases, leading to the availability of more work in the agricultural field. This situation actually brings about a scarcity of laborers in the fields, resulting in increased wages. Since there is more work in the fields, many more working days are available to villagers. This results in increments in the income of the agricultural laborers.[28]

Regeneration of Natural Resources

The regeneration of natural resources has occurred and the utilization of resources is done more judicially so that the future is assured for the village. This has led to the conservation of soil and water. The soil has become more fertile, and water levels have increased, leading to changes in the growing cycles and crop rotation and thereby increasing the growth of farm produce.[29] Due to grassland development, agro-based activities such as dairy farms and goat rearing have increased, and a secondary source of income (milk, meat) is made available to the farmers. The number of dairy animals has replaced the traditional indigenous cows and sheep due to the availability of good quality and quantity of fodder within the village itself.[30]

Rise in the Standard of Living and Development of Women

Since there is surplus produce in the villages, the annual income of the farmers has been augmented, giving them more purchasing power. This has led to the acquisition of more household assets. The environment has changed, giving way to new and permanent houses. The standard of living of the people has risen. They do not have to toil as in the past; more has emerged for less work. The people have more free time, which they are investing in caring for and training their children, attending village meetings, visiting relatives, attending entertainments, and resting from their labors.[31]

In order to encourage women to come forward to play their part in the developmental activities, self-help groups are formed in every village. When women see the economic benefits to their families, they readily come together to work in groups. As a social phenomenon, the men seem to have no objections to the women joining such groups. Through these self-help groups they are shown how to save money for unforeseen needs. All the self-help groups run micro-finance saving systems. As they come together and get used to the interaction, other kinds of activities begin. They begin to discuss issues concerning themselves and their households. In this way self-help groups become a powerful means for individual change and community development. As the women become aware of themselves, they also become aware that self-development is necessarily linked with community development. Thus, the "I" and the "we" are seen to be two interlinked aspects of the same reality. They become aware that their individual problems can be solved through the help of others, and this leads to their readiness to engage in cooperative activities. They have taken part in many income-generation projects, health improvement activities, community awareness training, and cultural activities—all done together through harmonious social relationships.[32] The micro-saving and financing projects take care of the contingencies of the villagers, and they no longer need to use the moneylenders to borrow money at difficult times with exorbitantly high interest rates.

Community Development

Watershed development is an immense program requiring huge efforts on the part of everyone. It combines a need for patience with the realization that authentic human development can occur. It starts with small interactions among the villagers and ends bringing multiple interactions among members of the whole village. It is an ongoing program. It gets better and better every day and opens the horizons of the people to new experiences. New approaches can be used and implemented for the spiritual and material betterment of people. It is a true revolution that spreads silently and steadily restores nature and humans to the original purpose of creation.

In short, the Watershed Development Programme is a true democracy implemented at the village level by the people, of the people, and for the people. It has brought about human ecological and natural resource regeneration that leads to the establishment of more human relationships among the villages, a cooperative attitude for development, the common good, a healthy lifestyle, and a higher standard of living. These advances have led the villagers to lead good and moral lives,[33] achieved by practicing their rights and undertaking their corresponding duties.

Conclusion

The discovery and implementation of the overall development of the people based on the judicial use, conservation, protection, and regeneration of their natural resources along with participation of the villages on democratic principles for their own authentic human development is the application of CST to concrete realities.

This method can be replicated in any place that has the same physical and natural features. In fact, this program is taken as one of the model programs by the Government of India, which now assists it financially with the help of its various departments and with the cooperation of NGOs.

This program helps in building human communities, promoting peaceful living conditions, and reducing caste differences.

Notes

[1] Giorgio Filibeck, *Human Rights in the Teaching of the Church: From John XXIII to John Paul II* (Vatican: Libreria Editrice Vaticana. 1994), 88.

[2] Benjamine Masse, *Justice for All: An Introduction to the Social Teaching of the Catholic Church* (Milwaukee: Bruce Publishing Co., 1994), 4.

[3] Pontifical Council for Justice and Peace, *Compendium of the Social Doctrine of the Church* (Vatican: Libreria Editrice Vaticana, 2004), no. 55.

[4] See Second Vatican Council, *Gaudium et Spes* (1966), nos. 32, 29, 25.

[5] Benedict XVI, World Peace Day Message, January 1, 2010 (Vatican: Libreria Editrice Vaticana, 2010).

[6] Vatican Radio India Desk, *Newsletter* (February 2010).

[7] Pontifical Council for Justice and Peace, *Compendium of the Social Doctrine of the Church*, no. 481.

[8] Ibid., no. 482.

[9] Ibid.

[10] Ibid., no. 484.

[11] Ibid., no. 486.

[12] Cf. *Gaudium et Spes*, no. 66; also cf. John Paul II, Message for the 1993 World Day of Peace, no. 3.

[13] Gazetteers Department, Government of Maharashtra, *Ahmednagar District Gazetteers*, rev. ed. (Bombay, 1976), 1, 12.

¹⁴ Several severe famines in this district have compelled missionaries to undertake relief works. Even now, due to lack of rain, there is a severe drinking water problem and the crops have failed in most parts of the district, requiring the government and other agencies to undertake relief work.

¹⁵ Social Centre, *In the Service of Small and Marginal Farmers and Other Weaker Sections of the Community*, 7.

¹⁶ Ibid.

¹⁷ *Annual Report of the Social Centre* (1998–99), 8.

¹⁸ Social Centre, *Impact Assessment Report on Bhagewadi Watershed Development Project*, 7.

¹⁹ *Annual Report of the Social Centre*, 5.

²⁰ Ibid., 5.

²¹ H. Bacher, *The Social Centre Ahmednagar in the Hitguj* (March 1980), archives of Pune Province.

²² Whenever Mr. Bade was called to give a lecture on watershed development and its effect on the village population and the environment on account of the implementation of the Watershed Development Programme in his village, he has made this remark. I have heard him say this myself when I took some villagers to his village on an educational demonstrative tour.

²³ Development Management Network Pune, *Action Research on the Process of Impact of Indo German Watershed Development Programme Chincoli Village*, 24. The report was prepared by the above agency to evaluate the impact of the program. The program is implemented by the Social Centre with financial assistance from Indo German Watershed Development Programme.

²⁴ *Annual Report of the Social Centre*, 4.

²⁵ Ibid.

²⁶ Often the members of a Watershed Development Committee are requested to accompany the social workers of the Social Centre to other villages in order to give witness to how the program has helped them and how it may help the other village communities.

²⁷ *Annual Report of the Social Centre*, 4.

²⁸ Ibid.

²⁹ Ibid., 1–2.

³⁰ Ibid., 2.

³¹ Ibid.

³² Ibid., 6.

³³ This may be inferred from the various evaluation reports of the Watershed Development Programmes.

7.

North American Culture's Receptivity to Catholic Social Teaching

John Coleman, SJ

In an article written for a larger symposium about the papal encyclical *Caritas in Veritate*, James Hug, SJ, says of that papal teaching: "Its vision conflicts head on with many American cultural assumptions." In particular, Hug thought that Pope Benedict XVI's view of the market, business, and politics might be, in places, hard for Americans to swallow. "The market must integrate more relational principles into its working. Trust and a sense of gift or gratuity in the relationships between producers and consumers need to replace cutthroat competition and a philosophy of *caveat emptor*. Creation of wealth is not businesses' only responsibility. Every business must recognize its responsibilities to all its stakeholders, including workers, clients, suppliers, consumers, local communities and the environment."[1] Just how amenable is North American culture to the presuppositions and philosophy of CST?

It is, admittedly, quite a tall order to try, succinctly, to adumbrate, fairly and adequately, a national or regional culture in a few paragraphs or pages without falling into oversimplifications or reductionisms. It is all the more difficult if one is attempting, as I am, to cover an entire region, North America, which includes both the United States and Canada. Canadian culture, as we will see in its place, has many important elements that differentiate it from the culture of the United States, although polling data generally suggest a wide convergence in attitudes between the two nations.[2] I will begin this chapter with a primary reference to the culture of the United States and how it may include key elements that diverge from some of the ordinary assumptions of CST (especially as CST incorporates a strong communitarian ethos around the core concept of solidarity). Second, I will treat of American receptivity to and contributions to CST. In a third section I raise up the specifically Canadian contributions to CST, which will help us segue to a larger question of the future of CST in the North American context.

American Culture as a Lens
to Receive Catholic Social Teaching

No culture is simple. Most cultures contain their own ways and methods of dealing with the basic antinomies of human life: individualism *and* community; spirit *and* body; continuity *and* change. Moreover, no culture is static. Every culture includes subgroups or subcultures such that, except for very primitive and isolated tribes, every culture is, to some extent, multicultural.[3] Cultures are quite fundamental to our identities and supply a core symbolic by which we see the world. Social scientists reinforce, for us, the sense of culture as a very salient reality. For the social scientist, culture provides the "deepest structures" (often enough, pre-verbal) and patterns for perceiving the world; conceptualizing identity; defining and then negotiating "reality." A culture is both verbal and pre-verbal, a matter of sensibilities. Anthropologists note how cultures, for example, shape our sense of bodily presence and integrity in the world. Thus,"space" (having room to do one's own thing, to pick up and move on, to achieve social mobility) has been very important in American culture (and also in the vast transcontinental Canada).

Anthropologist Clifford Geertz defines culture succinctly as "an historically transmitted pattern of meanings embodied in symbols." Citing another ethnographer, Geertz asserts that "a society's culture consists of whatever it is one has to know or believe in order to operate in a manner acceptable to its members."[4] In a cognate vein, a French anthropologist observer of American culture, Herve Verenne, notes that American culture presents any outsider with all the problems that those who live in the United States have to deal with, whether they want to or not, whether they agree with the American trait or not.[5] Cultures contain deep templates.

Cultures also include structures of relationship that reflect and shape the shared meanings and values. The historically transmitted meanings of a culture include underlying assumptions, taken-for-granted wisdom, and ways of looking at things that almost everyone, in a particular time and place, shares. While cultures are not static and constantly change, they are also not infinitely malleable. America could probably never accept an aristocracy, direct rule by the military, or a unitary religion. Cultures, in a sense, are cults (the cultivation of certain virtues and representative types), creeds, and codes.

Cultures cultivate idealized and typified images of the "good" or "successful" or "wise" man and woman. In *Habits of the Heart*, Robert Bellah and his associates suggest that from the mid-nineteenth century the "representative type" of the American was first, the entrepreneur (remember that Alexis de Tocqueville described American democracy as a "mercantile" or "commercial" democracy). Now, argue Bellah and associates, the therapeutic practitioner (in business or public relations, as much as in a psychological setting) and the manager predominate. In America, the manager type reinforces norms of technical rationality and the therapist type underscores consumerism and defines almost all problems in individualistic psychological terms. As Bellah and associates argue, in America the dominant cultural language and morality verge either toward utilitarian or expressive individualism.[6]

Cultures cultivate, as well, norms for the family, politics, interpersonal courtesy, and interaction. Americans, for example, eschew formal titles; they use first names and interact in familiar ways that often puzzle Europeans when the Americans fail to follow through in a way a true friend would. Some outsiders see Americans as friendly but not, often, true and consistent friends. Herve Verenne noted what he found to be an almost promiscuous friendliness among Americans, which they feel constrained to show in public, even to strangers.[7]

Cultures provide templates for typical gender and age behaviors and relations. Feminism is strongly present in American culture, for example, but Alexis de Tocqueville found, even in 1840, a kind of equality among the sexes in America that was absent in France. Americans do not especially honor the elderly. Cultures provide us with maps of who we are, where we have come from, where we need to go together. Cultural maps are both models *of* the world (descriptions of sorts) and models *for* the world (normative prescriptions).

I would argue that five salient themes dominate the American cultural ethos: equality, freedom, material abundance, better living through technology, and individualism. They get filtered through the institutional realities of democracy, technology, the free-market "myth" and partial reality, and a legal system based on adversarial notions in a pattern of common law that privileges individual rights and is relatively blind to anything like collective or cultural rights (these latter are, of course, a concern of CST). A culture never exists as a mere free-floating set of ideas and symbols. It interacts in and through institutions, such as education (in the US case, to provide upward mobility and to be governed by the ideal of individual achievement); the mass media (with a strong American mythos of a free press); and in the American economic system, based on market capitalism and consumerism. Justice, in America, is primarily defined in procedural rather than more substantive terms: equality of opportunity.[8]

The defining initial cultural matrix for papal CST (from 1891 through the late 1960s) was, of course, a Europe with strong social democratic traditions, stemming from European socialist and vigorous Christian Democratic parties. The United States barely ever had a socialist movement. Indeed, Robert Bellah once argued that there was a kind of "taboo against socialism" in the United States.[9] Many ethicists or political philosophers in the United States favor a view of the unencumbered individual as an autonomous chooser, cut off from essential relationality. This is, of course, diametrically opposed to the Catholic understanding of the human person as profoundly, and *essentially*, relational. So, strong notions of solidarity and communitarianism do not resonate as well in the United States as they do in papal social teaching. Moreover, many American political philosophers, seeing an essential pluriformity of the good and inherent conflicts about defining it, are often quite wary of Catholic notions of the common good as a shared sense of public good.[10]

A persistent notion of American exceptionalism, for its part, also makes the American culture code frequently somewhat adverse to the rich Catholic notions of inter-dependence and universal solidarity. From the time of the first Puritan landings, many Americans have seen their country as an exceptional city on the hill, a beacon for humankind. Herman Melville touches on this theme of American exceptionalism in his novel *White Jacket*: "We Americans are the peculiar chosen people—the Israel of our time; we bear the ark of the Liberties of the world. Almost for the first time in the history of the earth, national selfishness is unbounded philanthropy, for we can not do a good to America but we give alms to the world."[11] Americans, paradoxically, have believed that they—as a vast continental-wide expanse—were free to become whatever they imagined themselves to want to be and, simultaneously, an incarnation—in their Bill of Rights—of the idea of universal rights. National self-interest, more often than CST's sense of a universal common good, has driven American foreign policy choices.

American Consumerism

While consumerism as a full-blown cultural phenomenon in America only fully blossoms after the gilded age (circa 1880), very early on, even in Puritan times, the dream of America as a self-contained garden of affluence undermined the alternative religious and early republican ideals of plain living and the simple life. In a sense, consumerism is already an ingredient in the early strong emphasis in America on freedom of choice, a peculiarly voluntaristic evaluation of freedom as *simple* choice—*sacred*, precisely because of the choosing.

American culture privileges freedom as a societal value, and this reinforces consumerism. Consumerism also draws on the early ideal of America as a new Eden, full of material wealth and abundance. Connected with that Eden theme is the notion of Americans as the new Adam—without history, without a fall—which explains a certain "innocence" and lack of a tutored historical sense. The hardest thing for Americans to do is to reverence tradition.

By the turn of the twentieth century the anti-establishment Chicago economist Thorstein Veblen, in his classic *The Theory of the Leisure Class* (1899), already mocked Americans' love of money and conspicuous consumption. Without an aristocracy, he argued, and agreeing with what Alexis de Tocqueville thought to be an excessive and one-sided emphasis in America on equality of conditions, Americans, Veblen thought, could only find in conspicuous consumption a difference principle to set some people apart as those who had "achieved" or had merit. It became for Americans the only "legitimated" counterbalance to the stress on equality.[12] Wealth was seen to flow from individual hard work and merit. Later, in the mid-twentieth century, Robert and Helen Lynd, in their classic sociological studies *Middletown* (1929) and *Middletown in Transition* (1937), defined America as *essentially* a consumer culture.[13] What had, at the turn of the century, been true only of the rich had now spread to the middle classes.

To nurture and sustain itself, consumer culture relies on important structural elements in advanced capitalist society: the growing centralization of economic power among producers; the extended scale of bureaucratic control and market operations; the growing remoteness of controllers and decision-makers from local sites of decision; the strong role of an advertising industry; the packaging of family entertainment and sport. To be sure, a consumer culture has its decided strengths and weaknesses. It does increase choice and freedom. It helps material wealth to circulate and expand. Its prime weaknesses are both environmental (the cost to the earth of producing so much and disposing of so much waste) and human (the cost to the human who begins to see himself or herself as a kind of commodity or to judge value by having rather than being). In contrast, CST lifts up the environment and emphasizes human dignity as entailing more being than having.

There also exists a persistent, if somewhat subaltern, countercultural movement in America against the grain of this consumerism. David Shi's intellectual history *The Simple Life* tells the tale of a continual subversion, yet equally continuous reemergence, of an earlier American ideal of plain living: from the Puritan ethic with its anti-sumptuary laws, to the simple republican ideal of Jefferson, the transcendental plain living of Thoreau, and later of Walt Whitman.[14] During the Progressive Era there was a renewed thrust to cut against the grain of a consumer culture, with an ideal of discriminating consumption; consumer and producer cooperatives; uncluttered living; personal contentment; aesthetic simplicity in art and architecture; civil virtue; social service; and a renewed contact with nature. John Muir stands out in this era. So there do exist authentically American subaltern cultural resources to counter the dominant culture of consumerism. Andrew Del Banco stands in this counter-cultural line when he asks, sardonically: "Do we have the nerve to say of ourselves that a culture locked in a soul-starving present in which the highest aspiration—for those who can afford to try—is to keep the body forever young, is no culture at all?"[15] Nor is this ideal dead today. It can be found in American environmentalist groups and elsewhere among both religious and nonreligious groups operating in civil society. It is with this strand of American culture that Catholic notions of interdependence and the common good promise to find a deeper resonance.

American Individualism and the Romance with Technology

As with consumerism, America contains subaltern cultural strands more congenial to communitarianism than those espoused by its notorious individualism. In 1840 Alexis de Tocqueville had to coin this neologism—*individualism*—to describe the America he saw. American individualism has roots in American religion, the revival tradition of purely personal salvation, and in American concerns for freedom at home and abroad. The consequences for moral discourse in American culture of this individualism often have been catastrophic. Chaotic pluralism, unable to transcend individual choice and mere interest-group balancing, takes over.

Here, too, there exists an alternative authentically American cultural strand, found in populism and other social movements. Wilson Carey McWilliams has charted the byways of this American communitarianism in his classic study *The Idea of Fraternity in America*.[16] McWilliams shows how American novelists (such as John Steinbeck in *The Grapes of Wrath*), movie makers (especially Frank Capra in such classic films as *Mr. Smith Goes to Washington*, *Meet John Doe*, and *It's a Wonderful Life*), and public figures, such as Martin Luther King, Jr., tapped into and did not simply create an American variety of communitarianism. More recently Princeton sociologist Robert Wuthnow has argued that the American individualists still retain vigorous practices of voluntarism and cultivate a more solidaristic compassion.[17]

Nor does American public philosophy totally lack significant communitarian voices. Besides the two Catholic philosophers Charles Taylor and Alasdair MacIntyre, these include Michael

Sandel, Michael Walzer, and the distinguished sociologist Philip Selznick.[18] To be sure, fraternity or compassion in America must usually first pass through a filter that pays sufficient obeisance to individualism, but it is not absent, nor do we need to create it whole cloth. But it is perhaps symptomatic of American individualism that advocates for health-care reform chose to name a proposed governmentally operated competitor to private insurance companies a "public *option*." Europeans and CST would have more likely dubbed it a common-good reform or governmental guarantee of fundamental rights rather than an option. For CST, adequate provision of health care is a human right, not just a desideratum.

Much the same line of argument can be traced for technology, so deeply engrained in the American myth of taming the wilderness and turning it a garden of abundance through the machine.[19] Here, too, American culture rather one-sidedly stresses means, technique, procedure—even, often enough, a "quick fix" and a purely pragmatic solution—rather than substance and goals (which CTS lifts up with its more vigorous account of the good). Americans seem more content than CST with thinner notions of the good.[20] Yet, once again, there is an alternative American subaltern cultural tradition of doing things for their own sake, savoring what cannot be passed through a technical utilitarian calculus, for example, the famous American movement to save and preserve wilderness. Albert Borgmann, who has studied the history of technology in America, calls this alternative tradition "focal practice."[21]

To summarize, American culture is not the most congenial possible setting for CST. It lacks strong communitarian strands in the culture (although they are not absent). It is more strongly individualistic than CST. It tends to eschew the possibility, in a pluralist society that values freedom, of a genuine and not simply imposed "common good." It overly valorizes the market mechanism in economics. It still sees itself as a kind of exception to other nations. It does not value enough the new globalization of the economy and even culture. Yet, as a complex culture it does contain elements more congenial to the Catholic social vision. Moreover, American Catholics have not only received papal social teaching, but they have also significantly contributed to Catholic social thought.

American Catholic Receptivity and Contribution to Catholic Social Teaching

It would be fairly farfetched to claim that CST has made or left any major imprint on American larger culture and political philosophy. But it would be equally mistaken to deny it any influence. Over the years, arguably, American Catholic variants of CST have become, often by default, a major carrier, in American society, of the just-war theory (with its sense of a limit to engaging in both war and the ways war can be conducted, morally; a condemnation to any first use of nuclear weapons; a strong sense that war must lead to new international structures of peace). To be sure, many of the first recipients of CST in the United States have been largely immigrant in origins (often from less individualistic cultures than the United States). Early and yet not fully assimilated immigrant groups have usually been somewhat more sympathetic to calls for solidarity and a more communitarian ethos. American carriers of CST have also included important peace movements (for example, the Catholic Worker movement and Pax Christi U.S.A.) and, largely through seed funding by the Campaign for Human Development (financed through the National Bishops' Conference) of community-organizing groups, most of which have been of decidedly Catholic provenance or sustenance.[22]

It is not my intent in this chapter to do a fully rounded history of American Catholic reception of and contribution to CST. Others have given us very useful histories and accounts of this.[23] Probably because of the minority and recent immigrant status of American Catholics and fears of nativism, American Catholicism lacked a decisive voice in the nineteenth century and remained largely silent on the social justice questions of the Mexican War, slavery and abolition, and the Civil War; American

Catholics' first stance, at that time, was to demonstrate to a suspicious Protestant majority that they could be a loyal and good citizenry, in war or peace. Toward the end of the century Cardinal James Gibbons of Baltimore spoke out forcefully (and had some impact on the final coming to be of *Rerum Novarum*) in defending the Knights of Labor—the first major American labor organization—from an impending Vatican condemnation as a secret society. The Canadian version of the Knights of Labor was so censured by the church. Most immigrant Catholics were predominantly pro labor.

The first major American bishops' statement on issues of economic reform was the bishops' 1919 letter, a variant of an original document written by John A. Ryan, entitled "The Bishops' Program of Social Reconstruction." That document, actually much more influenced by the British Fabians than by the Vatican, did reference *Rerum Novarum* in its calls for greater productive efficiency, position against waste, opposing insufficient wages for working men, and large gaps in income and wealth in the United States. The incipient National Catholic Welfare Conference (an agency of the US bishops) wrote eighty-two documents between 1919 and 1950 on topics ranging from unemployment to secularism and social welfare. Especially noteworthy is the 1940 "Statement on the Church and Social Order" penned by John A. Ryan and influenced by *Quadragesimo Anno*.[24]

Over a long span, three men (John A. Ryan, John Cronin, SS, and Msgr. George Higgins) anchored, for the bishops, the section of the Catholic Conference that dealt with economic, social, and labor issues. In general, as Charles Curran has argued, these men "basically followed the same approach as the papal documents: a heavy natural law basis; a moderate reforming stance; a working together with all others for the common good; and an emphasis on change of structures rather than a change of hearts."[25]

Organizationally, from the 1930s through the early 1960s, American Catholics focused on (1) labor schools to train Catholic labor leaders (and fend off Communist influences on labor); (2) the Association of Catholic Trade Unionists (working within the secular unions) that emerged in 1937 and was of influence on the East Coast; (3) motivating and facilitating labor priests in a number of parishes and dioceses around the country; (4) specialist academic associations of Catholics, the Catholic Economic Association, and the American Catholic Sociological Association, dedicated, also in their respective journals, to applying CST to economics and sociology in the American context; and (5) a Jesuit commitment, through the Institute of Social Order at Saint Louis University, to further social research and action committed to applying papal social thought in the American context. Still, for most Catholics, CST remained, as the famous throw-away line has it, the church's "best kept secret."[26]

During World War II the American bishops remained conspicuously silent about the injustices of placing Japanese-American citizens in concentration camps, of the saturation bombing of German and Japanese cities, and of the use of nuclear weapons at the end of the war. In the 1960s American Catholics showed a certain prominence in the peace movement, opposing nuclear weapons, and the Vietnam war. In a guarded fashion the American bishops raised issues about the justice of the war in Vietnam and championed the right to conscientious objection, including selective conscientious objection to only some wars, for Catholics and others. But without any doubt the most important vital influence on American cultural values (and thus the most salient American Catholic contribution to CST) grew out of the two very influential bishops' pastorals of the 1980s: *The Challenge of Peace: God's Promise and Our Response* (1983) and *Economic Justice for All* (1986).[27]

What set these two documents apart from earlier and subsequent documents of the American bishops and from CST in other contexts besides America was their unique process. Subsequent documents have dealt, impressively, with issues such as ecology, immigration, health care, welfare reform, and the death penalty, but they have lacked the cultural impact of the two aforementioned documents. The bishops conducted, for them, a wide set of hearings among experts, secular and religious, on nuclear or economic issues, including non-Catholic moralists and other experts on technical issues. They followed a multi-tiered process in which preliminary drafts were circulated for discussion and feedback. They addressed not only general issues of universal moral principle but policy ramifications (for example, Can there be any legitimate first use of nuclear weapons? Is any use of nuclear weapons against a city ever justified? What kinds of agricultural and developmental policies should the nation follow? What levels of unemployment are morally tolerable?).

In these letters, more than evident elsewhere in the international church to that point, the bishops tried to integrate careful scriptural exegesis, ethical norms, and policy science. The bishops were conscientious in distinguishing between absolute norms of morality, which hold always and everywhere, and their prudent—if necessary for credibility and impact—application of the norms to real cases. This had the effect of actually enticing policy elites and influential journals and newspapers to enter into the arguments of CST. For both letters, but especially the letter on peace, the bishops' initiative fed into and drew upon already existing social movements (for example, a secular movement opposing the build-up and proliferation of weapons and the employment of new kinds of weapons during the Reagan presidency). The American bishops' strategy of open hearings, preliminary drafts, and feedback were replicated in the important joint Canadian and Western U.S.A. pastoral letter on issues of the economy and the environment related to the Columbia River basin.[28]

The American bishops had their critics, both at home and abroad, for the more democratic and participatory process they engaged in with these three letters. Some felt that the teaching authority of the bishops was compromised by the give and take (and, sometimes, pressure-group tactics) of public hearings; drafts with critique and comments; and final votes that engaged (at least informally), besides the bishops, other Catholic and non-Catholic constituencies in the outcome. Others, however, thought that this participatory process enormously enhanced the episcopal authority and gave impetus to the voice of CST in a wider cultural context. In any event, since 2001 no episcopal teachings on CST have engaged that participatory process.

In assessing the relative lack of impact of CST on American culture, political philosophy, and social science, Charles Curran proposes the following reasons for its lack of cultural influence: (1) American academicians tend to be very specialized. The kind of interdisciplinary efforts of the bishops to bring together moralists, social scientists, economists, foreign policy experts, and military experts is somewhat alien to the separate, specialized disciplinary enclaves of academia. (2) To some extent a secularist antipathy to the religious voice contributes to the Catholic isolation from culturally central policy decisions. CST continues, all too often, to be seen as a kind of theological, even sectarian (at any rate, non-neutral or "scientific") influence on a pluralistic, secular policy sector. (3) "Many people in the United States see the role of the Catholic Church as a political actor, trying to have its positions enshrined in law and public policy and not primarily as an intellectual interlocutor engaged in public dialogue about what is best for the country. Thus, before and even after the pastoral letter on the economy, the Catholic social tradition has had little or no influence on political philosophy and science."[29]

Despite often heroic and altruistic efforts to further justice for workers and immigrants, to expand US aid for international development, to fight for reforms of the penal and health-care systems, the Catholic bishops (both at national levels and at state levels through their Catholic State Conferences) also do, frequently enough, work for specifically Catholic institutional interests. It may be fairly hard, simultaneously, to be seen or to operate as a religious (albeit legitimate) interest group and also, at the very same time, as an impartial interlocutor for the public or common good. I suspect this dilemma for church voice (that is, an organizational actor with palpable self-interests also claiming to be above self-interest) is not only found at the level of national Catholic episcopacies but may redound also back to the Vatican.

Canadian Receptivity
and Contributions to Catholic Social Teaching

Despite some considerable overlap on attitudes, as shown in the World Values survey, between Canada and the United States, Canada is decidedly culturally distinct in many ways from the United States. The polities differ. Canada has a parliamentary system with a prime minister, not a president. Canada lacks that American "taboo against socialism," having spawned a home-grown (stemming largely from a religious background) socialist third party, the DNP, which is of some political importance. Although Canada did not have, as such, a Christian Democratic Party, as in Europe or Latin America, many French Catholic Canadians were imbued with principles and attitudes quite similar to those of the Christian Democratic Party elsewhere. Emmanuel Mounier was quite influential in French Canada. As an important intermediate-size power in the Commonwealth of Nations (consisting, mainly, of former British colonies), Canada is more poised than is America to see its role as an actor in an interdependent world of politics and development.

Canada's religious map also looks different from that of the United States. While quite diverse religiously, Canada's Christians are, overwhelmingly, found in only three mainline churches: Roman Catholicism, the Anglican Church, and the United Church of Canada. There are fewer Evangelicals, proportionately, in Canada (with their penchant for purely personal religion and an overly moralistic stance on politics) than in the United States. Catholics, in Canada, at some 50 percent of the population, are a more significant cultural force in that country than they are in the United States, where Catholics represent only about 25 percent of the population.[30]

Canada's strong—if disputed—founding myth of a covenant between the two nations, bringing together French Catholic and the English-speaking communities, meant that Catholics, in Canada, were never quite "originally" outsiders, needing to prove their cultural credentials. As a dual-language culture, Canadians are much more sensitive to the range of corporate (and not just individual) rights, which include language rights and a right to one's culture. These latter rights are fairly prominent in international CST yet seem somewhat foreign to the culture of the United States.[31]

Moreover, the Canadian Catholic bishops have produced over the years a truly remarkable set of documents treating social, economic, and political realities that stand out, worldwide, among episcopacies in its notable contribution to CST.[32] They have made it clear, as the Canadian bishops announced in a 1972 document, that "social justice in the church, in Canada and in the world will remain a major and consistent concern of this conference."[33]

The Canadian social documents can serve as a useful prism for illuminating continuities and changes in international CST. Many of the Canadian bishops' documents represent explicit responses to or more concrete applications of papal encyclicals, such as *Mater et Magistra, Populorum Progessio, Laborem Exercens*, or the 1971 Synod of World Bishops' document *Justice in the World*. Over time, Canadian social teaching shifted from its original natural-law-based catechesis of fundamental social rights and duties, often arrived at deductively, to an inductive and experiential sense of the social teaching as integral to evangelization, grounded in a deeper ecclesiology and articulating the theological motifs of sin and liberation. The Canadian bishops' documents mirror shifts, as well, in international CST from a focus on the common good as, primarily, a national reality to questions of international development and liberation. Remarkably, the Canadian bishops responded to the documents of the Latin American episcopacy at Medellín in 1969 as early as 1970. Canadian documents persistently link the social teaching also to special sessions of the United Nations on justice issues, programs for a new international economic order, and the environment.

Over time, one sees in the Canadian bishops' documents a more generous citing from economists and political analysts, including secular experts, than is usual in international CST. The Canadian bishops have spoken quite strongly—much more than the US bishops did in their letter on the economy—in referring to their own current economic reality as embodying "social sin" or of "a much larger structural crisis in the international system of capitalism." They say of Canada (and not only, as Pope Paul VI did in *Populorum Progressio*, for the Third World), "What is required is nothing less than fundamental social change."[34]

The Canadian bishops continually address post–Vatican II themes of an option for the poor and justice as participation. In a document entitled "New Power" and another remarkable document entitled "Northern Development: At What Cost?" the bishops demand that "we give the deprived a public voice and active role in decision making."[35]

In his 1971 apostolic letter *Call to Action*, Paul VI recognized that it is no longer possible to devise a totally unitary social teaching for the entire world church. Each local church has to apply the general principles of church social teaching to its own context. The Canadian bishops have consistently tried to do this. Because of the massive postwar influx of immigrants to Canada, the bishops have focused, on several occasions, on immigration and justice. They have dealt with Canada's native peoples (the First Nation) in several documents, raising the thorny question of internal colonialism in a developed land. They have focused on the unique Canadian development of widespread foreign ownership of corporations in their developed land.[36] The Canadian bishops have explicitly endorsed the Canadian Federation as a pact between two equal founding nations. They speak of Canada's "two great linguistic and culture groups" and "founding cultures." Episcopal endorsement of this disputed—yet crucial to Canadian unity—founding myth represents a critical contribution to a uniquely Canadian understanding of cultural justice.

Several elements stand out in Canadian CST. It consistently looks to alternative economic and social models. It seems untrammeled by the myth, so prevalent in the United States, that capitalism is necessarily and in principle benevolent. Hence, the Canadian bishops can speak of the inherent contradictions in the capitalist system. More clearly than in other social documents from industrialized lands, Canadian social teaching addresses some of the problematic roles of multinational corporations.[37]

The close ecumenical cooperation between the Canadian Bishops' Conference and Protestant groups in issuing joint statements on public issues is also noticeable, as is the bishops' insistence that it is not enough just to hand down principles from on high. They speak of the need to encourage "public debate about economic visions and industrial strategies involving choices about values and priorities for the future direction of the country."[38] Moreover, the Canadian documents represent a clear advance over Roman documents in moving beyond mere principles to some explicit guidelines for action for justice. This is something that only can be done, the bishops argue, in the context of a national church unit.[39]

The Canadian teaching urges the formation of groups working for effective change. Almost every recent document (which, in general, are kept short enough to place in the hands of people in the pews) ends with suggestions about what can be done about a given issue. One has the sense, also, that the bishops utilize religious educators to help draft clear and concise documents that speak to the citizenry and not only to policy elites. In "Ethical Choices and Political Challenges: Ethical Reflections on the Future of Canada's Socio-Economic Order," the bishops outlined a pastoral methodology for social teaching. Rarely in CST has such a methodology been as explicitly formulated as it is in this document.

> This pastoral methodology includes the following steps: being present with and listening to the poor; developing a critical analysis of the economic, political and social structures that cause poverty; making judgements in the light of Gospel principles; stimulating creative thought and action regarding alternative visions and models for social and

economic development; and acting in solidarity with community-based movements.[40]

This methodology, consisting of a strategy of "see-judge-act," puts more emphasis than is usual in CST on creative thinking about alternative models and actual solidarity with already existing social groups and movements working to bring about needed social change.

A Coda on the Future
of North American Catholic Social Teaching

It would take us too far afield to treat in any great length the future of North American Catholic social teaching.[41] At the least we probably need a much more extensive dialogue between CST and the regnant political philosophies in contemporary (particularly those in the orbit of what is often called Anglo philosophy, in contrast to the continental European philosophical thought) pluralist societies. Such a dialogue might, perhaps, make CST something more than our "best kept secret."

Besides national bishops' conferences in Canada and the United States and state conferences in the United States—which will continue to serve as teaching vehicles on the application and relevance of CST for multiple policy issues, such as penal reform, health care, immigration, the issue of political refugees, war-making potentials, and an armaments race—both Canada and the United States also have some grassroots and vigorous NGOs that work on issues of peace, justice, and the environment. They supplement and give local face to issues beyond the ken or reach of episcopal conferences. CST, I insist, has never been a monopoly of the papacy or episcopal conferences. These organizations are important. One thinks of Network (a Catholic lobbying group on bills before the US Congress that have an impact on the poor), various pro-life organizations, the Catholic Coalition on Climate Change. These are important vehicles for giving bite to and putting heft on the general principles of

CST. They have greater flexibility than bishops' conferences to forge coalitions with like-minded secular or other religious groups working on the ground on issues of justice. Much progress has already been made in introducing CST into the curriculum of Catholic schools. Especially notable are attempts to introduce courses on CST into Catholic law and business schools.[42]

While North America has significant resources and the imagination to enrich international CST, it will be challenged—as James Hug's remarks about *Caritas in Veritate* at the beginning of this chapter made clear—also to learn from the center of the world church, the papacy, which has many communication possibilities and unique resources to sift through global economic and environmental issues not available at a national level. The Holy See's recent persistent initiatives on the environment (especially Benedict XVI's several World Day of Peace allocutions) have been especially helpful, enlightening, and, surely, a challenge to complacency about the continued North American global carbon footprint.

Notes

[1] James Hug, SJ, " The Educator's Mission," *America* 201 no. 16 (November 30, 2009): 17.

[2] Two papers, available on the Internet, argue to a convergence of US and Canadian social attitudes. See Dr. Neil Nevitte, "The World Values Survey: Canada-U.S. Integration," the Canadian Institute on Governance, issued March 14, 2002. See also Rudy Fenwick and John Zipp (University of Akron), "Continental Divide or Continentalism? Divergent, Convergent or Parallel Trends in U.S. and Canadian Political Attitudes, 1990–2000," online. Fenwick and Zipp claim that 85 percent of the political and social attitudes measured by the World Values Survey converge or move in similar directions in both Canada and the United States.

[3] I treat of American culture in my essay "A Cultural Overview," in *Reading the Signs of the Times*, ed. T. Howland Sanks and John A. Coleman, 12–23 (Mahwah, NJ: Paulist Press, 1993); and in John A. Coleman, SJ, "Selling God in America: American Commercial Culture as a Climate of Hospitality to Religion," in *Meaning and Modernity: Religion, Polity and Self*, ed. Richard Madsen et al., 136–49 (Berkeley and Los Angeles: University of

California Press, 2002). Some of the themes in this essay will overlap somewhat with these earlier two essays on American culture.

[4] Clifford Geertz, *The Interpretation of Cultures* (New York: Basic Books, 1973), 11.

[5] Herve Verenne, *Symbolizing America* (Lincoln, NE: University of Nebraska Press, 1986).

[6] Robert Bellah et al., *Habits of the Heart* (Berkeley and Los Angeles: University of California Press, 1985). See also their other important book on American culture, *The Good Society* (New York: Alfred Knopf, 1991). *The Good Society* exemplifies how culture intertwines with institutions that embody it.

[7] Verenne, *Symbolizing America.*

[8] For several good attempts to delineate American culture, see Andrew Del Banco, *The Real American Dream* (Cambridge, MA: Harvard University Press, 1999); R. Lawrence Moore, *Selling God: American Religion and the Marketplace of Culture* (New York: Oxford University Press, 1994); Seymour Martin Lipset, *American Exceptionalism: A Double-Edged Sword* (New York: W. W. Norton, 1996). For American ideals of Justice as mainly procedural, see John Rawls, *A Theory of Justice* (Cambridge, MA: Harvard University Press, 1971).

[9] For Bellah on the taboo against socialism in the United States see Robert Bellah, *The Broken Covenant: American Civil Religion in a Time of Trial* (New York: Seabury Press, 1975).

[10] I treat of some of the American aversion to notions of the common good in John A. Coleman, SJ, "Pluralism and the Renewal of the Catholic Sense of the Common Good," in *American Catholics and Civic Engagement*, ed. Margaret O'Brien Steinfels (Lanham, MD: Sheed and Ward, 2004); and in John A. Coleman, SJ, "The Future of Catholic Social Thought" in *Modern Catholic Social Teaching: Commentaries and Interpretations*, ed. Kenneth Himes et al. (Washington DC: Georgetown University Press, 2004), 538–41. The best single treatment of the notion of the common good in CST can be found in David Hollenbach, *The Common Good and Christian Ethics* (New York: Cambridge University Press, 2002).

[11] Cited in Del Banco, *The Real American Dream*, 57–58.

[12] Thorstein Veblen, *The Theory of the Leisure Class* (Boston: Houghton Mifflin, 1973).

[13] Robert S. Lynd and Helen Merrell Lynd, *Middletown: A Study in Contemporary American Culture* (New York: Harcourt, Brace, and Company, 1929); idem, *Middletown in Transition: A Study of Conflicts* (New York: Harcourt, Brace, and Company, 1937).

[14] David Shi, *The Simple Life* (New York: Oxford University Press, 1985).

[15] Del Banco, *The Real American Dream*, 111.

[16] Wilson Carey McWilliams, *The Idea of Fraternity in America* (Berkeley and Los Angeles: University of California Press, 1973).

[17] Robert Wuthnow, *Acts of Compassion* (Princeton, NJ: Princeton University Press, 1991).

[18] Charles Taylor, *A Secular Age* (Cambridge, MA: Harvard University Press, 2007); Alasdair MacIntyre, *Dependent Rational Animals: Why Human Beings Need the Virtues* (Chicago: Open Court, 1999); Michael Walzer, *Spheres of Justice* (New York: Basic Books, 1984); Michael Sandel, *Liberalism and the Limits of Justice* (New York: Cambridge University Press, 1982); Michael Sandel, *Justice: What's the Right Thing to Do?* (New York: Farrar, Strauss, and Giroux, 2009); Philip Selznick, *The Moral Commonwealth* (Berkeley and Los Angeles: University of California Press, 1991).

[19] Leo Marx, *The Machine in the Garden: Technology and the Pastoral Ideal in America* (New York: Oxford University Press, 1964).

[20] Michael Walzer, *Thin and Thick: Moral Argument at Home and Abroad* (Notre Dame, IN: University of Notre Dame Press, 1994).

[21] Albert Borgmann, *Technology and the Character of Everyday Life* (Chicago: University of Chicago Press, 1984).

[22] For Catholic major influence on church-based community organizations, see Mark Warren, *Dry Bones Rattling* (Princeton, NJ: Princeton University Press, 2001) on the Industrial Area Foundation in Texas; Richard Wood, *Faith in Action* (Chicago: University of Chicago Press, 2002) on another faith-based community organization, founded by a Jesuit, known as PICO; Stephen Hart, *Cultural Dilemmas of Progressive Politics* (Chicago: University of Chicago Press, 2001) on another church-based community organizing group in the Midwest known as Gamaliel, founded by a former Jesuit. President Barack Obama got his start in community organizing as part of the Gamaliel network in Chicago.

[23] For comprehensive accounts of the history of American Catholic reception of and contributions to CST, see the accounts of Charles Curran, "The Reception of Catholic Social Teaching and Economic Teaching in the United States," in Himes et al., *Modern Catholic Social Teaching*, 469–92; and Todd Whitmore, "The Reception of Catholic Approaches to Peace and War in the United States," in ibid., 493–521.

[24] For the US documents (including those from the various US Councils of Baltimore in the nineteenth century) from the beginning of the Republic until 1983, see Hugh Nolan, ed., *Pastoral Letters of the Catholic Bishops*, 6 vols. (Washington DC: US Catholic Conference, 1984). Nolan's volumes include an important 1958 letter of the American bishops opposing racial segregation.

[25] Curran, "The Reception of Catholic Social and Economic Teaching in the United States," 472.

[26] Edward de Berri et al., *Catholic Social Teaching: Our Best Kept Secret* (Maryknoll, NY: Orbis Books, 2003).

[27] *The Challenge of Peace: God's Promise and Our Response* (Washington DC: National Conference of Catholic Bishops, 1983); *Economic Justice for All* (Washington DC: National Conference of Catholic Bishops, 1986).

[28] "The Columbia River Watershed: Caring for Creation and the Common Good" (2001). The text is available online or from the Washington State Catholic Conference. This letter is somewhat unique in that it involved, unusually, a joint letter by Canadian and Western U.S.A. bishops about a common ecological problem (involving fish stocks, urban development, farm issues, and ecological degradation in an important shared river basin).

[29] Curran, "The Reception of Catholic Social and Economic Teaching in the United States," 484.

[30] See Robert Bothwell, *Penguin History of Canada* (Toronto: Penguin Global, 2008); Roy McGregor, *Canadians* (Toronto: Penguin Global, 2008).

[31] Compare, for example, the arguments and assumptions about a more collective right to one's language and culture in the essay by the Canadian Catholic philosopher Charles Taylor (who is bilingual and lives in the Province of Quebec) with his respondents from the United States who resist non-individualistic understandings of rights in Charles Taylor et al., *Multiculturalism: Examining the Politics of Recognition* (Princeton, NJ: Princeton University Press, 1994).

[32] See E. F. Sheridan, SJ, *Do Justice: The Social Teaching of the Canadian Catholic Bishops* (Ottawa: Editions Paulines, 1986). The national Canadian Jesuit journal *Compass* (now defunct) published a symposium entitled "The Catholic Bishops and Canadian Society" based on the Sheridan volume (*Compass* 7, no. 2 [Summer 1987]). I contributed an essay to that symposium entitled "A Gift to the World Church," 19–23, from which I draw many of my comments in this section of the chapter.

[33] Document 30, no. 1, in Sheridan, *Do Justice*. A major point person for many years for the Canadian bishops on social and political issues is the economist William F. X. Ryan, SJ, founder of The Center of Concern and for a decade or so the secretary to the Canadian Bishops' Conference.

[34] For these citations, see Sheridan, *Do Justice*, Document 28, IIIa, for social sin; Document 55, no. 2, for the structural crisis in capitalism, and Document 40, no. 32, for the need for fundamental social change, not just change in the Third World.

[35] See Sheridan, *Do Justice*, Document 23, no. 15, and all of Document 40 on Northern Development.

[36] Sheridan, *Do Justice*, Document 49, no. 9.

[37] Sheridan, *Do Justice*, Document 42, nos. 16–17.

[38] Sheridan, *Do Justice*, Document 55, no. 26.

[39] Sheridan, *Do Justice*, Document 49, no. 15.

[40] Canadian Conference of Catholic Bishops, "Ethical Choices and Political Challenges: Ethical Reflections on the Future of Canada's Socio-

Economic Order" (1984), quoted in CCCB, "The Struggle against Poverty: A Sign of Hope in Our World" (Cambridge, MA: MIT Press, 1995), no. IV.

[41] I treat the topic of the future of CST more generally in "The Future of Catholic Social Thought," 522–44.

[42] Notable have been efforts at the University of Notre Dame Law School and at the School of Business of the University of Saint Thomas in Saint Paul, Minnesota.